American Advertising
in Poland

D1251943

American Advertising in Poland

A Study of Cultural Interactions Since 1990

JEFFREY K. JOHNSON

McFarland & Company, Inc., Publishers
Jefferson, North Carolina, and London

LIBRARY OF CONGRESS CATALOGUING-IN-PUBLICATION DATA

Johnson, Jeffrey K., 1972–
    American advertising in Poland: a study of cultural interactions
since 1990 / Jeffrey K. Johnson.
        p.   cm.
    Includes bibliographical references and index.

    ISBN 978-0-7864-3797-9
    softcover : 50# alkaline paper ∞

    1. Advertising — Poland.   2. Corporations,
American — Poland.   National characteristics, Polish.
I. Title.

HF5813.P7J64   2009
659.109438 — dc22   2008047502

British Library cataloguing data are available

On the cover: Polish flag, cola and burger ©2008 Shutterstock.

Manufactured in the United States of America

McFarland & Company, Inc., Publishers
  Box 611, Jefferson, North Carolina 28640
  www.mcfarlandpub.com

To my mom for always believing in me
and to Monika for loving and supporting me

Acknowledgments

Although my name appears alone on the cover of this book, I cannot take sole credit for its publication. During the process of creating this monograph I have been helped by a large number of people whose patience, generosity, and understanding have changed both me and my work. I humbly offer my gratitude to each of them.

I deeply thank my friends and supporters in Poland for helping me better understand Polish culture and society. Piotr, Dorota, Emila, and Ania Adamczewska provided much-needed support and assistance. A special thank you to my extended family, Krzysztof, Zofia, and Rafal Cieslak, for providing guidance and hospitality that helped to make this project possible.

I am lucky to have had a wonderful university committee that helped me in so many ways. I owe a debt of gratitude to Carrie La Ferle, Keely Stauter-Halsted, and Kirsten Fermaglich for how they assisted and pushed me in equal parts. An extra special thank you to Gary Hoppenstand, my committee chair, mentor, and role model who has given me more than I can ever express in words. As Isaac Newton said, "If I have seen farther, it is by standing on the shoulders of giants."

Many of my academic colleagues and mentors provided help, guidance, and assistance. Jane Neukomm, Gerda Ray, Kim Little, Peter Acsay, John Hoover, and Malcolm Magee all taught me how to find and trust my voice. Julie Wendy O'Connor, Tricia Jenkins, and H. Louise Davis were founts of academic and emotional support. Martyna Olszowska and Zbigniew Czapla have guided and helped me too many times to count.

ACKNOWLEDGMENTS

Michigan State University's American Studies Department, College of Arts and Letters, and Graduate School all supported this project with much-needed funding. Virginia Brock and Harriet Grossman at Coca-Cola, Bartosz Okulski and Małgorzata Skonieczna at Frito-Lay Poland, Dominik Szulowski and Jennifer Wong at McDonald's, and Robert J. Van Leer and Jeff Beckman at Levi's each showed professionalism and kindness that allowed this project to exist.

I especially thank my family that lovingly accepts the eccentric academic in their midst: Daniel, Rebecca, Alison, and Sophie Long; Amanda, Alexander, and Zoey Johnson and Louise Thompson; my parents, James and Brenda Johnson, who made me into the person I am today (few words in a book cannot repay your years of love and sacrifice but I hope it is a start); and lastly, to Monika Johnson for viewing and translating countless Polish advertisements, editing and proofreading my poor Polish, providing historical and cultural ideas, finding numerous mistakes, and for putting your heart into this text; without you this book wouldn't exist.

Contents

Introduction

As a high school senior in the 1989-90 school year, I watched as most of the former socialist nations of Europe moved toward capitalist-centered economies and the Cold War ended. Having spent my entire life accustomed to the nationalistic adversarial system of the Cold War, I grappled to understand what was happening and how I was now supposed to view the world. The enemy, the dreaded Soviet Union and its satellite states, was no more, and I, with many of my generation, was confronted with newly opened political and social voids. As with much of my former understanding of the world, I turned to popular culture to explain the new reality. It had been movies like *Red Dawn* and *Rocky IV* and television series like *Amerika* that had taught me to fear the Soviets and their minions, and I looked to the culture makers to inform me of how the new world functioned. Because few popular-culture references were immediately available, I was at first forced to rely on less trustworthy sources of information like newscasters and politicians. I remember my surprise and relief when I viewed a Cold War–inspired Pepsi television commercial one evening. The ad followed a teenage boy as he skateboarded through Red Square while rock and roll blared in the background and an announcer declared that, although Pepsi did not want to take any credit, things had started to change in the Soviet Union not long after Pepsi's soft drinks were introduced to the country. Even at the tender age of eighteen I understood what Pepsi was doing. It was not marketing itself as a soft drink, but rather as a keeper and exporter of American values. Much like the first Bush administration, Pepsi was taking credit for both a regime change and for spreading freedom around the globe. Pepsi was not only a product but also an agent of

1

social change. The soft-drink maker was wrapping itself in all things American (skateboards, rock and roll, and distrust of authority) and I was strangely both attracted and repulsed by the claim.

This television advertisement was the genesis of my interest in mythology, symbolism, and social issues within advertising. Although many of my university instructors attempted to purge me of my belief in the social importance of advertising, I was able to retain my conviction. While many academics study the business objectives or hidden meaning of advertising, I believe that advertising can be read as a text and that the narratives that are produced in advertising are of profound social importance. There is much opposition to the ideas of advertising's textual importance. Many scholars claim that ads are merely agents of commerce and contain little or no social value. I agree that almost all advertising is designed to sell products or services but contend that this does not limit its textual importance. The desired outcome of product sales does not impact the narrative structure that is utilized to achieve it. Advertising often uses stories, themes, myths, symbols, and other devices as cultural touchstones to form connections with viewers and to create an ongoing narrative. Scholars have successfully argued that nontraditional texts such as popular fiction, films and television can be read as narrative texts and advertising as a medium certainly falls within this increased understanding of narratives.

The narratives in advertising and other popular texts have spread cultural ideas and understandings throughout the globe. It is said that in the world the two most widely used English words are American gifts to the language: "OK" and "Coca-Cola." American products, movies, music, and culture in general are marketed to and consumed by mass audiences worldwide. The United States has built an empire based upon trade and exportation of its culture, and its future very much depends on its ability to continue this cultural expansion. However, the implications of cultural globalization are more far-reaching than American interests. The global economy and society of the twenty-first century demand that citizens embrace the world outside their nation's borders. The United States is important to the global community but the inversion of that statement, that the global community is extremely important to the United States, is as true or even truer. If the new global society and economy are to reach their maximum potential, then the participants must understand the role of U.S. culture internationally. My contention in this book is that often it is not merely American products that are being bought by international consumers, but rather a complex mixture of perceived pieces of the American way of life combined with local cultural symbols and mythologies. American merchants advertise their wares not as products but as culturally based lifestyle choices. Often, at first buying an American product becomes akin to purchasing a piece of the American Dream, whatever that dream means to the purchaser. When at first a teenager in Poland in 1990 bought a bottle of Coca-Cola, he was not purchasing a sugary, overpriced soft drink so much as a symbol of what he believed the ideal of America to be. Quickly though, this idea changed and the American product became transformed by the local culture, creating a blending of ideas and purposes. I propose that American brands and products do not always monolithically colonize overseas markets, as many have suggested, but often create partnerships with local cultures that transform both the brand and the culture.

To be clear, this study is not about the history of advertising in Poland or an effort to explain the ways that American products and their advertising have harmed or benefited Polish society. Rather, it is an attempt to locate and define various narratives that exist within Polish advertising for American products and to show how these narratives interact with local Polish culture and how these interactions affect both the products and Polish culture over time. In order to do this I will analyze Polish advertising for four American companies: McDonald's, Coca-Cola, Levi's, and Frito-Lay, from 1990 to 2007. These advertisements will be viewed as narratives and will be used to chronicle and understand the themes and mythologies that are present in various types of Polish ads. These advertising narratives reveal much about both Polish and American societies and their shared ideas, experiences, symbols, and mythologies.

Narrative Structure

Narrative structure is a much-discussed idea that forms the basis for most societies' stories and mythologies. Although many theories exist about narratives and their place within literature and society, few can argue against the idea that narratives are one of the essential elements of both local and international storytelling. Many different definitions of narrative and narrative theory exist but this reading will use the most basic. For the purpose of this study, narrative in advertising is present in any ad produced by or for a company or agency that creates a story, either within the ad itself or by interacting with local or international culture. This definition is necessarily broad in order to allow for the study of multiple types of advertising and associated narratives. Though many scholars would assert that a narrative must be a series of images or symbols that create a self-contained story, I am widening the definition to include seemingly static images or symbols that produce a story when placed into a cultural context. My assertion is that narratives can be created either by using the traditional multi-image storytelling structure or by showing a single image or physical structure that creates a complex story by interacting with culturally important ideas, symbols, and mythologies. This expanded definition is necessary in order to create a new framework that embraces objects that become narratives when placed within a cultural context. These cultural narratives often have gone unexplored in the past because they were thought to be too limited to be true narratives.

Expanding Narrative

The idea of reading advertisements as narrative devices follows a long tradition in popular culture of expanding the understanding of what comprises narrative structure and form. Into the mid part of the twentieth century, many scholars and lay people believed that the idea of narrative storytelling only included traditional written literature. Academic and social critics argued over the meaning of high and mass literature and many declared that only "real literature" should be explored as narrative. In the mid twentieth century John Kouwenhoven attempted to expand the academic notion of what was art, literature, and narrative by proposing that there were different types of art that should be judged on their own merits. Kouwenhoven claimed that seemingly common objects and buildings could be viewed in radically new ways and should be considered a unique type of art. Kouwenhoven asserted that the definition of art was much more fluid than commonly understood and that viewers and critics should reconsider how they judged artistic and seemingly nonartistic forms. Though these ideas were not generally adopted for several decades this was an early attempt to redefine art and the idea of narrative. It also served as the basis for many later notions of expanding the meaning of narrative structure and its uses in mass and popular culture.

While John Kouwenhoven provided an early foundation for the understanding of narrative structure in nontraditional texts, little changed until 1970 when Russel Nye published his monograph, *The Unembarrassed Muse: The Popular Arts in America.* The Pulitzer Prize–winning Nye created categories of arts and declared there to be merit in studying popular and folk cultures. By defining these areas Nye fashioned an opportunity to remake the meaning of culture and to use existing methods and understanding in new ways. This opened the door for narrative structure to be explored in new areas of popular and mass culture. Most scholars consider this to be one of the founding events in the study of popular culture and, more importantly, the beginning of a paradigm shift concerning how scholars viewed culture. No longer would narratives be thought of as merely limited to canonical literary works but the scope of their cultural significance would increase dramatically and would move into areas that many would have never considered.

Shortly after Russel Nye published *The Unembarrassed Muse,* several academics started to redefine the use of narratives in American and international society. One of the first was Stuart Kaminsky in his 1974 book *American Film Genres: Approaches to a Critical Theory of Popular Film.* In his work, Kaminsky expanded the definition of narrative and increased the ways in which the device could be explored. He no longer was limiting the idea of narrative to written texts but now included visual media like film. Expanding the scope of narratives to include visual forms was a watershed moment that opened the definition to many new views and usages. This expansion of the definition and study of narrative continued in 1976 in John Cawelti's book *Adventure, Mystery, and Romance,* in which he outlined the use of narrative in popular literature. While over three decades later it may seem obvious that detective, romance, and science fiction stories use a narrative structure, in the mid–1970s Cawelti greatly increased the idea of how narrative could be understood. The definition of high and low culture and art no longer seemed quite so clear and the standard for cultural forms that academics should study was increasingly less rigid.

The exploration of narrative structure in popular culture expanded into television in 1978 when John Fiske and John Hartley published their monograph *Reading Television*. By studying narratives in television, Fiske and Hartley extended the scope of the study of narratives to another area of popular culture. While narratives in film had already been studied by Stuart Kaminsky and others, television was still often viewed as a lesser storytelling device that offered little or no artistic value. Those social critics that wished to restrict the application of narrative study could protest that narrative was only found in art and literature that conformed to a traditional understanding. Although the definition of narrative was expanding, critics attempted to make it conform to previous notions of artistic value. Narratives could be found in popular literature because they were written stories that conformed to traditional rules and expectations. Likewise, film could contain narratives because it was an exceptional medium that occasionally produced "high art" like the highly artistic and complex film noir. The inclusion of television as a narrative medium marks a point in which it becomes nearly impossible to restrict the use and study of narratives. If television was worthy of scholarly study then what could not be considered a narrative? Because narratives were no longer limited to traditional art and literature their study grew to include many uncultivated fields and media. Soon formerly rejected areas like comic books, musicals, and advertising were being written about as narrative art forms. The idea of narrative had grown to include almost any format that could be used as a storytelling device.

This study of the narratives in advertising in Poland is very much within the above-described popular culture tradition of studying a medium's storytelling characteristics and attempting to define patterns, themes, ideas, mythologies, and symbols. By examining advertising narratives, one is able to begin to track and understand elements that are culturally significant within a society. When the narratives are produced by entities that exist outside of the realm of the traditional society, as with the American companies in Poland in this study, the narratives also offer an opportunity to understand how ideas, symbols, and mythologies are shared in an intercultural and transnational manner. The types of narratives that are created by the American companies reveal much about the producers and the intended audience. The narrative structure allows the viewer the chance to better understand cultural interactions and a way to witness the cultural transnational sharing that occurs when American companies enter a post-socialist economy. The advertising narratives provide clues to the nature and type of changes that occur within both Polish society and American companies and showcase some ways in which each party attempts to accommodate the other. These narratives offer a window into the cultural exchanges between producer and society, a view not often observed. This interaction can supply insight into the nature of globalization and transnationalism, and illustrate the complex relationships that occur on the local level.

Former U.S. Representative and Speaker of the House Tip O'Neill is reported to have said that "all politics is local." Increasingly, this statement is not only true of politics but also of international advertising and marketing. To declare international advertising a local affair sounds oxymoronic. What is international advertising, if not an attempt to sell products in a foreign place? When viewed this way, from the seller's perspective, it seems that international advertising is a tool that helps to create globalized markets and provide common goods and services to consumers worldwide. When considered from a buyer's perspective though, international advertising and marketing can be seen as an interaction between company and consumers that is used to explain how a product or service may be beneficial. Although some scholars would disagree with this characterization of advertising, it is important to note that advertising's purpose is to entice consumers to consume, and to do this there generally must be an understanding of the consumers' culture. While some companies have attempted to market in societies in which they have little knowledge, this often produces disastrous results. This study focuses on the choices that American advertisers have made locally in the Polish marketplace. By examining the narratives that are produced one is often able to understand how traditional ideas, symbols, and mythologies are blended with new ones and what is created from this amalgamation. It is in this set of choices and changes that we can see the formation of new international understandings, a more transnational society, and shifting local cultures.

Because American advertising narratives in Poland are the basis for this study, it is necessary to blend together understandings from the fields of advertising, history, and popular culture. This amalgamation of academic fields creates a unique vantage to view the issues of transnationalism and globalization. Though scores of works have been produced in each of these fields, very few studies, if any, have combined all three. This interdisciplinary approach allows one to utilize the methods and insights of each field in order to produce a new understanding of the issues as a whole. It has already been noted that narratives have been and continue to be explored and studied with the academic field of popular culture. This background concerning narrative usages helps one to form a basis for understanding how they will be used within this research. Likewise, it is important to have a foundation of knowledge about advertising and Polish history in order to grasp the many themes and mythologies inherent within the ads. In order to comprehend how and why ad narratives were created in the manner they were, one must have an understanding of what ideas and theories dominate the advertising field. Similarly, one must be aware of the basics of Polish history and culture in order to appreciate the themes and symbols contained within advertising geared for the Polish market. Without this background much of the tone, flavor, and meaning of the advertisements would be lost.

Advertising

Advertising theorists have long debated advertising's meanings and purposes. Scholars continually disagree about the nature of advertising and one of the most longstanding discussions is whether advertising is a mirror or molder of society. The basic question contained within this debate is whether advertising serves as a mirror of society's needs and desires or a molder that creates these wants and wishes. This argument is seemingly unending because it not only reflects one's understanding of advertising but also takes into account one's personal philosophies about life. This debate is important, though, because it helps one to define advertising and creates a context for viewing the advertising narratives that are produced. While one's view of advertising and its purposes are often as much personal as academic, strong scholarly arguments can be made for either side of the mirror/molder debate. Despite the fact that no universal agreements on these matters appear imminent, for the purposes of this study I am defining advertising as a method of interaction used in an attempt to encourage consumers to purchase or use a good or service. This definition is certainly open-ended and can be extensively argued but it sets the parameters of advertising without becoming too embroiled in the mirror/molder debate. In this study it is not necessary to decide the mirror/molder question but it is important to be aware of the basic question. When viewing advertisements as narratives the important elements are the themes, ideas, symbols, mythologies, and storytelling devices used. Although many issues concerning advertising can be contested, the above-mentioned elements will be this study's primary concern.

Because the study of narrative in advertising requires ads to be viewed as a type of literature, it also forces the viewer to negotiate the medium's artistic value. Although many producers, viewers, and even scholars of advertising declare it to be a utilitarian medium that is devoid of artistic merit, one must question this assessment if one wishes to study the narratives contained within. While advertising scholars such as Richard Pollay and Theodore Lewitt may argue over advertising's artistic status, I define advertising as artistic in nature because it meets the classification's minimum standards. The medium uses both visual and textual dimensions in order to change how the viewer thinks and feels. This definition will be rebuked by some as imprecise or unclear, and others will claim that it does not capture the spirit of what art is. The nature of these criticisms is exactly why I have chosen such a broad definition and why I define advertising as an artistic medium. Because art is so difficult to define and comprehend and since understandings of it are ever changing, it is imperative that we view the idea broadly. In keeping with popular-culture standards and tradition, I assign no hierarchical value to the advertising art in this study. I do not rank art as "high" or "low." Nor do I label it as either "good" or "bad." Rather, I assert that because advertising can be viewed as art it must treated with the same respect that other art forms enjoy. Many scholars would contend that advertising does not merit the label of art because it has no single inspired creator and its primary purpose is commercial. Though these criticisms may be valuable if one is creating an artistic hierarchy, they do not apply to a classification system that assigns no difference to "popular" and "high" art. Film and television shows are often the work of many creators that combine their efforts. Television often is sponsored by corporate entities and films are often shown in theaters to paying customers. While these are gross generalizations they do emphasize that the idea of the creator and the separation of art and commerce have no clearly defined boundaries. Because art is so difficult to define it is imperative that one judge each text on its own merit. When advertising is critiqued in this manner many will be surprised at the artistic narratives that are produced.

Advertising as Art

While this study focuses on narratives and advertising's literary value, those who produce advertising are not primarily concerned with its artistic merits. As previously stated, advertising's primary purpose is to create commerce. Advertising encompasses many forms, not just the conventional venues of radio, television, and printing advertising, but also lesser-considered categories like in-store, packaging, and architectural advertising. While some forms of advertising, like television commercials, may be more publicly well known, often many types are used in smaller venues or are employed together to form distinctive marketing campaigns. These campaigns serve to craft a message and their makers hope to create a unique image for the brand among consumers. This notion of "branding" is an attempt to give a brand a distinctive set of characteristics that will separate it from the competition. Often this means that the advertising must focus on more than just the functional virtues of the product but rather must create a product storyline. These value-expressive ads focus on more than merely utilitarian needs and instead attempt to connect to viewers on a deeper level. Branding allows a company to bond with a consumer in a way that goes beyond functionality and attempts to fill cultural, physiological, or psychological needs. Some scholars like Margaret Mark and Carol Pearson claim that good branding uses archetypal themes and creates narratives that tap into a shared culture (Mark and Pearson 3–6). The creators of ads don't usually attempt to be artistic in their efforts to create powerful brands and persuade consumers, but often ads become art inherently. Although advertising by its very nature is functional, it also often needs to be artistic to survive and be effective.

Culture

It is important to note that this study does not focus broadly on all advertising but specifically studies international advertising. Though this distinction may seem minor, it is significant because one of the most important elements in international advertising is the focus on both local and international cultural issues. Unlike many types of local or national advertising, international advertisers must preserve the often-delicate balance between a product's international brand recognition and the needs and values of a local culture. This means international advertising is inherently both local and global. While many would assume that international advertising is merely a different version of local advertising, it is often an amalgamation of different cultures and values. This has led many advertisers to conclude that because each culture has its own unique signs, symbols, and mythologies, campaigns should focus not only on the product but how it fits into the local environment. Advertising scholar Marieke de Mooij reinforces this point in her monograph, *Global Marketing and Advertising: Understanding Cultural Paradoxes*, writing first that "cultural values determine the way people think or their intellectual styles" (61), and then adding, "Understanding the concept of cultural and the consequences of cultural differences will make marketing and advertising people realize that one message, whether verbal or visual, can never reach one global audience, because there is not one global culture comprised of people with identical values" (61). This idea of cultural differences and cultural blending are at the heart of this study. Because companies and ad agencies work to appeal to the local consumer of American products, the narratives that are created display not only standard Polish cultural understandings but also the constant redefining of Polishness that occurs as society adjusts to outside influences. Polishness has historically been created by a number of factors both internal and external. Since Polish culture is not static, but is in a perpetual state of flux, advertisers' understanding of Poland must change as the society does. Ironically, international advertising and the products that it promotes may be one of the outside influences that are creating change within the culture.

Globalization, International, and Transnationalism

One of the most difficult problems when studying global culture is defining key terms. Because concepts like globalization and transnationalism have been both widely researched and written about there are countless differing definitions. As thousands of authors produce varying definitions that meet their research objectives and interests, it becomes difficult to understand the core concepts because so many nuanced perspectives survive. "Globalization" is possibly the most confusing of these terms, due to the sheer amount of notice given to the concept in academia, the mass media, and popular culture. Since globalization can be viewed from seemingly infinite perspectives, it is important when discussing it to provide both clarity and context. In this study I view globalization from a cultural perspective and see the term as defining a process in which a culture that is produced in one society is purposely transported to another by a state, corporation, organization, or agency. This broad definition intentionally only defines the process and says little about the many moral and ethical debates that surround globalization. Here it is stripped down to its most basic elements so that the study can focus on the advertising narratives in Poland. I also view transnationalism from a cultural perspective and use the term "transnationalism" to mean a social movement that loosens national boundaries and encourages cultural mobility. Globalization is a process that is generally due to efforts of organized corporate or organizational entities, while transnationalism describes how individuals and groups of people create grassroots social changes that transcend national borders. Additionally, the terms "international" and "global," when used in this book, describe a concept or entity that exists simultaneously in several nations or societies. McDonald's is an international or global company because it has restaurants in many different societies and nations. I understand that some will disagree with my definitions and others will find them lacking a certain perspective or emphasis. It would be impossible to please every reader with these definitions, so I have striven to find definitions that are both understandable and helpful without being overly dogmatic.

Country of Origin Effect

While marketing to local cultural standards and tastes is of great importance to many companies, international advertising also attempts to capitalize on widely held positive opinions about the producing nation. Internationally, some countries have acquired a reputation as being manufacturers of high-quality goods and additionally certain countries are associated with specific types of products or services. For example, the United States has credibility as a maker of blue jeans, Japan of electronics, and France of perfume. These same products produced in other countries or other products produced by the example countries may not have the same cachet. This is because a country is often associated with certain symbols and mythologies that frequently translate into an inherent marketing advantage for specific products internationally. Barbara Mueller labels this link between country and product "country of origin effect." She claims that "some countries have particularly positive associations with specific product categories." (31). These associations can lead to marketing ideas and advertising campaigns that capitalize on existing public perceptions. In Poland, American companies like Coca-Cola, Levi's, and McDonald's are closely associated with the United States and the many positive attributes of the country. This public understanding of the product and its country of origin produces free advertising and can create goodwill but it also can be limiting if the advertiser is not careful to create local impressions to coexist with those of the producing country. This means that American companies have to craft campaigns that speak of their products' American origins while simultaneously embracing the local culture. The positive qualities of the country-of-origin effect often must be measured and then blunted or amplified in advertising and marketing, depending on the implications. In Poland, McDonald's never attempted to mask its Americanness, but in several early advertising campaigns the company did try to present itself as changing to meet Polish cultural standards. McDonald's advertised itself as an American company that had immigrated to Poland and wished to respect the local culture. This provided a way for the fast-food giant to retain positive country-of-origin associations, while also conforming to Poland's culture. It also allowed McDonald's to determine what kind of advertising worked best in the Polish market. By contrast, when Levi's began advertising in Poland in the nineties, it more fully embraced its American heritage. The clothing maker capitalized on existing Polish/European mythologies linked to Levi's blue jeans. By understanding existing ideas and crafting advertising around these preexisting notions, Levi's was able to use the country-of-origin effect to its advantage. While this is sometimes possible, international advertising often involves a blending of both the local and producing country's cultures.

Finding Meaning in Advertising

If one accepts that the primary goal of advertising is to sell goods and services, and in order to accomplish this task international advertising uses themes, ideas, symbols, and mythologies from both producing and buying cultures, then one must ask how advertisers know that consumers are receiving the desired meaning. Furthermore, what meanings are created by consumers who view the ads? These questions are especially significant to acknowledge because they seek to determine why certain types of narratives are produced and how they are received. It is important to again state that the purpose of this text is not to research the process of creating ads, ad campaigns' backgrounds, or any steps in the decision-making process that led to the formation of the ads within this study. Likewise, very little audience-response data has been collected or researched in order to determine how consumers reacted to or interpreted the ads. Rather, this study attempts to read the selected ads as narratives that can be linked to cultural factors within both Poland and the United States.

Although this monograph does not examine the process of creating ads, and neither does it track their reception, it is important to understand how meaning in advertising is produced. Advertising scholar Grant McCracken notes that although companies work closely with advertisers to produce a text, the real meaning is provided by the viewer/reader. McCracken sees ad readers as the final directors who determine the ad text's true meaning (75–76). Katherine Toland Frith claims that meaning in advertisements exists at multiple levels and that one of the most important factors in understanding an ad is the cultural background and knowledge of the viewer/reader. Without the consumer provided cultural context advertisements would lose much of their meaning and they would be superficial (4–7). This means that one cannot understand an advertisement without understanding something about the viewer/reader's culture. This study conforms to this understanding of the meaning of advertising by attempting to place American ads in Poland within a Polish cultural context. Narratives of ads are viewed for cultural connections to Poland and are placed within the context of the society during the time period in which they were created. Furthermore, it is assumed that the ads' consumers have agency to interpret and create meanings that are both intended and unintended by the ads' creators. It is also assumed that by placing an ad within a Polish cultural context many meanings, both intended and unintended, will become clear. While no one is ever able to understand every meaning created by an advertisement in relation to its viewers/readers, the ones that are readily identifiable are assumed to be the most prominent and widely understood.

Polish Culture and History

In order to comprehend the cultural context of American advertising in Poland one must understand several important elements of Polish history and tradition. A rudimentary understanding of Poland's past is essential to understanding the nation's present. Additionally, it is valuable to appreciate historical ties between Poland and the United States and how these common bonds themselves manifest in the present. The widely recognized founding of Poland occurred in 966 and the country became a kingdom in 1025. Many Poles would argue that the Battle of Grunwald in 1410, in which the Poles defeated the Teutonic Knights, was a turning point that influenced subsequent Polish identity. Although of questionable historical importance, this battle became a rallying cry for Polish nationalism and is seen by many Poles as the start of a golden age. Of greater historical significance was the Polish-Lithuanian Commonwealth (1569–1795), an age of Polish expansion and importance. During this period Poland became a regional power, gained territory and authority, and then slowly declined. It is important to note the national pride and feeling of accomplishment that Poles still carry from this period. Outsiders often forget that Poland was once a large, powerful nation but Poles do not. Almost all Poles still remember the accomplishments of this era and recall Poland's former glory and greatness. The national poet Adam Mickiewicz, who was born in Belarus, refers to this period in what is perhaps his most famous poem, "Pan Tadeusz," writing, "*Litwo Ojczyzno moja, ty jesteś jak zdrowie.*" ("Lithuania, my motherland. You are like health.") Because Poland and Lithuania were once joined in commonwealth, the two names were used interchangeably and the idea of nationality was still less defined than today. At that time Poland was a large, thriving state, an idea that still resides in the minds of many Poles.

Romanticism in Poland

After years of political and territorial struggles Poland ceased to exist as a political entity in 1795. The Polish state finally succumbed to its stronger neighbors, Russia, Prussia, and Austria, and it was erased from the map. But Poland survived as a nation, and nationalism began to develop and grow across Europe during the early nineteenth century, the stateless Poles began to glorify their past and to stress the value of their homeland and culture. Polish language and culture became rallying points and Poles began to view themselves as a unique people who ought to fight the process of assimilation. Partially because Poland was a landless entity, a new Polish identity began to form. Many in Poland began to embrace the concept of romanticism, a late-eighteenth and early–nineteenth-century movement that emphasized the beauty of nature, the role of the individual, a break from classical ideas, a rebellion against many of society's rules, and an emphasis on nationalism. Romanticism differs from rationalism in that the romantics emphasize the expression of emotion and national culture whereas practitioners of rationalism attempted to avoid such things. Romanticism in Poland and other places was mostly expressed via the arts. The quintessential Polish romantic literary beacon of the nineteenth century is undoubtedly the aforementioned Adam Mickiewicz whose verse has challenged and inspired Polish nationalists for over a century and a half. National figures like Frederic Chopin and Marie Curie inspire Poles to value their culture and ways of life. Interestingly, one of the apparent negative aspects of Polish history, the constant tragic outcome of wars and political uprisings, served as point of pride for many romantics. Some religious-minded Poles saw the nation's misfortune as a sign that it was the Christ figure of nations and believed its suffering would lead to better things in the long run. Romanticism was a strong force connected with nationalism and it spurred many Poles toward a vision of a politically recognized Polish state. Cultural nationalism opposes the idea of civil nationalism where the nation is characterized by the political legitimacy of the state. In emphasizing romantic nationalism, Poles were declaring the nation to be a cultural entity not a civil/political one. This is an important distinction that would continue to be important in Poland.

Polish Nationalist Insurrections and Organic Work

During the early years of the nineteenth century, Polish nationalists pressed for immediate action in gaining an independent Polish state. These Polish radicals often operated within secret societies inside Russian Poland and over time their agitation led to numerous revolts. The most noteworthy of these uprisings were the November Revolt of 1830, the Krakow Revolution of 1846 and the January Uprising of 1863. None of these revolts produced a Polish state and ultimately each worsened social conditions. Though unsuccessful, they helped create the idea of Polishness, something that flourished. The blood of martyrs often waters a people's nationalism even if the dead patriots' deeds are of little immediate worth. As with most nations, Poland's nationalist tendencies were not only displayed by uprisings but also revealed in less dramatic ways. Following the revolts of the early and mid–nineteenth century, many Poles began to call for a seemingly more constructive method of acquiring a state, a process sometimes known as organic work. The general idea of organic work was to better Polish society through economic development, education, and modernization. Although authors like Stanislaus Blejwas claim that organic work has been a traditional part of Polish ideology since before the partitioning, most historians believe that it is mainly an idea that took hold after the repeated failures of the uprisings. This ideological dichotomy created interesting debates and theories about what was best for Polish culture. These theoretical inquiries were secondary, though, to the understanding that a Polish nation existed and that Polish culture contained many different philosophies and understandings.

The Polish dream of a state continued throughout the nineteenth and into the early years of the twentieth century. As organic work modernized the nation by promoting education and emphasizing the need for commercial viability and a strong infrastructure, the Poles continued to hope and wait. Finally, the social, economic, and political carnage that followed World War I created an opportunity to form a Polish state. This new Poland, created after the First World War as part of the Treaty of Versailles, lasted only during the interwar period, but it was the child of Poles who would not let their culture die. Notice the similarities between Polish nationalism and the American version of the same idea. Throughout the eighteenth and nineteenth centuries, much like many other European countries, Poland was creating a modern nation. In the United States the effort was much the same. The difference was that American nationalism was used to strengthen the state while the Polish variety was attempting to create one. While Poles rose up against the empires that they were divided among, the Americans fought wars to safeguard their nation and to gain territory and fortify it. The same sense of nationalism was at work, but it was adapted to the local need. This sense of common goals and understandings would be a recurring theme for generations and would play a large part in the future relations of the two nations.

World War II and the Cold War, 1939–89

The Polish state created in the aftermath of the Great War ceased to exist in 1939 when the country was invaded and overtaken by Nazi Germany, an action that marked the start of World War II. Although the Polish underground continued to fight against its German occupiers, the Nazi occupation did not end until the Russian Red Army took control of Poland in 1944. After the Second World War ended, a new Polish state was created under Soviet influence. This socialist Poland, known as the People's Republic of Poland, remained under Soviet oversight for over fifty years until the collapse of the government in 1989. Arguably, the two most important events from this period are the steadfast existence of Polish nationalism and the founding of the Solidarity labor union. While Poles were faced with many dark days during the socialist era, including a prolonged period of martial law, most stuck firmly to their traditions and values instead of shedding them as many of the authorities wished. Perhaps the Solidarity movement best exemplifies this idea of common Poles clinging to historical traditions and values. The labor union, created by shipyard workers in search of fair working and societal conditions, grew into an opposition political party that challenged the authority of the socialist government. Many historians claim that the foundation of Solidarity marked not only the beginning of the end of the socialist government in Poland but in all of Europe. One cannot over emphasize the importance of Solidarity and its symbiotic relationship with Polish culture and tradition. These traditions and cultural influences will later become apparent in many of the American ads in the post-socialist era.

Post-Socialism 1989–Present

In 1989–90, Poland's socialist government was replaced, the Communist Party was disbanded, and the country's constitution was rewritten. The Cold War ended and former socialist states like Poland had to quickly adjust to new social, economic, and political situations. In Poland these transitional years were marked by benefits and missteps. The country continued to embrace its traditional culture while welcoming new ideas and cultures like those of the United States. This period is hard to define because it is yet ongoing. What is certain is that post-socialist Poland has taken a middle path, being both nationalistic and yet also internationally focused. Poland's international political outlook can be seen in its becoming a member of the North Atlantic Treaty Organization (NATO) in 1999 and the European Union (EU) in 2004. These two organizations encourage international cooperation and the strengthening of transnational ties. Additionally, Poland has attempted to become a leader in Central and Eastern Europe. The best example of this is Poland's involvement in the Ukrainian Orange Revolution. During this upheaval the Polish government encouraged revolutionary forces and served as a bridge between Eastern and Western Europe. These political affiliations, combined with international economic and social ties, have created a new understanding within Poland of the country's place in the world. This expansion of Poland's international role is often sharply contrasted with the country's increased sense of nationalism. Recent years have witnessed the national election of the conservative Law and Justice Party (*Prawo i Sprawiedliwość*) and the outspoken desire by many to protect Poland's traditions from cultural invaders. In fact, the country's public vote for inclusion in the European Union was far from certain and many Poles can still be heard grumbling about the loss of Poland's heritage. This constant struggle between the forces of nationalism and internationalism appears to be one of the core elements of the new Poland and is one of the major themes that will be addressed in this study.

Social Ties Between the United States and Poland

Another important theme in this study is the relationship between the United States and Poland, two countries with a long history of political, cultural, and social ties. This relationship has produced numerous connections many of which persist. One of the most important is that the United States and its culture are often viewed by Poles as inspirational. Common ties that encourage exchange began with the first Polish immigrants coming to America in 1608 and settling in the Jamestown colony. Later, two famous Poles, Kazimierz Pułaski and Tadeusz Kościuszko, fought in the American Revolution and their efforts are still remembered in their homeland and in the United States. Both countries had early forms of democratic governments and the first two modern codified national constitutions. One of the most important historical factors in Polish-American relations is immigration. Poles have emigrated to America throughout Poland's history, but the largest movement happened in the late nineteenth and early twentieth centuries. It is estimated that more than 1.5 million Poles entered the United States from 1890 to 1930 (Davies, *God's Playground* 279). A sizable percentage of the Poles that came to America returned to Poland, either by design or necessity. This, combined with correspondence between immigrants and their families remaining in Poland, meant that many Poles developed a distinct impression of the United States. Letters between immigrants and families collected in William Thomas and Florian Znanecki's *The Polish Peasant in Europe and America* reveal that by the early twentieth century many Poles already viewed the United States as a vibrant place that offered both opportunity and inspiration. Numerous Polish writers expressed the desire to come to the United States in order to make money and potentially have a better lifestyle. Often writers would exchange information about America's living conditions (404), foreign policy (1094) and even its popular culture, such as the Buffalo Bill Wild West shows (1005). Even the Poles who wrote negatively about the country revealed in their protest that they were attempting to correct commonly held misunderstandings about how exceptional the United States was. In a letter written in the first decade of the twentieth century Jozef Dabrowski writes to his family, "Many people in our country think that in America everybody has much pleasure" (746). Although Dabrowski disagrees, he understands that many in Poland view life in the United States and American culture as something to aspire to. The United States was and is a model for what Poles can achieve and a symbol of what can be gained. Much time has passed between Dabrowski's letter and present-day Poland but the idea of the United States as role model survives in Polish life.

The idea of the United States as Poland's role model is an important element in understanding the U.S. position in Poland. The United States has welcomed immigrants from many European countries but the people of many of these countries do not appear to have overly positive feelings toward the United States. While France and Germany have long-standing historical ties to the United States, their people often do not seem to have a favorable opinion of the United States. Other factors too combine with the symbolic role of the United States to shape the nation's image in the Polish mind. When looking for commonalities between Polish and American history and culture the concept of romanticism comes to the fore. Both countries have long traditions of romantic nationalism that have displayed themselves in various ways during their respective histories. While American romantic nationalism has tended to manifest itself as an ideology in a stable country, the Polish version has had to adjust to the political culture of an often stateless or oppressed people. This has led to different forums and outlets of expression for each culture but a basic, deep-seated nationalistic romanticism is shared.

Polish-American Relations

The late nineteenth and early twentieth centuries saw the beginning of many shared experiences for the American and Polish people. As previously mentioned, one of the most obvious ways in which Polish-American relations were forged is with the arrival of a large wave of Polish immigrants to the United States. It is estimated that currently around 15 million people of Polish origin live outside of Poland and that 6.5 million of those live in the United States (Davies, *God's Playground* 279). Many of the Poles who emigrated did so in the late nineteenth and early twentieth centuries during the "New Wave" of immigration to the United States. Although most Poles emigrated to the United States for economic reasons, an unintended effect was the linking of the two nations. By the start of World War I almost every native of Poland knew someone living in the United States. Conversely, many Americans had also become acquainted with immigrants from Poland and in some cities and states Poles gained a degree of political power because of their large numbers. In places like New York and Chicago hundreds of thousands of Poles settled and became liaisons between Poland and the United States. Immigration strengthened the ties between the two nations and created citizens with common interests and understanding. The new American Polonia created a bridge between the two cultures and the aftermath of World War I served to strengthen the role the United States played in the Polish psyche, a precursor to present-day positive attitudes.

Wilson and Polish Nationhood

In the minds of many historians, one the first major events in twentieth-century Polish-American relations was President Woodrow Wilson's famous January 1918 fourteen-point peace plan for reorganizing postwar Europe. Point number thirteen specifically addressed Poland: "An independent Polish state should be erected which should include the territories inhabited by indisputably Polish populations, which should be assured a free and secure access to the sea, and whose political and economic independence and territorial integrity should be guaranteed by international covenant" (President Woodrow Wilson's "Fourteen Points").

Although the Versailles peace treaty was a political compromise between a number of countries, it is often Wilson's name that is linked with the creation of Poland, especially within Poland itself. It is difficult to exaggerate how much the creation of a new Polish state meant to the Polish people. The new state was the culmination of years of Polish efforts, but it is an American president who is often associated with the event, a historical note still well remembered by many in Poland.

Hoover and Interwar Europe

With Wilson's help a new Polish state was created, yet things were far from idyllic for the Poles. Some historians have noted the severe disadvantages that Poland faced during this era of the Second Republic. Surrounded by hostile forces, unsure of its territorial boundaries, having suffered massive infrastructure damage, its economy in shambles, Poland was in a precarious situation. It needed outside assistance to structure a workable political and economic system and to avoid entanglements with other European powers. Unfortunately, this political aid was not forthcoming and Poland was transformed into a virtual dictatorship. The United States, having succumbed to its own isolationist tendencies, often offered token political help like peace-treaty negotiations and economic planning but the American administration was striving only for order and stability within the region. The United States did offer economic aid, and the man who is most associated with this is Herbert Hoover. Although most present-day Americans would identify Hoover as the president during the start of the Great Depression, he had a long and distinguished career before he became the leader of the United States. Before the end of World War I Hoover was distributing aid to Poles as the head of the American Relief Administration and he continued the job after the war, as he led the Relief for the Allied and Associated Powers agency of the U.S. government. In this role Hoover is credited with saving the lives of hundreds of thousands of Polish children. Hoover became so renowned in Poland that a square and a monument were built in his honor in Warsaw. Hoover's place in Polish history provides an interesting connection between the two countries and part of a possible historical explanation for present-day American popularity in Poland.

Cold War

By the time World War II began, Poland already had established strong ties with the United States for reasons that have been previously noted. Wilson and Hoover had already become heroes in Polish minds when the next era of Polish-American relations began. It appears that a large percentage of the Polish populace continued to respect and admire the United States. Piotr Wandycz claims that when John F. Kennedy was assassinated thousands of Poles lined up at the embassy to sign a sympathy book and that when Robert Kennedy visited Poland in 1964 he met crowds of admirers (Wandycz 377–8). Although some contend that the United States ignored Poland or did not engage in a helpful foreign policy, maybe their complaint was not what the U.S. did or did not do so much as what it was. As noted before, the United States has often served as a social, political, and economic model for Poland. Additionally, during this period the United States was the enemy of the Soviet Union, which was thought of as the enemy by many Poles. Possibly, Poland's enemy's enemy was its friend.

In 1980 Poland was still dominated politically and economically by the Soviet Union and cut off from most of the non-communist world. The United States had very little contact with Poland as the Cold War began to enter into its final stages. Undoubtedly, the most important event of this era, and possibly the entire Cold War, was the rise of the Polish trade union Solidarity. This Gdansk-based workers' union rose to prominence by battling the communist government for political, social, and economic rights. Solidarity was an interesting combination of the radicalism of romanticism and the practical aspects of organic work that pressed for action but also tried to make infrastructural changes. Many historical commentators claim that the Soviet empire began to fall when Solidarity gained unprecedented concessions and the U.S.S.R. did little to combat it. Although the United States had little direct impact on the events concerning Solidarity, it did maintain a symbolic political presence. As always, it was the "other way" that stood opposed to the Soviet-controlled system. Because of the lack of direct involvement it is difficult to confirm what role the United States played in Polish life. It is known, though, that during and after the Solidarity uprisings the United States increased its propaganda about Poland. For decades the United States had been using tactics like the Voice of America radio broadcasts to send its message into Eastern Europe but now Poland became the center of the U.S. anticommunist strategy and dominated White House press briefings and Sunday morning talk shows. These factors may have served to increase awareness about Poland within the United States and to lend credibility to the Polonia that pressed for change in the "old country."

Post–Cold War, 1990–2007

New York Times columnist Thomas Friedman wrote a column in December 2003 in which he claimed that Poland was one of the few places left in the world that Americans were still well liked. Friedman asserted that Poland's geographical position, sandwiched between Germany and Russia, and its long memory of a violent history had pulled Poland toward the United States. He also quoted young Poles who stated that they liked the United States because as a world power it could help them politically and economically but also because of some intangible quality that the United States possessed (Friedman). This unknown factor was quite likely made up of more than one element but one can speculate that it at least partially entailed the symbolic role of the United States in Polish life. The U.S. role as a model for many Poles is important both historically and in explaining current Polish–U.S. relations, which continue to grow and change. In recent years Poland has participated militarily in the U.S.–led invasion of Iraq, been accused of providing the United States with secret prisons on Polish soil, engaged in talks about becoming a part of a U.S. designed and financed missile shield in Europe, and been a defender of American foreign policy. After the Cold War thaw, the United States and other countries began sending business and social advisors to Poland to increase cultural connections and promote economic opportunities. These efforts morphed into various programs and partnerships and helped to further strengthen the ties between the two countries. In many ways the story of the post–Cold War Polish-American relationship is one of respecting the past and exploring the future. Poles remember their country's historical ties with the United States and seem to wish to continue this special relationship. For its part, the United States is becoming ever more reliant on Poland to act as its ally in European matters and seems to value Poland as more of a peer than in the past. This can be seen as an expansion of the Polish-American relationship. While in the past the Americans seemed to be the dominant party, the new order appears to be one of increasing equality and mutual need. No one knows how long this relationship will continue or what parts of it will change, but for the time being the Polish-American partnership seems secure. This relationship and its history are an important part of this study of American advertising in Poland. It speaks to a cultural and social connection that is the framework for the exchange of ideas, symbols, and mythologies that characterize the narratives used in this study.

Summary

The subject of American advertising narratives in post–Cold War Poland is one that crosses national, social, and cultural borders. It also refuses to adhere to traditional academic partitioning and instead requires one to think interdisciplinarily by mixing the fields of advertising, history, and popular culture. Ideas and methods from all three of these disciplines are rarely combined, but doing so results in new ways of looking at traditional topics. Many studies have been written about international advertising, advertising as popular culture, transnationalism, and Polish-American relations. This study is different because it combines the theories and ideas of the three disciplines in an attempt to understand the early post–Cold War relationship between American advertisers and Polish consumers. An understanding of this relationship not only provides an appreciation of the situation within Poland but also allows one to view other perspectives on such issues as culture, nationalism, tradition, international sharing, and the constant changes that occur within societies. This work studies these issues by analyzing narratives within advertising produced by American companies for the Polish market in the period from 1990 to 2007. These advertising narratives offer clues about the complex international relationships between different cultures and help to explain how cultures interact and change. By exploring the intersection between American and Polish cultural symbols and mythologies in Poland one can see the fluid and ever-changing nature of national cultures. This not only sheds light on the Polish-American cultural relationship but also potentially onto other interactions between multiple cultures. In an ever-more-interactive and globalized world it is important that we begin to reconsider our views of culture and society.

1

In the Beginning:
Socialist-Era Advertising

An often-told Polish anecdote begins, "Do you know the difference between Americans and Poles?" The storyteller explains, "If an American's neighbor gets a better car than him then the first man prays to God, 'Please give me a nicer car than my neighbor's.' If a Pole's neighbor buys a fancy car, the Pole prays to God, 'Please destroy my neighbor's new car.'" This joke not only showcases some of the perceived differences between Poles and Americans but also provides insight into how some Poles identify themselves. As noted previously, Poland has a long and troubled history that has lead to feelings of both pride and bitterness among many of its citizens. Poland's history is one of the elements that makes the nation unique and some of this history must be interpreted in order to understand the present. The purpose of this chapter is to serve as a prelude to a study of post–socialist-era advertising for American products in Poland by providing an overview of several advertising themes during the Cold War period. Although many of these themes and ideas boast a genesis before the socialist era, this chapter will concentrate on Cold War–period advertising, both because of difficulties in finding standardized pre–World War II Polish advertising and with the understanding that socialist advertising often directly affected its artistic descendents. Attempting to discuss a subject so broad in a few pages is undoubtedly a fool's errand, which is why this chapter should not be read as an in-depth examination of Poland's socialist-era advertising, but rather as a brief assessment of several early advertising themes that have continued in Poland right up to the present. Because product advertising during this period was heavily censored, rarely creative, and often utilitarian, print advertisements designed by artists to sell socialist ideas and American films will be examined. These ads not only display many pertinent ongoing themes but also show earlier stages of the Polish interpretation of several American myths and symbols. In order to understand the product advertising that was produced from 1990 to 2007 one must comprehend the historical traditions that led to its composition. These print ads provide an opportunity to examine a small segment of Cold War Poland and help to define the ideas, myths, and symbols that become prominent in later advertising.

Socialist-Era Advertising — An Overview

Socialist advertising differs from its capitalist counterpart in several ways; chief among them is an understanding that exists about how advertising is to be conducted. Although there are many different views of advertising's role in a free-market society, most would agree that capitalistic advertising is generally a marketing tool that promotes goods or services in order to increase sales, profit or participation. In general, the average person views capitalistic advertising as a way for a company, corporation, individual, or group to sell a product. The role of the advertiser is vastly different in a socialist system where almost all advertising is coordinated by the government or an advising council. According to the Marxist-Leninist tradition, western advertising is wasteful and unnecessary, and helps to exploit the working class, so advertising must be approved by an official government body. Because a socialistic government agency is in control, the advertising decisions are not based on economic needs but instead political or ideological ones. In Poland, the Advertising Planning Council (APC) handled domestic advertising while Agpol oversaw ads connected with foreign trade. These agencies coordinated with local groups and organizations to determine what would be advertised, how it would be advertised, and what the budget would be. In this system there was little marketing research, most of the decisions came from government agencies or councils, and there appears to have been almost no campaign planning or strategic vision (Hanson 107–112). Additionally, very little product advertising was produced in Poland and most advertising was in the form of posters, billboards, or other exhibitions (Hanson 131–33). It is nearly impossible to comment on product advertising narratives from the socialist era because so little was produced, campaigns were virtually nonexistent, and storytelling was discouraged by the overseeing agencies. A relatively small amount of Polish product advertising was produced and most of it was seemingly generic and not a part of any running idea or campaign. Even in 1995, over five years after the collapse of the socialist system, Michael Muth, the managing director of German American Trade Associates, an international trade association, wrote that from his personal experience advising and training executives in Poland, Polish advertising was still very rough and many businesses did not understand the basics of advertising and marketing (Muth 2). Muth's account shows how many in Poland understand advertising differently than those in capitalist countries. These differences often stemmed from the previous socialistic system's role in advertising, and its various rules and agendas.

Polish product advertisement during the socialist era may have been strongly controlled, heavily censored, underutilized, and often utilitarian but at least one type that displayed high-level artistry and narrative was that of political and film posters. The idea of artistic posters in Poland probably dates back to the *Młoda Polska* (Young Poland) artistic movement of the turn of the twentieth century. Although originally used for artistic means, these types of posters were also soon utilized by both governmental and marketing forces (Boczar 16–21). The political posters were often used to promote governmental ideas or societal restructuring, and show a high level of organization and planning. These posters most resemble the western idea of an advertising campaign in their tone and coordination. They also utilized common themes and narratives in much the same way that product advertising does in later years. The film posters are Polish artists' interpretations of the themes within American movies, most notably westerns, which were very popular in Polish society. These posters represent one of the few forms of advertising that was not overly censored and that allowed the artist to show a Polish understanding of American myths and symbols. Both the political and film posters are excellent guides to understanding the styles, themes, and symbols of socialist advertising that would become even more apparent in later years. These ads display the proto-product advertising that would change into new advertising narratives after 1989.

Polish Nationalism

Political poster advertising has a long history in Poland, as it does in many countries. Posters were created at various times during the nation's past to encourage public support for political, social, or military objectives. Because of Poland's history of political instability and its often undesirable relationships with its neighbors, the nation developed a unique understanding of symbolism, advertising, and propaganda. Partially because Poland ceased to exist as a country from the end of the eighteenth century until after World War I, the nation became defined primarily by myth and symbol. Poles created anthems and poems about how the nation would never die and struggled to craft mythic and symbolic touchstones that would define a stateless nation. This creation of a mythic nation, that has been labeled an "imagined community" by Benedict Anderson (15–16) and referred to as the "invention of tradition" by Eric Hobsbawm (17–19), continued during the interwar years, as Poland regained statehood, and into the socialist era. Since Poles struggled to preserve their ethnic identity for many years, Polish society developed a strong sense of nationalism and a desire to protect its "Polishness." This yearning for a continuing Polish society is by far the most important theme in socialist-era Polish advertising. Although most nations can claim a certain level of nationalism, tradition, and cultural identity, Poland is unique because the nation's identity was shaped and strengthened by centuries of loss and brutality. Polish identity was formed by the struggle to exist and this battle to remain Polish continued to be the central theme of socialist-era advertising. In many ways advertisers, like the government and political organizations, used existing cultural ideas to market new concepts and ideas. Polish cultural nationalism defines advertising of this period just as it defines the nation.

Government and Communist Party Promotion

While Polish nationalism is the dominant theme in socialist advertising, it is presented in various ways by utilizing a number of sub-themes. One of these themes that is often coupled with the theme of nationalism is that of governmental and Communist Party promotion. At first glance, the idea of the government and party advertising sounds bland, uninspired, and unnecessary but in reality this promotion displays much about Polish society and Polish national identity. The Communist Party produced many posters that advertised its role in Polish society and its link to the nation's values and history. This declaration of Polishness in advertising would later be used by international companies like McDonald's and Coca-Cola as a tool to employ Polish nationalism in its promotions. The Communist Party, like later multinational corporations, declared the value of Polish identity and emphasized its place in Polish society. The party presented itself not as an outsider or as a new entity but rather as a product of Polish history and a valued member of the society. This theme of inclusive Polishness matched the doctrine that the party was the voice of the people and the representative of the state and nation. It is noteworthy that the Communist Party did not use ads to display its dominance in Polish society, but rather to show itself as a servant of Poland. The party was careful to market itself as a strong and powerful entity that bowed to the needs of Polish citizens. By declaring the Communist Party an integral part of the Polish nation, the advertising used Polish nationalism and history to promote an organization, a tactic that would also be used by advertisers in the post-socialist years.

The use of nationalism to promote the Communist Party is showcased in many posters during the socialist era. Several of these present striking images that strongly display the theme of nationalism. An excellent example is a poster created in 1974 by Karol Sliwka that shows a montage of photographs incorporated inside an outline of an eagle, the symbol of Poland, on a red background with white lettering. The images showcase Polish workers and industry and a caption in Polish reads, "The Polish Republic — the joint result of the work of our hearts, brains and hands" (Sliwka). The ad uses the ancient symbol of Poland, the eagle, and places all of the citizens, labor, and industry within it. The red and white used for the background and lettering are the national colors of Poland and the colors of the Polish flag. The poster is clearly linking the socialist Poland of 1974 to the mythic historical Poland of lore and changing the symbols for the benefit of the advertiser. In the ad everything in Poland exists within the symbol of the eagle. Land, commerce, politics, industry, and people are all included inside this historic symbol of Poland. This image connects the modern government to the values of the nation and portrays the Polishness of the leadership. The caption reminds the people that they are Polish and that they alone build the society and make it function. The socialist government is using historically important Polish symbols to declare that the nation exists because of the will of the people and that the people must aid the government. This advertisement is striking because it used historical Polish symbolism to create a modern connection between Polish society and its then current government. The symbols were altered to fit the government's vision of the modern Poland. This theme of using nationalism as promotion would be used many times by the government and later in product advertising.

In his monograph *The Power of Symbols Against the Symbols of Power*, Jan Kubik writes extensively about the Polish socialist government's attempts to revise and utilize historic Polish symbols to promote itself. While Kubik claims that this advertising did not always change public opinion, he demonstrates that the government knowingly created an advertising and marketing campaign to promote its Polishness and to change the meanings of many of the symbols (Kubik 36–41). Another advertisement that displays this theme of the government co-opting national symbols is a 1972 poster by Hubert Hilscher. The red-and-white ad shows a white eagle inside of a large heart seemingly cut from construction paper in a childlike manner. The caption reads, "There is nothing more precious than People's Poland" (Hilscher). Like the previous ad, this one shows a symbol of Poland (again the eagle) and a caption about the government's affection for the Polish people. As with the former ad, this one uses Polish nationalism and historical identity to promote and validate the socialist government. Furthermore the image is presented in a childlike manner that suggests a parental bond between Poles and the state. The creators of the poster understand the symbolic value of the image of the eagle within the nation. Much the same as Kubik, Hilscher says that the leadership of Poland exploited cultural symbolism in order to market itself as worthy. This is but one of many instances in which this occurs in Polish advertising in both socialist and capitalist Poland.

Coupled with advertising posters to promote the socialist government of Poland were ads that marketed the Communist Party. Since during most of the socialist era the communists controlled the only legal party in Poland and all governmental leaders were members, the government and the party were almost a single entity. In general, advertising for the national leadership was advertising for the party and vice versa. This interconnectivity meant that many of the posters advertising the Polish communists were very similar to the ads for the government. A good example of a Communist Party ad that associates itself with Polish nationalism is a poster created by Jarosław Jasiński in 1978. This ad features the massive red and white letters "PZPR" in the foreground and behind the smaller and faded letters "KPP" (Jasiński). The large letters "PZPR" refer to the *Polska Zjednoczona Partia Robotnicza,* the Polish United Workers' Party. The KPP is the *Komunistyczna Partia Polski,* the former Communist Party of Poland that later became the PZPR. By presenting itself as the larger image in the poster, using the bright red and white colors of Poland, and appearing in the front, the PZPR is identifying itself as the current embodiment of Polish politics and nationalism. By contrast, the KPP is relegated to the back of the ad, half hidden by the lettering of the newer party. The KPP also has faded coloring, which appears to have once been red and white before but no longer holds the vibrancy that it did. Additionally, the PZPR is lettered in thick substantial letters that resemble sculptures made of granite, while the KPP had thin elongated letters that seem slight and unimpressive by comparison. This ad markets the strength and vibrancy of the new offical party and shows its superiority over its predecessor. It also shows the PZPR as the political party of inclusion that united three different parties into one organization that represents all of Poland. The simplicity of the ad exhibits the importance of symbolism in Polish culture and society, as it is in most societies. No captions or taglines are used and no names, dates, or historical references are provided. All that is displayed are seven letters and a variety of colors and the viewer is forced to interpret meaning based on his or her understanding of the societal context. The sturdy and vibrant red-and-white "PZPR" evokes not only strength but also Polish nationalism and history. Poles are reminded that this party stands for the nation and has been formed out of lesser parties that were not as a capable as the PZPR. The red and white colors in the ad are of great importance: they are the colors of the Polish flag and often of Polish resistance. The party reminds the viewer of the failures of the past and then emphasizes the desirability of the current ruling party. Without using words of any kind, the ad invokes Polish nationalism, referencing a shared history and using understood symbolism to promote its Polishness merely through the use of the Polish national colors. This ad conveying the message that the party is a historical representative of Poland uses many themes and techniques that will later become prominent in product marketing.

Anticapitalist, Anti-western Advertising

While much of socialist-era advertising promoted the Polishness of the government and the Communist Party, there were also many other themes that were widely marketed during this period. One such theme that received much attention was the attempt to display via ads the weakness of capitalist nations, generally focusing on the United States. These ads portray a Cold War mindset in which the United States is seen by many socialist leaders as an enemy that threatens socialistic societies. Often the ads not only attempt to showcase the negative aspects of capitalism but also try to counter any potential sway that capitalism may have over the Polish populace. It appears that the authorities were relatively worried about the public's view of capitalist nations and created a campaign to "educate" the masses. This was a common practice among socialist countries at this time but this specific example is instructive because it indicates concretely that during the socalist era in Poland there was interest in — and possible affection for — capitalist nations like the United States. This idea that the United States was popular among many people in Poland during this time is confirmed by authors and historians, including Donald Pienkos and John Radzilowski, who show the strong bonds that still existed between the two societies. If the image of the United States and other capitalist states was desirable to many Poles then these anticapitalist advertisements provide an interesting reference to what authorities feared about images of the west within Poland. These ads show the government's worries about the public's desires for capitalism and the fears of the social problems that would follow, fascinating in contrast to later advertisements by companies such as Levi's and Frito-Lay that promote the very ideas that were outlawed during the socialist era.

There are several excellent examples of Polish socialist-era anticapitalist, anti–American advertising. A Polish political poster from 1952 is particularly interesting because it critiques the use of product advertising, showing a picture of a man wearing a sandwich board advertising shoes.

The stylish men's dress shoes are proclaimed to be "made in U.S.A." by "the Florsheim shoe company [in] Chicago." The caption reads: "*Amerykańska reklama obuwia*" (American shoe advertisement) (Lengren). The irony of the ad is that the man wearing the pictured sandwich-board shoe advertisement is himself not wearing shoes. The implication is that the capitalist system discriminates against the poor. This is meant to stand in contrast to the idealized version of socialism in which all members of society are equal and share equally the products that are produced. By highlighting perceived deficiencies, the attempts to market capitalism as an undesirable alternative to socialism in Poland. It portrays the United States and other western countries as being of poor quality and is intended to stop Poles from desiring a change. Although Poles at this time did not have many choices in government (or merchandise), they did have enough political power that the government felt it necessary to advertise social and political messages. This use of advertising to influence the competition of ideas and systems foreshadows later product ads that will encourage Poles to embrace capitalism.

Two other ads that highlight the advertising of negative aspects of the United States are a poster that displays racism and one that draws attention to three social ills within the capitalist nation. A cartoonish 1950s poster depicts a crude caricature of a black man being chased by a uniformed white police officer brandishing a nightstick. The men are exiting a building labeled "*lokal wyborczy*" (local elections) adorned with an American flag in which a dollar sign replaces the stars. The black man is yelling "*ratunku!*" (help!) and the caption at the bottom reads, "*w Stanach Zjednoczonych Murzyn mają ... Prawo Głosu*" (In the United States blacks have the right to speak/vote) (Ferster). This ad is intended to counter the U.S. branding as a nation of freedom and equal rights. By showing that African Americans are abused by the authorities and that citizens are not treated equally, the ad tries to discredit American Cold War assertions of moral superiority. The United States often claimed that socialist states like Poland were guilty of human rights violations and this ad answers such contentions by highlighting problems within the United States. This counterclaim portrays America as a racist society that does not adhere to its own basic beliefs. The ad implies that the United States does not really give African Americans the freedom of speech or the right to vote, and because of this it implies that the United States is not a free nation. It is important to note again that this type of counter advertising indicates that a symbolic understanding of the United States had already developed in Poland and that the authorities were attempting to change this popular image. While the ads themselves show the United States to be undesirable, the idea of America must have been perceived positively by a significant percent of the Polish population in order to make the campaign necessary. American symbolism and mythology appear to have been alive in Polish society during the socialist era.

Another ad that follows the same format also deals with the perceived differences between America rhetoric and reality. This 1983 poster entitled "*Symbol i rzeczywistość*" (Symbol and reality), contains three figures on a stark black backdrop. The background of the ad shows a white outline of the Statue of Liberty with cracks and missing pieces. The foreground displays two images. On the left a uniformed soldier identified with the words "U.S. Army" on his hat is labeled "*militaryzm*" (militarism). On the right a hooded member of the Klu Klux Klan is labeled "*rasizm*" (racism). This ad attacks the known American symbol of freedom and attempts to replace it with other less desirable ones (Mysyrowicz). While the ad's claims are much the same as previous one's, it deals specifically with American symbolism and its place in Polish society. The ad suggests that the Statue of Liberty is a well-known symbol of American freedom and desirability in Poland but the disheveled appearance of the icon indicates that it no longer represents those values. While many Poles may see Lady Liberty as the symbol of a free America, the poster claims that this idealized nation does not exist. Instead it offers new symbols of America that the creators deem to be more appropriate. This attempted rebranding of American symbols showcases the cultural inclusion of the existing ones within Poland. The Statue of Liberty is the ad's only unlabeled symbol and the only one that could be identified without a caption. The two new proposed symbols are counterarguments to the symbolic value of the Statue of Liberty. Without the American icon the poster would have little meaning and would cease to be understandable. Even while attempting to portray the ills of American life the ad reaffirms the cultural significance of American symbols and mythology. This demonstrates the foundation that will already have been laid when American companies utilize existing symbols for their ads in the post-socialist years.

Another subject of anti-western, socialist-era advertising is the North Atlantic Treaty Organization (NATO). This military organization founded in 1949 and composed of many western nations was designed to protect its members from the communist bloc. Because NATO was anticommunist by design it unsurprisingly was worrisome to communist states such as Poland. Two anti–NATO advertisements reflect the Polish government's concern about the organization and an attempt to rally public support against it. The first ad, from 1983, designed on a light-blue background, displays the acronym "NATO" in huge dark block letters in the center of the page. Resting on the letters near the top of the page is a black military jet with two attached missiles. The jet is drawn to resemble a bird and is used in contrast to the poster's other symbol, a white dove with an olive branch in its mouth that is located at the bottom left of the ad. Next to the dove is the caption "*Zagrożeniem pokoju*" (threat to peace). The war plane/bird represents NATO and the dove symbolizes either Poland or the larger eastern bloc. The caption and the graphics indicate that NATO and its member nations are militarily aggressive and that Poland is a peaceful bystander ("NATO Zagrożeniem pokoju"). This portrayal of the situation differs greatly from the western version that was often broadcast into Poland by media such as Radio Free Europe. In the western ideal, NATO is a non-aggressive body that seeks to protect the world from the communist threat. The point to note about this ad is not the argument between the two societies but rather the need to develop a counter–NATO campaign within Poland. One might assume that as members of a socialist nation Poles would already harbor anti–NATO sentiments. The advertising campaign indicates that some Poles did not view NATO negatively and that counter–NATO marketing was undertaken to correct this. This again displays the idea that western culture was viewed positively by some Poles even during the socialist era, an idea that would be used in later advertising.

Another anti–NATO ad, also from 1983, displays similar characteristics and themes. This darker-blue poster shows an imposing cluster of black missiles falling from outer space toward the Earth. The missiles are labeled NATO and they are arranged to resemble a dark ominous cloud that is approaching from the distance. The caption at the bottom directly states, "NATO *aby zniszczyć ziemię*" (NATO will destroy the Earth). This ad uses the same themes and ideas of the previous one, that NATO was an aggressive and destructive force that endangered a peaceful Poland and the planet itself ("NATO *aby zniszczyć ziemię*"). This understanding of NATO as a threat again highlights the apparent dichotomy between the government's views of the west and the understanding among many in Polish society. While the government created advertising campaigns against western ideology and influence, many Poles continued to produce their own understandings of American/western symbolism. This is evident not just in the work of numerous authors but also in the repeated need for anti–American, anti-western advertising. Each of these posters reminds today's viewers that these campaigns' creators were marketing against a perceived established mindset. These ads were intended to change minds and to vilify western countries, to change the ingrained positive feelings that would be used by some American companies after the socialist era ended.

Social Advertising

One other type of social advertising that predominated during Poland's socialist era was a government attempt to correct a perceived social ill. While this public service type of ad exists in many countries, it is instructive to view the types of issues that were addressed in Poland. Much can be learned about Polish society by understanding what items and actions the authorities wished to ban and what behaviors were deemed to be undesirable. Ads often used humor, scare tactics, or logic in an attempt to change some part of Polish society. Such social advertising employed many of the same methods as later post-socialist product advertising. It was also oriented to the same end, since both social and product advertising create campaigns in an attempt to change society. Social advertising purports to do so for the common good; product advertising's purpose is profit, even though the methods used are similar. While the outcome that the Polish socialist government desired is different from that of McDonald's or Levi's, the campaigns have much in common. In this sense, the social ads present a useful background and a helpful reference for comparisons with later advertising.

Alcohol

Social reconstructive advertising targeted many issues and behaviors in socialist Poland that ranged from serious to mundane. Five notable ads from this period address drinking, and attempt to curb the use of alcohol and to change the drinking habits of Polish citizens. Each of these ads focuses on a separate issue concerning drinking and utilizes a different tactic in order to combat it. When viewed together the ads display a complex campaign that used Polish cultural ideas and symbols to market a proposed social change. This type of marketing is a forerunner to many later product ads in its use of Polish culture. The first ad shows a bottle of alcohol with the neck replaced by a glass snake. The caption that reads "*nie ulegaj pokusie*" (don't yield to temptation), together with the alcoholic serpent, causes the viewer to connect drinking with the biblical story of the temptation of Adam and Eve ("Nie ulegaj pokusie"). This tale from the book of Genesis would undoubtedly resonate with many in the predominantly Catholic nation. It is interesting that the socialist creators of the ad would rely on religious references, which indicates that even during this period advertisers understood the need to appeal to implicit Polish cultural references and symbols. While the advertisement attempts to change part of Polish culture (drinking), it does so by employing other engrained elements and mythologies. The advertisers use some parts of Polish culture to try to alter others. This method of advertising foreshadows the methods that many multinational corporations would later use when they attempted to change Polish buying habits by promoting new products with Polish ideas and symbols.

A second socialist ad that concentrates on the theme of drinking in Poland examines the consumption of homemade alcohol. *Bimber* is a well-known alcohol in Poland that is especially popular in rural areas and mountainous regions. This strong liquor resembles moonshine and is regarded by Poles to be strong and cheap vodka. Because the drink's production is unregulated, it has historically been illegal, though widely available. During the socialist era, alcohol was often expensive and difficult to buy, and *bimber* was a popular alternative to mass-produced spirits (Pietrzak). Since *bimber* was generally illegal, the authorities had cause to worry about its usage and to warn the public about its potential harm. An early socialist ad from 1945 displays a hunched, pale, blind man contrasted against a dark purple background. The word "*Bimber*" appears in black graffiti-like letters at the top of the page and near the bottom is the caption, "*Przyczyna Ślepoty*" (Causes Blindness). The purpose of the ad is to show the undesirable side effects of using *bimber* and to attempt to reduce its production and consumption ("Bimber").

In this ad, the state again highlights its authoritative role but does so without a religious connection as in the previous poster. This time the advertiser presents itself more as a concerned parent who wishes to warn citizens about societal dangers. Besides *bimber* being a type of alcohol that would generally be known only to Poles, most of the poster is generic and could be used in almost any society. The ad addresses a negative effect of alcohol in Poland but both the problem and the marketing are universal. Many societies have campaigned against homemade alcohol, and an often-used deterrent is to promote the fear of alcohol induced blindness. This ad exemplifies a transnational subject with a specific societal appeal. While the producers of this ad focused on Poland, they borrowed symbols and mythologies — like the unfortunate man blinded by alcohol and the darkness that surrounds him — that have a broader history and appeal. This marketing idea of taking a universal image and having it represent a campaign will be used often by international companies that will use global ideas to market locally. The artist that created this ad may not have intentionally used international ideas but the universal appeal of the ad showcases an early version of transnational symbol sharing.

A third ad from this period that focuses on alcohol in Poland is a poster that addresses the issue of drinking and driving. This darkly colored ad displays the pale face and hand of a man as he partakes of alcohol while gripping the steering wheel of a motor vehicle. The red-lettered caption: "*Źle tankujesz*" (Filling up badly). The obviously pun in this ad is the connection between filling up a car with gasoline and filling up a drinker with alcohol. This joke is even more meaningful when one learns that the Polish word "*tankujesz*" means not only to fill a car with fuel but is also slang for getting drunk. This clever use of popular language to discourage drinking and driving also shows an intimate understanding of Polish sensibilities. Unlike the previous ads that attempt to vilify alcohol, this one chooses humor and language to emphasize its point. In selecting this approach the advertisers expressed an implied connection with the average Pole and his or her lifestyle and customs. Often ads from the government or the Communist Party contained large words and official-sounding verbiage. By comparison, this ad used the common vernacular and in doing so made it sound less threatening and authoritative. While the first ad equates the state with religious authority and the second ad sounds like a stern parent, this poster takes the tone of a helpful person who worried about a neighbor's safety. Although the state is far from being an average neighbor, it is attempting to declare its common Polishness and show itself to be not only the leader of society but also a member. This marketing device is very similar to ones that will later be used successfully by American corporations such as McDonald's and Coca-Cola. These companies will market themselves as average members of the Polish community and good neighbors. Often they will advertise their products as helpful additions to society and they will market lifestyle changes with the implication that these will better Poland. While these ads differ from their socialist predecessors in many ways, they also share many of the same methods and themes, and even sometimes intend the same outcomes.

Two final ads from this period that concentrate on different aspects of alcohol in Poland view the subject from a commercial perspective. These ads highlight the adverse effects of alcohol consumption at work and in one's personal money management. The first ad is a black-and-white drawing of a target with bullet holes in the bottom quadrants. The caption reads, "*kto pije—źle pracuje*" (someone who drinks — works badly). Although it is not clear what kind of worker fires a gun (police officer? soldier?), it is understood that alcohol has adverse affects on performance ("Kto pije"). The ad's simple message is that one should not drink on the job because it is harmful to everyone. It is not unusual that this ad focuses on work because labor is the often stated foundation of the socialist system. The government and the party frequently declared that workers were the basis of the nation. This poster is an extension of socialist policy and a restatement of the importance of labor to society. It also uses an extreme example to showcase how important common labor is. Although most Poles will not use a firearm at work, it is a very striking visual to see how alcohol affects performance. This is very much like the governmental advertising that was described earlier in that it shows the central role of the government in people's lives. It also is a suggestion to Poles to think of themselves not only as individuals but also as members of a larger society. This marketing approach uses national pride and solidarity to sell the idea.

Another ad that uses a similar approach shows a young couple driving a Polish Fiat 126p on vacation. The car's roof is loaded with luggage, camping gear, and sports equipment, and the oval "PL" sticker on the back identifies the couple as Polish. Black letters placed on the poster's blue sky read, "*Nie piję, bo zbieram na:*" (I don't drink, because I am saving for:). The poster and the caption present a cheerier outlook than many of the other alcohol themed socialist advertisements ("Nie piję"). Instead of threatening, cajoling, or showing negative consequences, this ad presents positive outcomes that can be gained by not drinking. The ad reminds Poles that they can do other things with the money that they might otherwise spend on liquor. Like the advertisement that warned people to not drink at work this ad is concerned with alcohol's role on the economy. Both ads want people to change their behavior in order to achieve positive economic consequences. If people do not drink at work then they will be more productive and if people save their money and buy things other than alcohol then it will help the economy and people will have more and nicer possessions. This call to help Polish society by helping oneself is often used by marketers and informs viewers of a "win-win" situation. By being responsible, it is suggested, citizens/consumers not only make good choices for themselves but also for society as a whole. This shorthand version of Adam Smith's idea of the "invisible hand" would seem to have no place in a socialist economy but it is used in this ad nonetheless. These two posters contain elements of product advertising that will be seen in Poland after the end of socialism. Companies such as Frito-Lay and Levi's will encourage Poles to make healthy personal choices that will also benefit society. This type of "everybody wins" marketing is most evident later but can be seen much earlier during the socialist period.

Advertising Change

Although most of the advertisements studied thus far have focused on established Polish symbols and traditions, another type of ad is intended to create and market new symbols and mythologies that are not widely recognizable within Polish society. This differs from the previously discussed liquor ads because at the time of the ads alcohol was already a known commodity that was well established in Poland's culture. These ads attempted to change the perception of certain types of alcohol (*bimber*) and some activities associated with it (driving, overspending, and working while intoxicated) but these were only corollaries to the substance itself. Even the ad that attempted to demonize drinking was not creating new ideas or symbols but was rather appealing to ancient symbols related to the Christian church. Many in Poland already understood the intake of alcohol to be a potentially unhealthy activity and the ad was presenting little new information. This idea of inventing new cultural symbols will be used much more in post-socialist advertising by companies that wish to become a part of Polish society but have new ideas and products to introduce.

Solidarity

The most obvious example of symbol creation in socialist-era advertising is the nongovernmental ads produced by the Solidarity labor union. Solidarity ("*Solidarność*" in Polish) was the first noncommunist trade union in socialist Poland. It was created by shipyard workers in Gdansk in 1980 and is credited by many as being one of the major causes of the end of communism not only in Poland but in all of the Warsaw bloc (Ash 41–44). Although Solidarity produced many interesting ads, arguably the union's most important cultural symbol is its logo. The logo, which was designed by young artist Jerzy Janiszewski, spells out the word "*Solidarność*" in red letters and tops the "N" with a red-and-white Polish flag (Weschler 111–13). Like many great symbols, the logo is powerful in its simplicity and has become easily identifiable not only in Poland but throughout the world. The red letters are both powerful and communal and the script is strong yet messy, all adjectives that could be used describe the union itself. The letters' hue reminds Poles of their much-esteemed flag but also of blood that was shed for the Polish nation. The Solidarity logo became the symbol of the Polish worker because the union marketed itself as an entity that remembered the state's past atrocities and wished to make a better life for the Polish people. The Solidarity logo is a simple icon but an important symbol because it was able to link itself to Poland's history, memory, and mythology.

The Solidarity logo became a Polish symbol by advertising the union as both opposition to the socialist government and keeper of the Polish nationalist tradition. Solidarity presented itself as the heir to the established Polish institutions of romanticism and political uprising. The trade union often referenced the 1944 Warsaw Uprising against the Nazis, the

1956 uprising in Poznan, the 1970 massacre at the Gdansk shipyards, and the protests of 1976 in order to gain legitimacy (Weschler 116–118). Because of Poland's past political and military struggles the nation's mythological past was an important element in the growth and development of Solidarity. Historian Norman Davies notes that tradition plays a much greater role in Poland than in other nations and labels the importance of this tradition "echoes of the Past" (*Heart of Europe* 312). Solidarity was able to become part of this Polish tradition/history/mythology by comparing itself to these culturally important periods and events. The union marketed itself as an extension of an established Polish identity and tradition. Solidarity branded itself not as a new force but rather as a logical and necessary product of Poland's past and present. Although examples of this marketing are legion, three early Solidarity advertisements can be seen to display the manner in which the trade union used Polish history and culture to become a symbol of the nation.

A 1980 print ad demonstrates how Solidarity linked itself to Poland's tradition and the uprisings of the past. This simple poster features a large black ship's anchor situated on a white and red background that is reminiscent of the Polish flag. The Solidarity logo is placed in large letters over the upper portion of the anchor. No caption appears in the ad and no explanation of the political nature of the ad is provided (Beller). Most non–Poles would be unsure how to construe the poster because nothing in it seems political. To an outsider the ad is confusing; it has little or no meaning because no context is provided. Almost all Poles, though, would understand that the anchor was a symbol of the protestors that were killed in the Gdansk shipyards in 1970. One of the founding goals of Solidarity was to convince the authorities to build a lasting monument to the fallen laborers, and so the trade union is often associated with this event (Dobbs 35). This objective of commemorating their fallen radical comrades and allying themselves with Poland's historical rebelliousness helped to brand Solidarity as the heir to Poland's activist past. By using Poland's historical mythology to brand itself as both radically and yet traditionally Polish, Solidarity was able to brand itself as an opposition party that was uniquely Polish. This was accomplished because the leaders of the trade union understood Polish society and culture and were able to utilize this knowledge to their advantage. This is not unlike major corporations that brand themselves with desirable images by connecting to various desirable qualities within a culture. Levi's is able to declare its brand rebellious and fun because it connects itself to traditions and mythologies from the American past. Solidarity did much the same thing and because of it became a recognizable brand.

Another poster that illustrates Solidarity's effort to become a symbol of Polish nationalism and radicalism is a 1981 ad that showcases both Polish history and symbolism. The ad again uses Poland's national colors of red-and-white by focusing on a red and white eagle wearing a crown. The Solidarity logo dissects one of the eagle's wings and the bottom of the reads, "Maja 1. Maja 3" (May 1. May 3). As previously noted, the eagle in the poster is the stylized symbol of the Polish nation, and the dates refer to the socialist labor holiday May Day (May 1) and the Polish Constitution of May 3, 1791, that is claimed to be the first modern codified national constitution in Europe. Both holidays were official celebrations in Poland that started during the communist regime, and to the non–Polish viewer the ad would seem to carry no political ideology that differed from the state-sanctioned version (Wieckowski). To one familiar with Polish culture and tradition, though, the image of the eagle in the ad is both subversive and politically important. The symbol dates back to 1295 when King Przemysl II ordered that the eagle be the coat of arms for the entire kingdom of Poland. After the socialists came to power following World War II, the crown was removed from the eagle's head in order to symbolize a change of political systems. Many Poles, including members of Solidarity, resented this change and wished for the symbol to be restored to its original appearance. The crowned eagle is a link to Poland's history and mythology and Solidarity uses it in this ad to show opposition to the government's underappreciation of Polish history. Solidarity is branding itself as a symbol of Poland's true past and a guardian of the nation's history. The government may have tried to change Poland's symbols but the leaders of Solidarity were attempting to restore what they saw as their nation's history. By fighting for a historical symbol Solidarity emphasized its Polishness and worked to become a symbol of its own.

Another advertisement from 1981 again displays how Solidarity used historic Polish mythologies and culture to become a symbol for the nation. From a distance the ad appears to be a red-and-white Polish flag with several words printed across the bottom. When inspected more closely the red part of the flag is revealed to be a large group of Polish workers that are so numerous that they blend together. A Solidarity logo appears in the top right corner. The caption states, "1 Maja. Święto Solidarnosci Robotniczej" (May 1. Holiday of Labor Solidarity). The ad has taken a socialist holiday (May Day) and a cornerstone of socialism (the labor movement) and declared them to be under Solidarity's control (Lewandowski). As previously shown, laborers were often used in state-sanctioned propaganda to declare the Polishness of the government. Solidarity was using the same kind of ad as the government and the Communist Party and was declaring itself the voice of Polish labor and by extension of the Polish people. The importance of this idea cannot be overstated. Solidarity was challenging the authority of the government and claiming itself to represent the nation. The trade union was attempting to express the importance of the past in the present and to assert its supposed authority. In ads like this one, Solidarity attempted to brand itself as an anticommunist symbol and as the successor to historic Polish radicalism.

In the short term this advertising campaign did not produce the desired effect for the union. By late 1981, General Wojciech Jaruzelski and the socialist government had declared a state of martial law in Poland and Solidarity was soon outlawed. During much of the early and mid–1980s the movement had to operate underground and so it could not advertise in the same manner as before. Solidarity remained in the minds of many Poles and others in much of the world, however, and would eventually come to the forefront again in the late 1980s. By that point the trade union had already entrenched itself as a Polish symbol of opposition and radical political thought. Solidarity accomplished this at least partially by recognizing and advertising its links to a mythologized Polish history. The union incorporated Polish symbols, ideas, and history and in turn Solidarity became a symbol itself. The trade union branded itself as a symbol of what Poland believed it had been, could be, and wished to be again. Although the importance and the outcomes are very different, Solidarity used many of the same advertising techniques that international corporations would later use to establish brands in Poland. While few would argue that the McDonald's and Coca-Cola logos and brands of as historically politically important as Solidarity's, one has to consider the shared method that each of these brands used in advertising in order to become culturally and symbolically important in Poland.

Western Film Posters

While the government, the Communist Party, and Solidarity were creating advertisements that used many of the same themes and techniques as later advertisers, another type of ad was being produced that helped to define American culture for several generations of Poles. One of the most symbolic types of advertising in socialist Poland was the film poster for American westerns produced by Polish artists. These posters were created to advertise American western films but were crafted using Polish ideas and understandings about the United States. This culturally Polish advertising about an American product provides a unique opportunity to not only examine one form of Polish advertising but also to study Polish views of American myths during the socialist era. While many types of film posters were produced in Poland, the western genre contains specific myths, themes, and symbols that were appropriated by Polish society in ways different from any other type of motion picture. The American West intrigued Poles and formed the basis for many cultural understandings about the United States. Many of these ideas about America and its culture formed the basis for the advertising of American companies like Levi's and Coca-Cola. These western film ads were precursors for advertising for American products and many of the same themes and ideas can be seen in each type of ad. Many of the corporations that advertise in post-socialist Poland sell products by using ideas about America that are evident in these advertisements from the socialist period.

The mythic vision of the American West has a long tradition in Poland, extending back into the nineteenth century. Poles heard tales of the expansive frontier and the mythic figures of the cowboy and the Native American. Historian Frank Fox argues that Poles value the strong individualism, freedom, and fight for national independence present in stories about the American West and often associate their own historical struggles with the American version. Fox also contends that the myth of the American West was so prevalent in Poland during the nineteenth century that several noted authors, like Henryk Sienkiewicz in his famous historical novel *With Fire and Sword*, may have based parts of seminal Polish literary works on American history and mythology (Fox 75–80). In the late nineteenth and early twentieth century many Polish immigrants in the United States wrote home about the myths of the American West and helped to cement these ideas further into the Polish national consciousness (Thomas 1005). By the time the socialist era, began the myth of the American West was well established within Poland and often served as a mirror to Polish historical ideas and events. American western films were often viewed with this background in socialist Poland, both as a product of an exotic and mythic nation and as a reflection of Polish society. It is within this context that Polish artists created film ads for American westerns that not only explored American themes and ideas but also questioned the place of these themes within Polish society. This idea of American symbols and mythologies being placed into Polish society will become prominent later in the post-socialist era.

Arguably, the most important Polish advertisement that uses American western themes is not an ad for a film but uses an image from one. The ad in question is a Solidarity poster that advertises important government elections in June 1989. The ad features Gary Cooper from the film *High Noon* dressed as a western sheriff, complete with cowboy boots and hat. Above his star-shaped badge Cooper wears a Solidarity logo and in his right hand is a paper marked "*wybory*" (election). Behind the sheriff's head is a large banner version of Solidarity's logo and the caption at the bottom exclaims, "*W Samo Południe 4 Czerwca 1989*" (At High Noon 4 June 1989). The entire ad is produced in black and white except for the two Solidarity logos which are the expected red and white. The picture of Cooper is a striking image of strength and individuality; the actor/sheriff is captured in mid-stride and appears almost capable of walking off the page and creating order within Polish society (Sarnecki). While this poster does not advertise a film, it does support the view that American western symbols and myths were of high importance even during the socialist era when such things were discouraged and that the elections might bring Poland closer to an American-style political and economic system. Solidarity chose a character from an American western to promote elections that redefined the Polish political system. Several noncommunist Solidarity candidates ran for office in a power-sharing agreement and, though it was unknown at the time, this marked the beginning of the end of the socialist government. In this context it is extraordinary that an American western sheriff was selected as the symbol of opposition to the government. Since 1980 Solidarity had been creating advertising that used symbols and imagery that connected to Poland's historical and mythological culture.

In using the *High Noon* image for such an important event the advertisement's creators validated American symbols and mythologies and gave them equal cultural standing as Polish symbols. This remarkable advertisement legitimized the idea that American culture in general and the west in particular reverberated within Polish culture. Poles had taken an American image and myth and redefined it as culturally Polish. This process was a harbinger of the cultural appropriation that would become standard during the post socialist era when Poles will create a new Polish culture comprised of transnational elements.

The *High Noon* image in the Solidarity poster projects a statement of rugged independence and individualism, two traits associated with the American west in Poland. Solidarity — and the Polish voters who elected the union's candidates — accepted the American symbols of independence and individuality and transformed them into Polish icons. This cultural appropriation is not a random event, though, but rather one of a series of examples of the importance of the American west in Polish advertising and society during the socialist era. As stated before, the most obvious example of these advertisements are Polish posters for American western films. These ads contain multiple examples of American mythologies being recultured to conform to Polish needs. The process of cultural acquisition will continue and expand in the post-socialist era as more international cultures are introduced into Poland, making these early Western film posters essential for an understanding of American advertising in Poland. The most notable symbol of the western film posters is the classic American hero, the cowboy. As shown in the Solidarity *High Noon* poster, the cowboy often symbolized individuality and freedom in advertisements and by extension in Polish society. In the ads the cowboy is usually posed in a self-confident or aggressive manner that visually assures the viewer of his strength and conviction. He is the essence of masculinity, self-reliance, and self-determination in a nation in which circumstances have often restricted such things. In Poland the cowboy is not just a character but rather a symbol of a better life. Examples of the cowboy in western film posters are vast but several good instances of the typical cowboy look and pose are posters from *Ride the High Country* (1968), *The Tall Man* (1965), *Tom Horn* (1982), *MacKenna's Gold* (1969), and *Missouri Breaks* (1978). (The dates given are for the Polish release, not the original U.S. release.) Each of these ads shows an image of a stereotypically strong and independent cowboy.

This image resonated in a nation that often was not allowed political, economic, or social choices, and it became a symbol of freedom and individuality. In such a way, the cowboy became a Polish emblem and not only an American one, by providing a cultural outlet and symbol for a nation that required one. This idea of American symbols being utilized by Polish culture would be seen again numerous times in later years.

While the image and mythology of the cowboy was expressed much the same in Poland as in the United States, the symbols that surrounded the western icon were often interpreted differently by Polish audiences. These emblems may have started as American but soon were culturally acquired by Poles and in the process their meanings were often transformed. One of the most obvious and notable examples of this transformation is the role of the gun in westerns and the related advertisements. Generally, in American culture, the gun serves as peacekeeper, equalizer, and a symbol of personal responsibility and individuality. The use of the gun can have dramatic and horrible consequences, and the user can be either hero or villain, but the gun itself is neither good nor evil, rather it is a tool. This idea brings to mind the famous anonymous quotation, "God created men. Samuel Colt made them equal." Or the often used, "Guns don't kill people, people kill people." The sentiment was that guns provide people with an opportunity to be more free and individualistic, even more human. Polish ads for westerns show a different view of the symbolic role of the gun. In these ads guns are often portrayed as menacing, intimidating, and unnatural. While the cowboy who uses the gun may be viewed as honorable or heroic, the weapon itself carries none of these distinctions. If most Americans understand the western gun as a tool of individuality, many Poles see it as a weapon of violence and aggression. The general Polish understanding of the gun is not surprising, considering the nation's history armed struggles against better-armed foes that often did not end well for Poland. While the battles that have been fought on American soil are distant memories, Poles are encouraged to remember the epic struggles in their homeland and to fear the weapons that were used in them. A difference in the interpretations of symbols can be seen in any two societies but what is important to note in this example is the cultural appropriation by Poland. The Poles have selected which symbols they wanted and have interpreted them in ways that best suit their cultural needs. The cowboy remains very close to the American understanding but the gun is morphed into a symbol that better reflects Poland's desires and understandings. Note that the Poles have not been forced to take the American versions of these symbols but rather they have chosen what best meets their societal needs. This cultural borrowing and reconfiguring has existed for centuries in Poland but after the socialist era it will be much more prominent in an increasingly globalized society.

A large number of ads for American westerns exhibit the symbolic Polish use of the gun as aggressive and threatening. Notably displaying this usage is a poster for 1973's *Shoot Out* that features a drawing of a pistol as viewed from slightly below. The revolver is poised to fire over the viewer's head as the viewer looks upward, inspecting the weapon's barrel, cylinder, bullets, and shooter's finger tightly gripping the trigger. The handgun in this advertising is ominous, filling most of the poster and resembling an airplane or a battleship's turrets more than a pistol. The background of pink-and-orange polka dots on lime-green background adds a circus-like feel that makes the weapon even more surreal in its dangerousness (Krajewski). The gun is not portrayed as a tool but rather as an unnatural hazard that should be feared. The Polish translation of the film's title reinforces this understanding of the gun's symbolic meaning. The title, *Odstrzał,* refers to the amount of animals that a hunter has killed during a given hunting season. This Polish idea of predatory behavior is very different from the equal-opportunity killing suggested by the original American title. The original American poster for the film displays a three-on-one gun battle and the tagline reads, "Three guns against one determined man!" ("Shoot Out"). This ad proclaims that the guns have made the fight "fair," while the Polish version focuses on the deadliness of the gun itself. The Polish poster creates a frightening idea of humans hunting each other for sport while the American version portrays rugged individuals fighting for honor and justice. Two different understandings of the symbol of the gun met the needs of two individual cultures.

One other Polish western ad that displays the symbolic use of the gun is 1972's *Soldier Blue,* a film focusing on relations between Native Americans and settlers. The Polish poster illustrates the waist, legs, and feet of a man wearing cowboy boots and spurs. On his right side hangs a rifle, with a drop of blood falling from the stock (Młodożeniec). Like the previous poster, this one does not show the gun's owner; he appears to be only a footnote to the weapon itself. It also does not reveal anything about the plot or storyline of the movie. The focus of the poster is the rifle and the droplet of blood. The undeniable message of the poster is the deadliness of the rifle and the carnage that it produces. The connection between gun and blood is not often made on American posters or in the westerns themselves, which have often being criticized for their portrayals of bloodless shootings and killings. The symbolic American role of the gun as a tool of individuality is lessened if the weapon is associated with gory deaths or bloody battles. Polish symbolism encourages such displays, though, and rejects the American understanding of the antiseptic killing power of the gun. In Polish western mythology the gun is a killing machine and must be feared, even though its use is sometimes necessary. While Poles accept the American version of the cowboy, they transform the gun into a symbol that better meets their cultural needs, one that fits with Polish history and tradition. This cultural adaptation of an American symbol showcases the complex equilibrium that exists between the two cultures. While many will accuse the United States of cultural imperialism during the coming years, in truth the situation is not that simply defined. In the socialist era and in the later capitalist years, symbols and mythologies were promoted, acquired, refused, and adapted according to Polish cultural needs. Advertising would serve as a vehicle for much of this process but would remain one of many factors. In truth, there are such a wide variety of cultural needs and desires at work that it is difficult to point to only one reason for cultural and social change.

One other example of an American western symbol that has been adapted to meet Polish cultural needs is that of the Native American. While much has changed about America's understanding of Native American roles in U.S. history in the past thirty years, for many years they were regularly portrayed in a negative and hostile light. Native Americans were often viewed as lazy savages and an impediment to social progress and the nation's Manifest Destiny. These ideas frequently were reproduced in films where the Native Americans portrayed the villains and the settlers or cowboys the heroes. This stereotypical view was a standard element of the mythology of the American western for many years and while this may be changing it still is highly associated with the genre. By contrast, this bias against Native Americans does not appear to be present in much of the Polish understanding of American western mythology. Historian Francis Fox claims that Poles identify with Native Americans because both groups have been displaced and forced to submit to the rule of outside powers. In stories or films Poles see much of themselves and their history in the Native Americans' plight (74, 80). This adaptation of the Native American as a symbol highlights the way in which Poles create new meanings out of borrowed symbols and mythologies. This affiliation with the Native American is evidenced in many American western film ads. Often the films portray Native Americans in a stereotypically negative manner but the Polish posters choose to assert the opposite viewpoint. The Polish artist and viewer interpret the symbol of the Native American differently than the symbol's American creators, and in the process Polish culture creates a Polish understanding of an American mythology that is often very different from the traditional American version.

Many film advertisements from this period showcase the Polish conception of the Native American and its symbolic use. One such ad is a 1958 Polish poster for the musical Western *Annie Get Your Gun*. The film itself is a lighthearted musical comedy that offers little political commentary concerning Native Americans. The Polish poster by contrast, is disturbing in its cheery depiction of a world gone awry. The ad illustrates a cheerful Annie Oakley dressed in white, surrounded by a circle of three men. Two of the men are cowboys and stand at of her sides while a smartly dressed man lies underfoot and a Native American floats above her head. In Annie's right hand is a rifle that is pressed against the Native American man's face as it is also gripped by his left hand. The characters are brightly dressed and each seems blissful, even the Native American that appears to be in the process of putting the rifle in his mouth. The rifle is at odds with the rest of the poster and makes the viewer uneasy about a world that is so causal in its use and acceptance of guns. The firearm transforms the picture into a statement about a society in which the gun has created a carnivalesque hierarchy that does not follow the natural order. The floating Native American appears to be willfully taking the gun into his mouth, unaware of the consequences. This may be a reference to smoking the peace pipe after the signing of a soon-to-be-broken treaty or an allusion to the consequences of the gun on Native American life (Stachurski). Both interpretations would appeal to Poles, a people who felt wronged by both allies and enemies. No matter which version one chooses, the Native American appears superior, sympathetic, and wronged. He rests on higher ground both morally and physically and has no ill feelings or guile. This is contrasted by the well-dressed capitalist under Annie's feet that is at the lowest rung of the poster's hierarchy. The Native American is the victim in the advertisement's narrative, an unsuspecting casualty of a society gone haywire. This understanding of the Native American is vastly different from that of 1950s America and is in contrast to the musical silliness of the film itself. Very few films or television shows of this era would portray the Native American as victim or even sympathetically. This Polish version deviates from the then standard American mythology in a way that mattered to Poles. The nation sympathized with the Native America and in doing so redefined an American symbol to meet their unique cultural needs.

One other ad, from 1965's *How the West Was Won*, shows another image of the Native American being victimized. This poster focuses on half of a bright red mask with green, yellow, and blue feathers. A large black gun presses against the mask/face, with the barrel sticking out of an ear. This image, coupled with the film's title, creates a grotesque statement that the West was won by abusing Native Americans (Treutler). If the gun symbolizes the European settlers/pioneers and the mask is a symbol of Native Americans then the statement of the ad is undeniably that Native Americans are victims. As in the poster for *Annie Get Your Gun*, the Native American is shown as the injured party in the morality of the West. This Polish version of the mythology of the West differs greatly from what was then the common American idea of Native Americans as savages or enemies. Because Poles thought they understood the plight of this distant people, Polish mythology and symbolism embraced them. While this act unto itself sounds ordinary, it is remarkable. Poles were able to take a foreign mythology, understand it not only as presented but also in terms of their history and culture, keep what seemed valuable, discard what was unneeded, redefine and alter what could be improved, and incorporate what was created into Polish society. During much of this process, internal and external forces such as the government, the party, and Radio Free Europe attempted to stop or influence its reception. Amazingly, Polish culture adapted these outside symbols and mythologies to meet its needs and was able to remain Polish and yet not become stagnant. Polish culture was shown to be both strong and flexible, two traits that would be tested after the end of socialism.

Summary

At first glance, it would appear that Polish socialist-era social and film advertising has little connection to later international product advertising and marketing. Advertising during the socialist era was generally government regulated and often claimed to be produced for the betterment of society. By contrast, product advertising's goal is often thought of as being to entice viewers into buying more merchandise and it generally relies on public opinion to shape its marketing campaigns. These contrasting approaches and desired outcomes leave many to believe that ads from the two eras lack commonalities. In reality, socialist-era advertising provides an underexplored foundation of themes, symbols, and methods that are widely used in modern-day international product advertising. While the subjects may have changed, the underlying ideas have not. Many of the themes and techniques that are used by companies such as McDonald's, Coca-Cola, Levi's, and Frito-Lay were utilized by advertisers in socialist Poland. Socialist-era advertisers understood the importance of historical tradition, symbolism, and mythology in Poland and used each effectively in their ads. They also grasped the importance of declared Polishness and crafted ads that linked the advertiser and the nation. Additionally, the advertisers comprehended the importance of western/ American symbols and mythologies and attempted to (re)define and regulate their use. These ideas and themes have been used extensively by American companies in Poland and in many cases serve as the main advertising strategy. When McDonald's markets itself as a good Polish neighbor, it is using one of the same marketing strategies that the Communist Party did. If Levi's declares itself to be a symbol of the American west, it is retreading advertising ground already traveled effectively by Solidarity. Although few corporations in Poland would comment kindly about the socialist system, each owes a debt of gratitude to the era's advertising, which displayed the types of themes and ideas that work in Polish marketing. Ironically, in many ways the underpinning for the capitalist product advertising was created in the socialist years.

Social Print Advertising

Ad Title	Date	Theme
Amerykańska reklama obuwia	1952	Anti-western
Bimber	1945	Social change
KPP-PZPR	1978	Party propaganda
Kto pije	Unknown	Social change
NATO *aby zniszczyć ziemię*	1983	Anti-western
NATO *Zagrożeniem pokoju*	1983	Anti-western
Nie piję	Unknown	Social change
Nie ulegaj pokusie	Unknown	Social change
Solidarity, High Noon	1989	Political change
Niebieski żolnierz	1972	American symbolism
Odstrzał	1973	American symbolism
Polska Rzeczpospolita Ludowa	1974	Governmental propaganda
Prawo Głosu	1952	Anti-western
Rekord Annie	1958	American symbolism
Solidarity, Anchor	1980	Political change
Solidarity: Eagle	1981	Political change
Solidarity, People	1981	Political change
Symbol i rzeczywistość	1983	Anti-western
Wszystko nad czym pracujemy	1972	Governmental propaganda
Jak Zdobyto Dziki Zachód	1965	American symbolism
Źle tankujesz	Unknown	Social change

2

McPoland

Expatriate Polish writer/translator Stanisław Barańczak, when discussing the cultural differences between Polish and American cultures, writes, "the color of Eastern Europe is gray (with occasional flashes of red on national holidays). America has no single color; it is brilliantly multicolored, pluralistic, and bold even in the first impression it makes" (9). In many ways this definition of America could also have fit the McDonald's restaurant chain as it entered Poland — bright, colorful American company hoping to immigrate to a colorless Eastern Europe. When McDonald's entered the Polish market in 1992 it not only brought a new restaurant chain to Poland but also introduced the Poles to an American cultural icon. McDonald's is one of the most recognizable American companies worldwide; the popular fast-food restaurant that has more than 31,000 outlets internationally has become a powerful symbol of America (International News Archive). No matter if one views McDonald's as a symbol of global commerce's ability to promote peace and understanding, as Thomas Friedman does in his monograph *The Lexus and the Olive Tree*, or as many others do, like George Ritzer in *The McDonaldization of Society*, as a symbol of economic colonialism, few can argue the power of the brand. In many places worldwide the concepts of McDonald's and the food it serves are used almost interchangeably with the notion of the United States. This cultural interconnectivity has been showcased recently by protests against McDonald's restaurants in places like France and Mexico and has caused many to wonder if the product can continue in a world in which many have a hostile perception of the United States. McDonald's, for its part, has long embraced a marketing strategy that promotes strong community ties and local versions of its menus. For example, McDonald's India relies heavily on vegetarian and chicken items and has a food entitled the "McCurry Pan" while McDonald's Japan serves many seafood dishes (McDonald's). These elements of American culture mixing with local cultures is an important part of McDonald's international strategy in many nations, including Poland.

Advertising in Poland

Although McDonald's has been expanding internationally since the 1960s, it did not found its first restaurant in Poland until June 17, 1992. The restaurant that opened in Warsaw was McDonald's' first venture into the nation of almost forty million people. As of 2007, there were 213 Polish McDonald's locations and only thirty-four were in the nation's capital, Warsaw (McDonald's Poland). The rapid expansion of McDonald's in Poland during this fifteen-year period is credited to many factors, including increased international development into the newly opened Polish state, Poland's desire for American culture, and the trendiness of the fast-food giant. It can be argued that advertising played a substantial role in all of these factors and many more. When McDonald's was first introduced in 1992 it was the advertising and marketing mission to ensure that McDonald's became a strong and profitable brand in Poland. In order to do this the fast-food chain was not merely content to sell burgers and French fries but rather wanted to market mythic visions of a new Poland with strong ties to the past. Before this could be attempted, though, advertisers and marketers had to understand what would appeal to the Polish consumer and how Polish society was different from the United States. Although these sound like straightforward questions, in actuality they can be viewed in multiple ways and have many different possible answers. McDonald's could not afford to treat Poland as just another market but had to understand the society and craft a business approach that addressed the needs of the culture.

Some Polish advertising scholars, such as Elzbieta Lepkowska-White, argue that because advertising is relatively new in Poland, the society's understanding of it is not as advanced as in "western" countries like the United States. This means that in the early 1990s American companies needed to learn if ideas and concepts could be easily transferred from the United States to Poland (76–80). In order to appreciate Polish society, data was collected to help identify what kind of consumers resided in the nation. One way to measure customers' needs and desires is a cultural framework designed by social scientist Geert Hofstede that identifies five important cultural dimensions within a society. When these five dimensions are compared between nations, one can begin to partially understand how consumers in a particular nation may react to an idea, concept, or product. Studies have shown that Poland is comparable to the United States in some cultural dimensions, so certain types of advertising appeals should be transferable, but others probably will not work. One major difference between the two societies is demonstrated by a category that Hofstede identifies as the Uncertainty Avoidance Index (UAI) which measures a "society's tolerance for uncertainty and ambiguity [and] ultimately refers to [a] search for Truth. It indicates to what extent a culture programs its members to feel either uncomfortable or comfortable in unstructured situations" (*Poland-Polish Geert Hofstede*). Societies like Poland with a high UAI tend to be very structured and have a need for rules and regulations, possessing little tolerance for ambiguity. Hofstede links this need for structure to Poland's overwhelmingly Catholic population and claims a correlation between the religion and the societal value. This also may be a cultural remnant of the numerous authoritarian states under which the Poles have been subjected. By comparison, the United States scores very low on the UAI meter and thus is much more open to new ideas and products. This data is important to advertisers and marketers because they believe nations like Poland that score high in UAI are more open to traditional practical appeals and less likely to be swayed by new symbols (Mueller 138–140). This means that advertisers would need to display a new product's useful virtues while linking to ideas that already predominate within the culture. Although new products can be successfully marketed in Poland, Hofstede's cultural dimensions suggest that the ideas of trendy and "new and improved" do not work well in Poland in the long term unless they are connected to known and valued cultural symbols and ideas.

Along with Hofstede's cultural dimensions, another method that can be used to understand Polish society is the study of psychographics. Also called Interests, Attitudes, and Opinions (IAO), this marketing-research method determines how a particular group feels about values, interests, attitudes, or lifestyles. After questioning a section of the population, researchers are able to identify what percentage of the population falls within six major personality/lifestyle categories: Traditionalists, Family Managers, Aspirers, Idealists, Free Spirits, and Isolationists. This demographic breakdown is helpful to advertisers because it assists them in understanding what messages are likely to attract consumers and which may offend buyers. In Poland the psychographic research reveals that a large portion of Poles are conservative and traditional, and thus want products that appeal to old-fashioned values. Conversely, the data also displays that there is a sizable percentage of the population, about 42 percent, that could be convinced to buy new nontraditional items. Additionally, around 27 percent of the Polish population desire new and innovative products that break from the norm (Senft). While to the lay reader this may seem like useless information, it in fact is telling because it showcases Poland as a traditionally minded society with certain liberal tendencies. The data outlines what advertising and marketing approaches will probably work best in Poland and what kinds of things different groups of Poles will most likely desire. This profile is also very helpful when trying to understand the various themes contained within advertising narratives produced for the Polish market because it allows the viewer to identify the probable mindset of both the ads' producers and audience.

Additional understanding of the nature of Polish advertising comes from observational data collected by marketing and advertising scholar Marieke de Mooij. Corroborating the studies described above, de Mooij finds that Polish society is more traditional than the United States and many countries in Europe. She also notes, "Polish culture is reflected in a respect for elders and in strong family values in both adapted international and indigenous advertising. I have found large family groups in television commercials. Polish people are individuals, but not extreme" (280). De Mooij goes on to state that advertisers need to respect the well-defined Polish gender roles and that although Poles like practical products and advertising they also enjoy humor in their ads. She finishes by stating that "the need for the traditional, for roots, is reflected in the frequent use of folklore, nostalgia, and historical drama" (281). De Mooij's understanding of Polish advertising agrees with most of the results of Hofstede's cultural dimensions and the psychographic studies. Poland is marked as a conservative society that values practicality and normalcy. For advertising to work in Poland it needs to abide by the Polish standards and to understand the consumer who it is attempting to sway. The advertiser should understand the ideas, symbols, and mythologies that are an important part of Polish culture and attempt to integrate these into advertising narratives. It is with this understanding and framework that I approach my narrative exploration of Polish advertising.

Architecture as Advertising

Because Poland was in an immense state of flux in the early 1990s, many of the ads from that period have been lost or are difficult to locate. This makes it difficult to say for certain how McDonald's approached the Polish market in these early years but several generalizations regarding this period can be made. First, it is known that McDonald's intentionally concentrated its efforts on the capital city of Warsaw, which probably means that the company was attempting to gain a presence in Poland while operating in the nation's most inviting market. Generally, a nation's capital is best equipped to support a new product like McDonald's because of a more diverse population and higher level of commercial activity. Additionally, Warsaw is politically, socially, and economically the most important city in Poland. Because of these factors, Warsaw would be the logical place for McDonald's to begin its Polish operations. As much of the advertising and marketing research has noted, Poland is a traditional-minded country that would appreciate the newness of McDonald's for a short time and would quickly need to know how the product connected to the lives of its citizens. In other words, McDonald's could not rely on being "cool" and "American" for very long and would quickly have to present itself as being partially Polish. While the term "Polish McDonald's" may sound oxymoronic, it does express the need for a multinational corporation like McDonald's to connect with the local culture and to be accepted as part of the community. One type of advertising that is readily available from this period is the signage and architecture from the McDonald's restaurants themselves. At first glance these permanent advertisements may seem pedestrian and unimportant but in reality they are significant advertising narratives that reveal much about the communication between Polish society and McDonald's. These architectural narratives speak to the relationship between the community and the corporation, and create a well-chronicled text that is waiting to be read and explored.

In the monograph *Golden Arches East: McDonald's in East Asia*, James Watson writes that McDonald's is symbolic of more than fast food, and claims that "McDonald's symbolizes different things to different people at different times in their lives: Predictability, safety, convenience, fun, familiarity, sanctuary, cleanliness, modernity, culinary tourism, and 'connectedness' to the world.... One is tempted to conclude that, in McDonald's case, the primary product is the experience itself" (38). In order to create this experience, McDonald's tightly controls its restaurants and strictly manages every aspect from kitchen to bathroom. One thing that is often overlooked by the lay person when considering McDonald's is the aesthetic design of individual restaurants. Although Americans frequently think of the fast-food restaurants as generic mass-produced spaces, in truth many contain unique designs built to appeal to the local populace. In Poland this desire to make McDonald's both unique and comfortable is apparent, as many of their locations attempt to marry the west with local culture. An excellent example of this is the first Polish McDonald's opened in Warsaw in 1992. This restaurant is located near a collection of rather gray and dreary communist-era buildings. The bright, shiny, glass-and-metal McDonald's serves as a stark contrast to those building that surround it. The two-story glass structure looks more like a train station or modern museum than a fast food restaurant. The front entrance is situated under a lofty glass arch with the Golden Arches logo placed at the top to beckon prospective customers. Metal tables and chairs are positioned in front of the restaurant to provide hungry Poles with a European street café setting that is popular in major cities. This modernistic design situated among architectural relics of Poland's past brings to mind Norman Foster's design for the glass dome that tops the ancient stone structure of the German Reichstag. To many Poles, though, it may be an allusion to a well-known interwar monograph, *Przedwiosnie* (Before Spring), by Stefan Żeromski. In the most famous section of the book, entitled "Glass House," a boy is given a vision of a rich and prosperous Poland in which all citizens live in glass houses. This story represents a vision of a bright future that was possible during the transition of the interwar years but never came to pass (*Część I — Szklane Domy*). When commenting on the design of the glass McDonald's, many Poles have expressed a possible connection to Żeromski's work and his idea of glass houses. Because *Przedwiosne* is required reading to pass the Polish high school exit exam, numerous Poles have read the book and remember its main themes, which connect to the new possibilities that the restaurant chain could provide. As Polish society was in transition in the early 1990s, a large, new, glass McDonald's could symbolize the lost promise of the interwar years and the nation's possible second chance. It seems improbable that McDonald's had Żeromski's novel in mind while designing the glass restaurant but the corporation did want to be a combination of traditional and modern to Polish customers. This idea of mixing traditional and modern elements and creating a new entity out of structures from the past is one of the restaurant chain's primary themes in Poland. In this restaurant — and in most Polish McDonald's — elements of American culture blend with Polish culture to create a new entity, a McDonald's that Poles can consider their own.

It should be noted that McDonald's' strategy of designing restaurants to fit native customs and tastes is not unique to the Polish market. Across the globe McDonald's often attempts to use local ideas and designs when creating its outlets. This even holds true within the United States where a neon encased McDonald's can be found in New York's Time Square and a McDonald's that stretches across an interstate exists in semi-rural Oklahoma. What is important to understand is that in Poland McDonald's has built numerous restaurants that advertise both McDonald's' foreignness and inclusiveness, an absolute necessity for a new product that wishes to be more than a passing fad. In essence these outlets act as concrete narrative texts that urge the viewer/reader to understand the chain's purposes in Poland. Three examples of McDonald's outlets that have managed to be new yet traditionally Polish can be found in the Polish cities of Warsaw, Krakow, and Zakopane. Each of these locations attempts to reflect the local environment and to define McDonald's as a new Polish citizen instead of a western colonizer.

Warsaw

As previously mentioned, as of 2007, the capital city of Warsaw was home to thirty-four McDonald's locations and was the site of the first

McDonald's in Poland. One of the most impressive of the company's restaurants is located in a historic and touristy part of Warsaw that is within walking distance of many notable attractions. The surrounding architecture is distinctly Polish in its beauty and grandeur. Although much of Warsaw was destroyed during World War II, a large portion of the city, including this area, was rebuilt to match its prewar condition. In order to advertise its presence but respect its surroundings, McDonald's had to build an outlet here that was forceful enough to be noticed but traditional enough not to be an eyesore. At this location McDonald's crafted what it has called "*Karczma Polska*" (Polish Tavern/Inn). It was created to resemble a traditional rural drinking establishment that would often serve as a neighborhood's center. The roof was crafted from special tiles made to bear a resemblance to rural Polish architecture. The inside was decorated with special arts and crafts to make the McDonald's feel like a Polish tavern. Additionally, a garden was fashioned adjacent to the restaurant to provide the sense of nature that would likely accompany an authentic Polish tavern. A first textual glance, this McDonald's may appear unimpressive and of little narrative importance. International companies often borrow native ideas or copy elements of local culture. What is important to understand is the conversation that the restaurant helps to create between McDonald's and Polish society. McDonald's is attempting to use the institution of the tavern/pub as a vehicle of inclusion. Although the importance of the tavern seemingly has diminished in the United States in recent years, in Poland local pubs and bars have highly respected social significance. Pubs are not merely locations to drink and meet members of the opposite sex but are often gathering places that serve as meeting areas in which communities are formed and upheld. Especially in smaller cities and rural communities, pubs often become one of the main institutions. Though it may be a stretch to compare Polish taverns to Quaker meetinghouses, the pubs are often the community nurturing "third places" that researchers like Ray Oldenburg claim are disappearing from many societies. In creating a fast food restaurant that copies the form and style of a traditional Polish meeting place, McDonald's is attempting to establish itself as a friendly cultural presence. The restaurant itself serves as a text that highlights the process of McDonald's becoming more Polish while still retaining its important American characteristics (McDonald's Poland).

Krakow

A second location that serves as a narrative of McDonald's' advertising in Poland is in the beautiful city of Krakow. Long known as the cultural hub of Poland, the historic city of Krakow also has become a popular tourist destination. Much of the city has been updated to serve the tourist industry's needs and often the time-weathered stone of ancient buildings can be seen covered with brightly colored advertising. One of the most important places in Krakow, and in many towns in Poland, is a large market square known as "*rynek*" in Polish. The *rynek* often serves as the central business district, entertainment center, and meeting place for larger towns or cities. The *rynek* is such an important concept in many Polish communities that it is often one of the first words that a visitor to Poland learns and one of the few he/she will not translate while speaking his/her own language. (While it would be strange to use Polish words like *tak*— yes — or *kapusta,* cabbage, in English sentences, many a tourist or expatriate can be heard to say, "I'll meet you later at the *rynek*.") Arguably, Krakow has the most beautiful *rynek* in Poland, an ancient, cobblestoned jewel that in 1978 was one of the first places in the world to be placed on UNESCO's World Heritage list (World Heritage List). Because of its historical and cultural importance, most Poles are extremely proud of Krakow and the city has a revered status within Polish culture.

In the mid–1990s McDonald's renovated a building on Florianska, one of the grand streets leading to the *rynek*, and there opened a restaurant. The outlet is within sight of the *rynek* and sits next to a Krakow landmark known as the Florian Gate. In other words, this Krakow McDonald's is located in a historic building that lies in the heart of the city and is adjacent to some of the most important symbols in Poland. When building this restaurant McDonald's had to be certain to use it to advertise to the public that it was trying to become a part of the Polish community and not merely a foreign interloper. Unlike the previously mentioned Warsaw Karczma McDonald's, the company did not attempt to reproduce the style of a Polish landmark, instead it attempted to change as little as possible. The Florianska McDonald's showcases the beautiful building while serving as a host to McDonald's. While the entry-level dining room and ordering stations are noticeable for their spaciousness, the true splendor of the building is evident in the multi-level gothic basements dating back to the thirteenth and fourteenth centuries that now serve as dining rooms. The restaurant's placement of tables, chairs, and other dining accoutrements serves to enhance the presence of the historic building. McDonald's clearly chose to build their restaurant around the needs of the building. While one could argue that McDonald's had little choice or did the only logical thing, that does not change the fact that the corporation's use of the restaurant served as an effective advertising narrative. The McDonald's entry into the Krakow market displays how restaurants can create advertising narratives that reassure and attempt to form cultural ties. While the Warsaw Karczma McDonald's attempted to model its restaurant on a Polish cultural symbol, the Krakow Florianska outlet chose to conserve an already existing structure. In doing so, the Krakow McDonald's became a part of the existing neighborhood and signaled to the Polish people that it wished to live within existing Polish boundaries. In selecting to preserve Polish culture, McDonald's respected the neighborhood surrounding the *rynek* and Poland's historic past. If Warsaw's Karczma McDonald's was an attempt to create a restaurant that connected with Polish culture, Krakow's Florianska location shows an understanding of how to live and work within Poland (McDonald's Poland).

Zakopane

Another McDonald's that displays the characteristics of architectural advertising being used in Poland is a restaurant in the mountain town of Zakopane. This quaint village on the Slovakian border is a favorite among Poles that enjoy its natural scenery and historic past. The town has a cultural style that to many Poles beckons back to a fairy-tale tradition of hard-working yet poor mountain folk. This belief combined with Polish culture's affinity for natural settings has caused Zakopane to become a top vacation destination for Poles. When McDonald's built a restaurant in Zakopane in the mid–1990s the corporation had to be certain to advertise that it was a member of the mountain community without becoming clichéd or overbearing. Although this may sound like the same style of restaurant advertising as in Warsaw and Krakow, it was much different. In the Karczma Warsaw McDonald's, the corporation recreated a rural symbol in an urban setting while in Krakow, the company kept a local building in its natural style. In Zakopane, McDonald's had to combine the two ideas in order to signal to Poles that the company was serious about being a member of the community. It is one thing to have a McDonald's in a major city and quite another to have one in a place that symbolizes nature for many Poles. McDonald's hired a local folk artist to design the Zakopane restaurant in a mountain style. The location emphasizes the use of wood, stone, and painted glass and even boasts a fireplace. In many ways this seems to be McDonalds' strategy for acceptance in the Polish market, emphasizing the chain's connection to the Polish community. This restaurant was designed by Poles, for Poles, and respected the local traditions and environment. This is in no way an endorsement of McDonalds' practices but rather a description of how McDonald's marketed and advertised itself by using its restaurants as tools in its early days in Poland. One cannot say for certain if these strategies have worked for the fast-food giant but it is important to note that McDonald's has grown considerably in the Polish market and only six years after opening its first Polish outlet in Warsaw it opened its one hundredth Polish restaurant on April 25, 1998 (McDonald's Poland). This certainly is not proof that the chain's early plan was successful but it does strongly suggest the possibility.

It should be noted that McDonald's has designed and created several restaurants in Poland that embrace the local culture. These locations conform to Polish norms while retaining McDonald's international elements. By blending its international elements with local cultural understandings McDonald's not only exists within Polish culture but also redefines and changes some parts of Polish society and culture. The previously examined marketing data indicated that most Poles were slow to embrace new concepts but also many valued new ideas when they were linked to Polish culture. This appears to have worked with McDonald's Poland where the company has changed to meet Polish expectations and in turn many Poles have adjusted their cultural practices to include McDonald's. Possibly the most important indicator of this change in Polish culture and customs is the rapid growth of McDonald's in Poland, which indicates that a sizable number of Poles are eating at the restaurants. Another indicator of this change, though, is media stories that describe new and transformed customs and habits. One such newspaper report from the *Warsaw Voice* in 2004 describes the change from traditional, Polish-style, inexpensive dining to McDonald's-style fast food. The article interviews Poles who compare a traditional Polish milk-bar restaurant to eating at McDonald's. Those interviewed indicate that there is room for both styles of food in Poland but McDonald's is providing something that the milk bars do not. Zuzanna Roszkowska, a student from Warsaw, is quoted as saying that she appreciates the cleanliness of McDonald's, which is often not a priority in Polish milk bars. She adds, "Besides, I think it's great that all the products served by a given chain look exactly the same in all its outlets around the world. In other restaurants completely different dishes may be found under the name 'pierogi,' prepared and served in diverse ways. [But] a hamburger is always a hamburger. Besides, you don't have to wait too long for your food at McDonald's, which can't be said about all the milk bars" ("Cheap Eats"). Although many may disagree with Roszkowska's desire for culinary conformity she does showcase a change in Polish desires and habits. McDonald's conformed to Polish norms in order fit into Polish culture but it also changed the ideas and values of at least some Poles in the process.

McDrive

While McDonald's was advertising its immersion in the Polish market with the design of its restaurants, it also was attempting to change the way that Poles thought about themselves and their culture. Before 1990, few individuals in Poland owned automobiles and many of the vehicles were used for business purposes. As the economic system changed, car ownership became more common and society began to reflect this growing trend. While figures from as late as 1999 show that Poland's per capita car sales were still a low .014, the rate of growth did increase dramatically. In the nineties car sales in Poland grew faster than any other country in Europe. From 1992 to 1998 automotive sales in Poland grew at a rate of 17.6 percent a year, which made it the eighth largest automotive market in Europe. Although Poland does not have anywhere near the per capita car ownership as the United States, the market is increasing dramatically and experts expect that trend to continue (Tutak). During this period of change toward more of a car culture in Poland, McDonald's was in some ways at the front of this trend. Because before 1990 personal ownership of cars was often literally a foreign concept to Poles, the idea of the drive-through restaurant was virtually nonexistent. During the 1990s, McDonald's often advertised its food as cheap and fast and opened many locations near highways or major roads with drive-throughs, which were called "McDrives."

It appears that McDonald's attempted to adhere to a strategy of opening two kinds of restaurants in Poland. First were the neighborhood locations like the ones mentioned earlier in places like Zakopane, Florianska Krakow, and Karczma Warsaw. As noted, these locations advertised the chain's willingness to become Polish and adapt to the local culture. Additionally, McDonald's created restaurants in areas near highly trafficked roads or highways that would give drivers easy access to fast food. This means that McDonald's could not only be seen as a local eatery but also as a provider of new kind of food service for those who owned cars. A television commercial from 1996, titled "McDrive," emphasizes these themes. It shows a man going to buy a new car from a dealership. The man measures the driver's side window and then tests the car by reaching out the window and pretending to take something in his hands. The commercial cuts to the man in the McDrive taking a McDonald's bag from the attendant. His family is shown happily eating McDonald's food and then his son whispers something in the man's ear, which causes him to go back through the McDrive and order more food. The commercial ends with a close up of the McDonald's McDrive sign and the announcer stating, "McDrive — you can eat without getting out of your car!" ("McDrive"). This commercial seems to indicate that McDonald's wanted to change Poland's ideas about cars and food. Dining no longer had to be a meal in a restaurant or at home but could now be achieved in the car. The name "McDrive" is now used in Poland for the concept of the drive-through. While this may seem minor, it is of great importance because an American company created a word in Polish that is used for a type of service no matter what company provides it. Additionally, the word references the original company's name, so that company will always come to mind when the consumer thinks of the service. This is what McDonald's was able to do with the "McDrive" in Poland. McDonald's added a word and a concept to Polish culture that continues to be linked to its company. In doing so, it was able to become a symbol the growing car culture and to advertise itself as both modern and a measure of success.

Polish Tradition

By the late 1990s, McDonald's restaurant designs and business practices had made McDonald's a recognizable brand in Poland, with well over a hundred locations in the country of almost forty million people. Important locations in major cultural spots had provided McDonald's with marketing and advertising that helped to establish its closeness to the Polish community. Its McDrive locations gave Polish consumers another view of the company as new, trendy, and exciting. As the new millennium approached, McDonald's found it necessary to not only build its image and brand in Poland but also to solidify itself and to become an even more important part of the nation. One way that the company attempted to accomplish all of these objectives was by television advertising that promoted its restaurants' multiple purposes. The ads from the period 1996–2007 reveal many of the themes and ideas that the fast food company used in Poland. One of the most important themes is much the same as one projected by the architecture and decor of many of the urban McDonald's restaurants in Poland, the idea of tradition versus modernization. A January 2000 television commercial (commonly known in Poland as a "*reklama*") utilizes this theme. The *reklama* entitled "Wies-Mac" markets a McDonald's sandwich called "WiesMac," unique to the Polish market. The word "*wies*" roughly translates as "rural" or "country" and is often used when referring to a traditional rural Polish lifestyle. The *reklama* features a family of stereotypical city dwellers arriving to visit a family that lives in the Polish countryside. The city family consists of a man, a woman, a boy and girl who arrive in the country with all the accoutrements of an urban lifestyle (fancy car, trendy clothing, skateboard, headphones, etc.). They are contrasted with a country family in traditional village attire who are surrounded by the symbols of the countryside (farming implements, livestock, rural architecture, and crops being harvested). To make things even clearer, the city folk announce their presence by less than subtly exclaiming, "Good morning! We are from the city." A sign on the barn reading "*Agroturystyka*" suggests that the members of the city family are agri-tourists trying to experience a back-to-nature way of life. In recent years this type of agricultural tourism, in which urban dwellers spend a short amount of time with a rural family in order to experience a traditional Polish lifestyle, has become ever more popular (Agro Wakacje). Shortly after the city folk arrive in the *reklama*, the rural hosts run out of food and the man of the house is sent to find more. He goes to McDonald's and orders WiesMacs, explaining to the woman taking his order that, "[as usual] I need WiesMacs for the city people." A picture of the WiesMac is then displayed as the announcer comments, "fresh country vegetables, cheese, new sauce, and two hamburgers." As the man leaves, the viewer sees that the McDonald's is surrounded by tractors, and the announcer exclaims, "WiesMac conquerors the city." This *reklama* wishes to connect McDonald's food to the purity and good taste of the countryside. In the ad, the wise rural dweller understands the value of McDonald's and the last line shows that the ways of the country have "conquered the city." While many would see this commercial as a sign that an international urban lifestyle has changed rural Poland, the ad promotes the opposite understanding of the situation. Instead of being seen as a multinational corporation that is forcing its products on Poland, McDonald's is declaring that traditional Polish values have affected the fast-food chain ("WiesMac").

Another *reklama* that plays on the theme of traditionalism in Poland is one from February 2002 entitled "Dziadek" (Grandfather). It features a granddad at play with his grandson. The older man astounds the youth with the timeless trick of pulling a coin from behind the youngster's ear as the child asks, "Once again, Grandpa, okay?" The grandfather looks at the amount of money in his hand and responds, "no, I have enough now!" and then leaves to go to McDonald's. The ad ends with pictures of McDonald's sandwiches, showing how inexpensive they are. The *reklama* is using a stereotypical situation between grandfather and grandson, and adapting a McDonald's product to fit. Although the humor in the ad is that the grandfather does something unexpected (leaving once he has enough money) the joke is only funny because the situation is so familiar. McDonald's employs the traditional family structure to sell its products in Poland and in doing so declares its kinship with Polish culture ("Dziadek").

"Mother's Day," a *reklama* from May 2005, uses the traditional family to an even greater degree. Throughout the commercial no words are spoken and the only sound heard is soft piano music, as pregnant women and mothers are shown in various situations. As each woman is revealed, words appear on the screen in Polish to describe the circumstances. For example, a pregnant woman is presented pushing a bicycle down a street and the caption reads, "I'm hopeful." A pregnant woman's stomach is displayed, along with the words "I'm strong." A man kisses a woman's pregnant stomach and the screen reads, "I'm proud." An expectant woman walks slowly in a manner suggesting that she is about to deliver, while a caption states, "I'm ready." A woman is shown in labor and then her newborn baby clutches her finger to the words, "I'm heroic." As the screen goes black a caption reads, "I love you, Mommy," then the golden arches logo appears and the words "I'm lovin' it." Nowhere in the ad is McDonald's mentioned except for its logo and slogan at the end. The commercial is an obvious example of the corporation selling symbols rather than food. McDonald's is attempting to sponsor motherhood and wrap itself in the glow of the traditional family unit. In this *reklama* McDonald's is using one of the healthiest and most natural symbols available (motherhood) to link its food to those same qualities. This idea connects McDonald's to important symbols within traditional Polish culture and promotes the company as valuing many of the same things as ordinary Poles ("Mother's Day").

McDonald's as Polish

Another theme that becomes prevalent in McDonald's advertising from 1996–2007 in Poland is that of McDonald's being a Polish product. While this may appear similar to the previous theme of tradition in Poland, it is quite different. McDonald's uses Polish tradition in its ads to convince Poles that its products meet their cultural needs. Early restaurant architecture and decor as advertising used symbols of tradition to market McDonald's as being Polish-like. Marketing McDonald's as a Polish product is the next logical step in the campaign. It takes McDonald's from being an outsider that is respecting Polish traditions to a company that is a genuine part of Poland. In essence the two themes, while different, are interconnected. As noted, McDonald's continued to use the theme of Polish tradition in their advertising through 2007, so the marketing of one idea does not impede the other. The major question that arises is how can McDonald's market itself as Polish after only entering the market a few years before? While very few Poles would identify McDonald's as a Polish company more would see the fast-food giant as a part of Polish society.

As more than one hundred restaurants opened and the aforementioned McDrives became commonplace, McDonald's became a very normal part of Poland. If the word "normal" does not entirely seem to fit in the previous sentence it is because it is being used as many Poles would use their version of the word, "*normalny*." In the United States "normal" often has a rather bland and uninspiring connotation. To label something normal is to call it average, common, or ordinary which is less than exciting for many individualistic overachievers. In Poland, *normalny* generally means not that something is average but rather that it is of good quality. To tell a person that he or she is "normal" in the United States would likely be akin to a nonstatement (or a medical diagnosis), while in Poland it would be a compliment that means the person is someone the speaker can identify with. (To be told that one is "very normal" by a Pole is an honor, the Polish equivalent of the Southernism "good people" or the Yiddish "mensch.") If McDonald's truly became a "normal" part of Polish society then that meant more than just average, it meant that many Poles deemed it as acceptable.

Some advertisements that helped to market McDonald's as culturally Polish are instructive as to how this theme is used. An early untitled *reklama* from 1997 shows a child's birthday party at the restaurant. At the beginning of the commercial, children and adults eat McDonald's food and sing the traditional Polish birthday song, *Sto lat*, as a large birthday cake topped with a McDonald's logo is presented. After the children run off to play in the multistory restaurant, the adults enjoy the McDonald's food and atmosphere and act like children celebrating a birthday. The ad then outlines the quality of ingredients and excellent preparation that go into Chicken McNuggets as "a reason why every occasion is good to visit our restaurants." The *reklama* finishes with a slogan, "Let's meet at McDonald's." Although the setting of the commercial is a child's birthday, from the tone of the ad it appears as if McDonald's is not a natural place to hold such an event. The ad informs the viewer that all occasions are good to come to McDonald's, which seems to indicate that the idea is not already widely accepted. Also, because the commercial mainly focuses on the fun that the adults are having and the quality of ingredients (hardly a child's concern) it appears to be aimed at influencing the adult market. While it is common for McDonald's to hold children's birthday parties around the world, it appears that in 1997 it was not an ordinary thing to have a party at

McDonald's in Poland. The restaurant chain was attempting to change that, and this commercial seems to be laying the groundwork for changes to come. McDonald's was not a valued member of Polish society in 1997 but the company was attempting to alter this ("Untitled").

If the 1997 commercial appears to attest to the continued foreignness of McDonald's in Poland, then a January 2001 *reklama* displays another attempt to change this situation. This commercial, titled "Quality," chronicles the life of a McDonald's' French fry in Poland from farmer to customer. The ad, which features no dialogue, appears to be a stylistic precursor of the Mother's Day commercial that was discussed earlier. It starts with a shot of a field of potatoes as a man picks them, and the name of the town in which this takes place, Bobrowniki K. Leborka, is shown in a stylized handwriting on the screen. The man, dressed in a checkered shirt, is then shown holding a potato, and the name "Jan Nowacki" appears. He throws the potato to a worker loading a truck with bags of potatoes, and the name "Marcin Szylko" graces the screen. The truck is opened in a factory in the town of Leborle where a man inspects it, and the name "Pawel Malesymink" is shown. A McDonald's truck is driven to a restaurant and the city name of Wolica appears. A McDonald's worker, identified as Adam Kozlowski, catches a plastic bag of uncooked fries, and after they are prepared another worker, Piotr Zawanda, gives the French fries to two children, Kuba and Stas. The ad ends with the McDonald's logo and the slogan "We know our products from the cradle" ("Quality").

The first thing to note about the commercial "Quality" is the use of a potato-based product as its theme. The potato has long been a staple of the Polish diet and a large part of the economy. The United Nations Food and Agricultural Organization ranked Poland as the seventh largest potato producer in the world in 2005 (UNFAO). The World Potato Congress estimates that 10.5 percent of available arable land in Poland is used for potatoes (World Potato Congress). Even the word for potato in Poland, "*ziemniaki*," holds special signifigance because it is derived from the word "*ziemi*," meaning "soil" or "earth," which may indicate its importance in a historically argicultural society. To many Poles the potato is a symbol of agriculture and a traditional Polish lifestyle, and its usage in the ad reflects a deep connection to Polish culture. Additionally, the commercial obviously is attempting to demonstrate how McDonald's' French fries in Poland are grown, inspected, packaged, shipped, cooked, served and eaten by

Poles. While the company may be foreign, everything associated with French fries, and other products by inference, is Polish. The names of the places where the product is produced and consumed are familiar, the names of the people and the way they look and dress are recognizable and the product is already culturally Polish. Nothing in the commercial would indicate that McDonald's is a foreign company. Rather it appears that in Poland McDonald's is managed, operated, and patronized by Poles. In this way the ad attempts to infer that the company is at least partially Polish and has made a substantial transition to become part of the local community.

Just as the commercials from 1997 and 2001 attempt to showcase McDonald's as being more Polish, a television ad from January 2002, called "Skoki," tries to display the chain's Polish traits to the viewer. In the commercial a ski jumper, dressed in red and white, attempts to successfully complete a ski jump while his competitor, dressed in yellow and red, pulls even in mid-air and invites the first jumper to McDonald's. The ad ends with the two men eating together at McDonald's, still dressed in their ski clothing. To understand the underlying message of this commercial one needs to understand that in the early years of the twenty-first century a Polish ski jumper named Adam Małysz became incredibly popular in Poland and still remains a national sports icon. Małysz, an Olympic medalist and three-time world champion, is a consistent subject of talk among Poles and a source of pride for the nation (Cristodero). One of the main reasons that the skier is so popular is because of his friendly, unassuming manner and his underprivileged rural background (Adam Małysz). In the commercial, the first skier is dressed in red and white, the national colors of the Poland and ones that Małysz himself sometimes wears. The other skier is wearing a yellow-and-red ski suit, the standard colors of McDonald's restaurants and the ones that McDonald's mascot Ronald McDonald generally wears. In this context it is easy to see the red-and-white clad ski jumper as a symbol of Poland and the yellow-and-red dressed athlete as a representation of McDonald's. The two symbols meet in midair and Poland is invited to a McDonald's establishment to share a meal and honor the nation's success. In this way McDonald's is linking itself with a Polish hero and attempting to celebrate his victories with Poland. By doing this McDonald's is trying to become a part of the culture and share the nation's triumphs and defeats. McDonald's created an advertisement that few outside of Poland would understand in order to display to Poles that company understands and respects the local culture ("Skoki").

In 2003 the company produced another ad that endeavored to display McDonald's as being Polish. The *reklama* titled "McKielbasa" shows a man with a grill on the side of a highway, selling Polish sausage or kielbasa from a roadside stand. As cars stop to buy a kielbasa the stand's owner silently waves the would-be customers down the road. He then closes his stand and drives to a nearby McDonald's to get a McKielbasa, and the commercial ends as he is eating the sandwich. To understand the commercial one needs to know that kielbasa stands are a fixture near highways and large roads in Poland. Many Poles consider the sausage to be a Polish dietary staple and delicacy and often stop at a stand to get this very Polish food. In the ad a kielbasa stand owner, the keeper of a Polish gastronomical tradition, is deferring to McDonald's and admitting that the restaurant makes a better sausage than he does. In such a way, in the ad, McDonald's has become more Polish than the roadside cook. The restaurant has mastered a Polish delicacy in a way that only a Pole can, and now makes it as well as or better than many other Poles. McDonald's has not only designed a sandwich based on a popular Polish meal but now claims to be able to prepare it better than Poles. The restaurant chain is asserting that it not only is Polish but that it is better at being Polish than many people in Poland ("McKielbasa").

In "Potato Print," a May 2004 television commercial, McDonald's continued its theme of announcing its Polishness. This ad is reminiscent of the 1997 untitled commercial in which the adults enjoy a child's birthday party at McDonald's because it also portrays the restaurant as a cultural institution and not just an eatery. In "Potato Print," McDonald's advertises a two-day craft workshop for children in which they can participate in "crazy T-shirt stamping" by using a potato stamp and paint to make designs on a T-shirt. The beginning of the ad shows children creating their T-shirts and at the end a young child named Kasper uses his shirt to blend in with the wallpaper and hide from his dad. Much like the earlier commercial, this one encourages families to visit McDonald's but unlike the previous ad the new one does not attempt to promote the good qualities of McDonald's restaurants. The new commercial does not market the restaurant or declare a list of its advantages. That is assumed to be prior knowledge in the ad. Before, McDonald's was marketing itself to parents who would bring their children to the restaurant. Now the restaurant is appealing to the children. Mostly likely this means that McDonald's had become a known and accepted entity and no longer had to advertise its basic qualities. In 1997 it had to appeal to customers who knew little about it, but in 2004 it was already a member of the community. Now both children and adults presumably understand McDonald's qualities and see the restaurant as a viable social option, a substantial change seven years ("Potato Print").

Internationalization

While early on McDonald's introduced itself to the Polish market by utilizing Poland's tradition and attempted to gain acceptance in the community by emphasizing its Polishness, it also understood that one of the primary purposes of advertising and marketing is to change customer taste and behavior. It would not be enough for McDonald's to adjust to Polish culture and tastes, Poles would also have to adapt to international ideas and tastes. While the company did not wish to be seen as a corporate cultural colonizer, it also could not accept the role of Polish imitator. McDonald's needed to be both foreign but friendly to Poland, trendy yet traditional, international but non-threatening. McDonald's had to find (or create) customers that wanted new experiences and longed for a change. In other words McDonald's needed to become more Polish, but it also needed Poles to become more international.

In early advertisements, like the previously mentioned "McDrive" from 1996 and 1997's birthday-party ad, it is clear that McDonald's is an outsider that is trying to become part of the Polish market. In these early commercials, McDonald's was admitting its foreignness but was attempting to showcase its respect for Polish culture. McDonald's was trying to become more Polish and to blend into the community. But a substantial change can be seen from the first commercials in 1996 until the last ones of 2007. While McDonald's was unique and unfamiliar in 1996 it had become commonplace in ten years. Part of this was probably accomplished by the campaign to make McDonald's appear more Polish, but just as influential was Poles becoming more accepting of international culture. A perceivable change is evident in the McDonald's commercials starting in

2002, when the ads begin to focus less on Polish society and more on Poland's place in the world. Before, ads concentrated on the company's place in Poland and how the company fit into the nation's culture but starting in 2002 many commercials identified Poland as a growing member of the international community and showed McDonald's serving as a bridge between the nation and the world. In other words, from 1996–2001, McDonald's appears to be mainly working to become a part of Polish society, but from 2002–2007, the corporation, having already established its influence in Poland, began attempts to connect Poland to the outside world.

It is difficult to ascertain why the focus of McDonald's advertising seemed to change in 2002. Certainly, there were still commercials that focused on the company's place within Poland but the majority seemed to be more internationally focused. One explanation for this shift is that McDonald's advertising was deemed to have worked well in establishing the company in Poland so it moved on to its next strategy. Also, McDonald's was moving to a more internationally focused advertising approach in many countries at this time. The international "I'm lovin' it" campaign was being introduced and the company was connecting its advertising operations in many countries. Additionally, and probably most importantly, Poland was in the process of joining the European Union, which was changing the way that Poles thought about themselves and the world. A combination of these factors most likely led to this change in McDonalds's advertising in Poland. The company saw that their place in the Polish market had progressed and that Poland's place in the world was changing, and used the new campaign as an opportunity to grow in the market.

Scholars often debate whether advertising acts as a mirror or a molder of society. Although few answers to this question have been agreed upon, it does seem evident that the new transnational approach of McDonald's in Poland was at least partially inspired by world affairs. A wave of internationalism was beginning to sweep through countries like Poland and McDonald's seemed to be in position to benefit. In 1999, a number of central and eastern European countries, including Poland, joined NATO. Founded in the midst of the Cold War to provide security against the Soviet Union and other communist countries in Europe (including Poland), NATO expanded its rank in 1999 to include many of its former adversaries. As Poland joined NATO it not only gained a military alliance with many countries, primarily the United States, but it was also taking a greater role in the international community. Political scientist George Sanford comments that NATO membership was a possible first step for Poland to gain substantial political power in Europe and the world. He sees Poland's future role as that of a bridge between eastern and western Europe and as a representative of each (92–94). If NATO membership marked a perceivable beginning to Poland's internationalist approach then the nation's entry into the European Union (EU) further expanded the notion. As the EU expanded in 2004, Poland was the largest of the new EU countries and potentially one of the most powerful. Scholar Kerry Longhurst quotes then Polish president Alexander Kwasniewski as saying that Poland's new role in the world after September 11, 2001 was to "act as a leader to coax Eastern nations into the Western camp and to persuade the West to accept them" (53). Even then U.S. Secretary of Defense Donald Rumsfeld's controversial comment that the United States was interested in New Europe and not Old Europe conveys the idea that Poland was growing in international stature. It is in this environment that McDonald's started its new international campaigns, one in which "new" Poland seemed on the verge of an international revival.

As previously mentioned, 2002 seems to mark the international transition of McDonald's Polish advertising. Like many transitions, this year does not mark a total change but rather the beginning of what later can be perceived as a new path. Some commercials from 2002–2003 either combine the ideas of tradition, Polishness, and transnationalism or focus on the former ideas from the past. Examples of these ads, already described, are "Quality" (the potato ad), "Skoki" (the ski-jumper ad), and "Dziadek" (the grandfather and grandson ad). While some ads show links to the old themes of tradition and Polishness, others are almost entirely international in tone. An example of this is a commercial titled "Engel," starring Jerzy Engel, then head coach of the national football team. The ad begins with a shadowy figure walking down a long outdoor corridor at night as emotional, percussion-based music plays. The man walks into a dark stadium and the lights theatrically illuminate, one after another. The unidentified man, dressed in a long coat, suit, and tie, reveals his face for the first time and he begins talking about his guidelines for life. "Football, that's my whole life," he says in Polish. As he plays with a soccer ball, he continues,

"I believe in what I do. I always try to do everything the best way possible." The camera shows a close-up of his face as he says, "I demand quality." Then as he turns his back to the camera and leaves the stadium, he finishes: "After the game...." The screen then goes black and displays the McDonald's logo entwined with the FIFA (soccer association) logo and the message that McDonald's is a sponsor of FIFA. Interestingly, the most important parts of this ad are never stated. Engel is never identified by name and his job as coach of the national soccer team is never mentioned. Engel is so well known in Poland that it is unnecessary to identify him to the viewer. As in most European countries and elsewhere in the world, international soccer is sport bordering on religion. The Polish team is an obsession to a large number of the nation's fans and holds a revered status within the country. In this way, the ad focuses on an important symbol of Polish society and then links itself to that symbol. The commercial does more than declare its Polishness though; it also subtly connects Poland to the idea of internationalism. Certainly one understands that Engel is endorsing McDonald's but the company and the coach are also endorsing the idea of international soccer. This ad aired near or during the World Cup of soccer in 2002 and served as an identification of Poland's presence in the world. Soccer is certainly a national obsession among Poles but it is also one that links Poland to other countries and creates an international framework for both Poland and McDonald's ("Engel").

Another 2002 *reklama* that shows this gradual transition into the theme of internationalization is titled "McPolska" and it also connects to the 2002 FIFA World Cup. In the ad a group of men run down an empty street to get home in order to watch the World Cup. Each of them has been to McDonald's and is now rushing home in time for the game. The ad ends with a shot of a McDonald's outlet and the word "*Futbolmania!*" next to the golden arches and the FIFA symbol. This ad features a sandwich called the "McPolska" (McPoland) but references Poland in no other way ("McPolska"). In much the same fashion a commercial from 2004 titled "Olympic Weeks" shows a Polish woman that the viewer thinks to be an Olympic athlete but is later revealed to be delivering food to an elderly man. The ad promotes Greek-themed food products (since the games were held in Athens in 2004), the Greek Mac and the Greek salad, but nothing is mentioned of Poland. At the end of the commercial, the golden arches and the Olympic rings are displayed together and the corporations declares itself to be, a "proud partner" ("Olympic Weeks"). Both the World Cup and the Olympics gave McDonald's opportunities to promote itself as international while still appealing to a local audience. These large international events are valued as chances to show nationalistic pride while embracing a transnational existence. By using these revered forms of internationalization, McDonald's is able to take safe steps toward marketing itself as an international brand. In such a way the company can still appear to be a local entity but one with an international scope.

Perhaps a series of "I'm lovin' it" commercials from 2003–2004 best express the theme of internationalization in Polish McDonald's ads. These ads show quickly intercut footage of urban dwellers from around the world interacting with their environments and enjoying McDonalds' food as a Polish rap plays in the background. Although a few denizens of the ads are distinctly Polish, many of the people featured are either of a generic nationality or clearly non–Poles. While the footage for these ads was apparently used in many different national markets, the background rap was produced for Poland. The song's lyrics are mostly nonsensical observations on the problems and joys of everyday life, like "my car, downtown culture, have to go, my office is calling" and "surprises break my sleep sometimes but I know that my babe likes what I do." The ads' lyrics are of little importance but their style and the technique of the photography are. The video is produced as a montage of rapidly moving clips that is reminiscent of an MTV video. Besides emphasizing the international aspect of McDonald's, the commercial also markets itself to a youth audience. These ideas are a departure from many of the previous ads that appear to be geared toward an older, more traditionally Polish audience ("I'm lovin' it"). This is possibly because McDonald's believed that the valuable youth market would be in tune with internationalization more than an older audience would. The "I'm lovin' it" commercials demonstrate a belief that both Poland and McDonald's are part of a larger international community that share a number of core ideas and values. In the ads, McDonald's is portrayed as representing the things that all people wish to have: excitement, friends, and fun. In the commercials' idealized global society these common items bring peoples together and are the bonds that remain. This idea of an international society does conform to a stereotypical youthful view that sharing common values can unite the peoples of the world. All of the world citizens in the ad dance and display youthful excitement as the Polish rapper announces how good life is. In such a way McDonald's is declaring that the young generation of Poland will be internationalists and the company will begin to emphasize its transnational presence. This is a significant transition for a corporation that had spent over ten years trying to appear as Polish as possible.

It is important to recognize that although McDonald's was attempting to become part of an internationalist change in Poland, it was doing so from a position of strength rather than weakness. As evidenced by how the company presented itself in later ads, by 2002 McDonald's had become a visible part of Polish life. While it might be foolhardy to argue that McDonald's had become Polish in many citizens' minds, the ads' tone and composition suggest that the corporation had become a part of Polish society. While, like many businesses, McDonald's found it necessary to continue to aggressively market itself, it no longer had to explain the basic idea of what it was and what it did. McDonald's was no longer a visitor to Poland but an immigrant that shared many ideas and customs with the society. This is important because, as Poland's international status increased, McDonald's was Polish enough to be both local and international. In many ways McDonald's and Poland had grown together and were expanding into the international community as partners. The international-themed ads' narratives suggest that many were aimed at a young audience that had scarcely ever known a Poland without McDonald's. A sixteen-year-old in 2003 would have been age five in 1992 when McDonald's first entered the Polish market. Though it may have taken a few years for McDonald's to open an outlet in their town, these young Poles would have almost certainly had childhood contact with the restaurant. It is to these customers that the international ads are aimed because in some ways McDonald's helped to train them to be part of a transnational world. McDonald's, along with other international brands, helped to develop the concept of international culture and to sell it to primarily younger people in countries like Poland. By becoming part of the Polish community and offering choices to the local population, McDonald's changed and grew with Poland in a way that is not entirely controlled by either. Although McDonald's is undoubtedly using the advertising and marketing strategies that best serve the company's needs, it is doing so in cooperation with a Polish society that is also deciding which direction is best for its culture.

2. McPoland

By the year 2007, McDonald's commercials were increasingly international in theme and tone. The advertising appears to embrace Poland and McDonald's increasing focus on transnational connections and emphasizes international ties. One example of this is the previously discussed "Mother's Day" ad from 2005. This commercial that shows scenes of pregnant women and childbirth promotes traditional family values but also does it in an international context. The ad contains women of multiple nationalities and ethnic backgrounds, promoting the idea of motherhood and its link to McDonald's. The ad not only expresses McDonald's connection to families but also sets this theme in an international context. The company is not only emphasizing Polish families but rather all families in the world and how the concept of family is a shared value. Another ad from 2005 celebrates World Children's Day, a holiday in some countries. Much like the Mother's Day ad, this one plays background music while scenes of children and families are shown. In the Children's Day commercial, though, the music is provided by American recording artists Destiny's Child and the band travels from location to location to view children around the world. The narrator explains that by coming to McDonald's and donating money a customer can help give children around the world a secure future. The Polish customers are encouraged to give money at local McDonald's to help children in Poland and the entire world ("World Children's Day"). The ad contains a mixture of local and international; the music and musicians are international yet locally known and consumed. The children in the ad are from many places in the world but their problems and pleasures are the same as those of children in Poland. McDonald's is an international company that operates locally and wants to help not only Polish children but all children. In these two ads the elements and themes are a mixture of local and international. In the past, each would have included something to make them seem more Polish. In 2007 McDonald's was able make the ads both local (without referencing Poland) and international. This shifting and blending of themes and ideas reflects the changes in both McDonald's and Poland from 1992–2007. As McDonald's marketed its goods in Poland it had to constantly change in order to conform to what many Poles needed and desired. The company had to become a recognizable and accepted part of the Polish community. Although McDonald's understood what it wanted to accomplish in Poland, the company needed to work within boundaries of Polish culture and society. This means that although McDonald's helped to change Poland in many ways, these changes were generally directed and accepted by the Poles themselves. The residents of Poland forced McDonald's to adhere to the standards of local society and to offer culturally desirable goods and services.

Summary

There is an often-told story of a Japanese couple that bring their daughter to the United States for vacation. While in the United States the family passes a McDonald's outlet and the daughter announces, "Look, they have McDonald's here too, like in Japan." While this may seem comical to those who know that McDonald's is an American-based company, it displays the point that international brands like McDonald's have become a ubiquitous part of children's lives worldwide. This cultural familiarity with its brand is one of McDonald's primary goals around the world and in the Polish market in particular. After introducing itself to Poland in 1992, McDonald's quickly attempted to define itself as a company that understood and respected Polish culture and values. This is evidenced by the architectural advertising that was built into restaurants in historic places like Warsaw, Krakow, and Zakopane, and the reoccurring theme of Polishness in McDonald's commercials. These advertisements attempted to brand McDonald's as a western company that understood and respected Poland. Although one cannot say for certain how well this strategy succeeded, later commercials display a familiarity with the products that, coupled with McDonald's rapid growth and sustainability, seems to indicate a fairly high level of success. In other words, a large amount of people appear to have accepted McDonald's as a viable part of the Polish community. One can debate if McDonald's advertising acted as a mirror or molder in Poland but it seems clear that the corporation became widely received within Polish society. Around the year 2002, the corporation appears to have altered its approach and instead of solely focusing on its image as a good Polish citizen, it expanded its identity to also be considered more international. This transition closely followed trends within Poland that marked the nation as more viable internationally and more open to transnational exchanges. As 2007 ended, Poland was a member of NATO and the European Union, and becoming internationally powerful, and McDonald's was promoting its Polishness as well as its international standing. In many ways this is a story of how McDonald's was able to have its cake and eat it too. An American company was able to establish itself in Poland in 1992, display itself as culturally akin to Polish society, and then expand itself to promote its international status. In a world in which image is terribly important, McDonald's seems to have marketed itself into Polish culture as both a local and international brand.

McDonald's Television Commercials

Ad Title	Year Produced	Themes
Dziadek	2002	Traditionalism
Engel	2002	Internationalism
I'm lovin' it	2004	Internationalism
McDrive	1996	Cultural Change
McKielbasa	2003	Polish McDonald's
McPolska	2002	Internationalism
Mother's Day	2005	Traditionalism, Internationalism
Olympic Weeks	2004	Internationalism
Potato Print	2004	Polish McDonald's
Quality	2001	Polish McDonald's
Skoki	2002	Polish McDonald's
Untitled	1997	Polish McDonald's
WiesMac	2000	Traditionalism
World Children's Day	2005	Traditionalism, Internationalism

3

Levi's: Rebellion in a Size 6

A much-repeated story among English-speaking expatriates living in Poland begins, as a many do, with a young American noticing a beautiful Polish girl in a local bar. In this version the hero downs a few shots of liquid courage, approaches the young woman, and tries to communicate in broken Polish. Finding the young lady's English superior to his Polish, they carry on a slow conversation. The Polish girl informs him that she respects the United States and especially likes America's beautiful levees. The young American asks her to repeat herself and again the girl tells him how much she likes the levees. The young man tries to understand if he has enjoyed one Polish beer too many or if he has meet someone with an interest in civil engineering, and asks what she likes about levees. Her answer, that they are well designed and look good, confuses him even more. Unable to converse easily about rivers, floods, levees, and dams, the conversation dies and the two part ways. The next day, when talking to his friend, the young man learns that "levees" is the Polish pronunciation of "Levi's"—the girl was talking about blue jeans.

Much like McDonald's and Coca-Cola, Levi Strauss & Co. is one of the most recognizable brand names in the world. Levi's was founded in San Francisco during the Gold Rush of the 1850s. The company began making denim clothing, especially blue jeans, for laborers who needed rugged work wear to meet their demanding lifestyles. Over time, Levi's became synonymous with the concept of jeans and the individualistic, youth-oriented lifestyle that the clothing came to represent both in the

United States and abroad. Internationally, Levi's became a symbol of freedom, rebelliousness, and individuality, and the jeans were especially valued in communist Europe where both the product and the ideals it represented were in short supply. Although Levi's were not officially marketed in the Eastern Bloc, the jeans were a well-known product that was coveted by many. American travelers to the USSR were told to bring cartons of Marlboro cigarettes and Levi's jeans to trade with locals hungry for both western products. In Hungary, often described as the most western of the Warsaw Pact nations, a thriving black market sold Levi's jeans to customers willing to pay high prices. In communist Poland, consumers who agreed to pay outlandish prices could purchase jeans at a chain called Pewex that specialized in western goods. Even before Levi Strauss & Co. officially entered these countries in the early 1990s, its products were already understood and desired by many.

Levi's in Poland

Levi's jeans are unique among the products discussed in this book because they are the only nonfood and non-beverage product, and thus have a much longer shelf life than McDonald's food, Coca-Cola drinks, or Frito-Lay snacks. In theory, a pair of Levi's jeans can be stored for decades and then used or resold with the promise of the same quality or value as when they were made. This long shelf life meant that Levi's jeans could be sold in communist Europe even if they were not officially being marketed because they would not expire during the length of time it took to travel through underground channels. Additionally, Levi's jeans are by definition a clothing item that has the dual purpose of utilitarian usage and fashion statement. Levi's are comfortable and nice to wear for one's personal satisfaction, but generally more importantly they also make a statement about the wearer. The jeans symbolize many things to observers and often their opinion of the wearer changes after connecting the owner to his or her Levi's. In other words, people who owned a pair of Levi's in communist Poland probably became the objects of envy of many because of their association with the product. This linkage between ownership of Levi's and elevated social status is most apparent when speaking to middle-aged residents of Poland. Most Poles have a story of how much he or she wanted a pair of jeans and how Levi's was the most desirable brand of all. Many reflect that Levi's were symbolic of individuality and the west, both in the political and historical sense. One woman in her forties from the industrial region of Silesia tells of a girl who was the first in her elementary-school class to own a pair of jeans, and to this day, over thirty years later the woman is still associated with being the first to have jeans in the storyteller's mind (Cieślak). This desirability of jeans in general and Levi's in particular is important because it helps to demonstrate the market that existed prior to the company's entrance in Poland. Unlike McDonald's, Coca-Cola, and Frito-Lay, which often had be both simultaneously western/international and Polish, Levi's main selling point when entering Poland was its product's connection with the west and the concepts that went along with that. Levi's did not need to make itself more Polish or make Poland more western; instead it needed to promote the idea that Levi's jeans were universally desirable.

Levi Strauss & Co. opened its first factory in Poland in 1991 and began to sell and market its products in the country not long afterward. As mentioned before, even prior to 1991 Levi's had a presence in the Polish market, which often is credited to the product's appearance in American film and television. Many popular American films and television shows featured jeans-wearing characters which made jeans exciting and desirable. These entertainment vehicles preceded Levi's official entry into Poland and helped to create demand before the product was readily accessible. Additionally, many Poles had families in the United States and England that sent them jeans as gifts. After Levi's entered Poland in the early 1990s, the company's market strategy was to sell jeans from Levi's stores and thus promote its brand as being exclusive. European television commercials were often used alongside print ads specifically designed for the Polish market. This created a campaign across Europe that could be tailored to a specific country or market. This means that Poland's Levi's ads had many of the same themes that were used across Europe and the United States, which helped to cement the universal appeal of the product. In the early stages of its official arrival into Poland, Levi Strauss did not wish to become more Polish but rather the company wanted to market the universal appeal of its apparel.

The makers and advertisers of Levi's jeans found themselves in a unique and almost oxymoronic situation internationally and especially in

Poland. Levi's is a brand with a tradition as a western icon and an anti-establishment product. Levi's jeans have a long history as a product of the American west and as a symbol of rebelliousness in the fifties and sixties. This link to the past provides apparent documentation that the company has always produced products for rebels and renegades. The advertising website AdForum remarks that this strategy in European advertising of noting Levi's legacy started because of the brand's less-than-stellar reputation. AdForum states, "When Levi's first came to us in the early 1980's the denim market was in decline. There was no brand leadership in the market and Levi's were seen as old persons [*sic*] jeans. Being an American brand, Levi's was associated with Ronald Reagan, Dinasours [*sic*] of Rock and fat tourists. In product tests, consumers found Levi's 501s unattractive" (AdForum). Because of this preconception, the marketers focused on Levi's past as a strength and a chance to use American mythology:

> [Bartle Bogle Hegarty, Levi's advertising agency's] solution for the 501 was to celebrate the authenticity of the Original Jean. Our aim was to focus on the 1950s when Levi's 501 was adopted as a badge of youth rebellion and cool. We developed a Mythical America far from contemporary reality and captured the enduring values of youth: sex, rebellion, freedom and individuality whilst luxuriating in product detail. The brand territory we identified for Levi's was Originality and the Big Idea was The Original and Definitive Jean, a positioning which Levi's still adheres to today [AdForum].

Levi's advertising focused on a mythical American past, a good America that countered any negative contemporary images of the United States. In such a way, America was not a nation as much as it was an idea. Paradoxically, the primary audience for Levi's ads was teenagers and young adults, a group generally uninterested in history. This means that Levi's had to embrace its past and mythological heritage, while courting a youth audience, not an easy task for any marketer. Many Levi's ads focused on the iconic nature of the brand, while placing the product in a contemporary youthful setting. The ads often included attractive scantily dressed characters who seemed to lead exciting and desirable lifestyles. Although these characters were often stereotypes or clichés, they also were timeless ideas that seemingly appealed to young viewers. The themes of good times and overt sexuality were frequently used in advertising, and Levi's mixed them with elements of the past in an attempt to create a classical brand that continued to be modern.

Levi's European commercials from 1992 to 1994 are good examples of the company's agenda to mix the present and the past to create a seemingly timeless brand that would appeal to a foreign market. Though created in the United Kingdom, these television commercials were some of the first Levi's advertising in Poland and served as an official introduction to Levi's as American myth. The ads are groundbreaking in their use of music and plot ideas, often appearing more like sixty- or ninety-second films than television commercials. Each miniature motion picture introduced characters, established a storyline, and generally ended with a plot twist in around a minute. Because of the language barrier, most European Levi's commercials contain little or no dialogue and instead relied on a soundtrack of recognizable, popular music. This created a commercial that appealed to consumers weaned on MTV-style videos and action-driven films. Levi's cultivated the notion that its ads were more than "just television commercials" by listing its past ads on its Web site and including such information as director, actors, music, singers, and plot summary. By creating these short film commercials, Levi's was declaring its marketing to be smarter and fresher than its competition, which in turn stated that the company held these same values. Levi's embraced its past mythology as rebel and used that image to declare itself both contemporary innovator and current radical. This message would appear to especially appeal to early 1990s Poland, a country that was being widely introduced to Levi's jeans for the first time and that may have held many of these ideas about the United States in its collective memory.

Two television commercials that showcase Levi's usage of its American mythological rebelliousness to attract contemporary customers are ads from 1992 entitled "Swimmer" and "Night and Day." "Swimmer" depicts an idealized version of 1950s high-society America, replete with fancy garden parties and lush lawns. The narrative follows a muscular, shirtless young man running through a series of backyards and diving into multiple swimming pools while wearing only his Levi's jeans, as Dinah Washington sings "Mad About the Boy." The young man finally jumps into his girlfriend's pool and they end the commercial diving off of a high board together, her wearing a swimming suit and him still in his Levi's jeans. The ad finishes with the tagline, "The more you wash them the better they get" ("Swimmer"). The quirky nature of the commercial mixed with the mythologized America of the past as its setting provides Levi's an avenue to declare its history of nonconformity. All of the characters of the commercial are stereotypical Americans of lore: the well-dressed home owners that watch the young man run from pool to pool, the servants that wait on the American nobility, the young girl dressed in debutante pink that falls for the young man from the wrong side of the tracks, and said young man that fights both the oppressive nature of society and the monetary elite. This seems to reference the modern American fable of the rich girl and the poor rebellious boy and mirrors much of the style of 1987's *Dirty Dancing*, a film popular among Poles of the younger generation. The mythological loner/rebel/antisocial young man of the ad undoubtedly was designed to appeal to a young audience that identified with the character in theory if not in practice. Levi's was marketing to a Poland that had just escaped the communist era and was embracing the rebellious idea of independence. By setting the ad in the 1950s, Levi's could create a safe level of rebellion during a bygone era in an America that may have never existed. Levi's was hoping that young Poles desired a mythologized American brand that could provide an impression of rebellion that had been denied to Poland during the socialist era.

Another 1992 Levi's commercial, "Night and Day," relies on the mismatched lovers theme but with a storyline that closely resembles the fairy tale "Cinderella." In this ad, a young woman hurries down the stairs of an office building as a clock strikes midnight. On the way down she loses a shoe and is pursued out of the building by a man. On the street, a biker stops between the woman and the man and drops a pair of Levi's jeans before disappearing. Later the woman searches the town for the jeans' owner and after asking many men, finds him — a handsome mechanic ("Night and Day"). Like the previous ad, this one uses a well-known tale in a new way to sell Levi's jeans. The fairy tale of "Cinderella" is European in origin, but the modern corporate setting and the American product of Levi's seems to embrace a western or American attitude. The commercial carries the same theme of rebellion but recasts the neo–Cinderella as a motorcycle-riding man and the jeans as the new glass slipper. The woman is the pursuer who takes control of her life, not conforming to an antiquated system of rules. She finds happiness by being aggressive rather than passive and thus does not conform to the stereotypical woman's role. By doing this she is rebelling against the past and much of society. In the end, this rebellion proves to be fruitful because she is able to acquire what she desires and prove herself to be independent. By creating this ad, Levi's was again declaring the rebellious and individualistic spirit of its company and products. To many, the ideas of individuality and rebelliousness are symbolically linked to the United States, mythologized land of freedom. Its pioneering spirit was reflected in blue jeans. This usage of the mythology of the past allowed Levi's to use its corporate and product history in a way that appeared fresh and modern instead of tired and antiquated. In Levi's mythology the company is serving the same role that it always has, keeper American individuality and rebelliousness. Although Levi's is connected to the past it is a product of the individual and not of society. This message would be especially powerful in Poland, where historical ties to the United States and the recent past gave special meaning to the struggle between individual and society.

Rebellious American Mythology

While companies like McDonald's and Coca-Cola attempted to become a part of Polish society by accentuating shared values, Levi's endeavored to gain market share by showcasing its Americanness. A number of commercials from 1993 to 1995 display how Levi's continued to use both the brand's historical importance and a mythologized America in contemporary European advertising geared toward a youthful market. Although the commercials differ stylistically, each of them chronicles a bygone era of American life and how it relates to Levi's jeans. 1993's "Campfire" displays picturesque John Ford-like cinematography as several cowboys pose for an attractive female photographer in what appears to be the early twentieth century southwestern United States. As Johnny Cash's "Ring of Fire" plays in the background, the ad artfully presents the clash between the American west and the modern United States. In a scene that brings to mind Frederick Jackson Turner's famous remarks about the end of the frontier, the cowboys are photographed in their natural habitat. While posing for the picture a young man sits too close to the campfire and the metal rivet in the middle of his jeans overheats, causing him to leap into the air and scream (and provides a new context to the background music). The ad ends as the cowboy, on horseback, tips his hat while watching the woman drive away toward the expansive horizon, with the tagline, "1941 saw the end of the notorious crotch rivet. 501. The original jean" ("Campfire"). Much could be made of the presence of the attractive cowboy and photographer and the sexual symbolism of the young man's crotch being on fire. While the sexuality of the ad certainly is an important element of the commercial, more important is the link to a mythologized American west. As discussed in chapter two, the cowboy and the American west provide a heavily symbolic and mythological image of the United States to Poles. The cowboy, the symbol of individuality, the rebellious loner living by his own code of conduct is both well known and highly appreciated in Poland. By associating itself with the historical coolness of the American cowboy, Levi's is able to it claim that it has always been a brand of rebels. In doing so, Levi's is not only linked to the time and place but also becomes a part of the mythology itself. This means that to many Poles, Levi's becomes a part of the American western legend.

Levi's produced other ads in this series that used much the same formula, showcasing a rebellious, historical, American archetype as in the commercial "Campfire." 1994's "Creek," follows a family of religious American pioneers that seem to undertake a family picnic in the American west during the mid nineteenth century. While the parents partake of lunch, the two daughters dressed in bonnets and cumbersome dresses frolic in the wooded mountain region and eventually see a handsome young man seemingly bathing naked in a lake. After seeing the shirtless man washing himself, the girls find his Levi's jeans hanging on a nearby tree and wait with both longing and shock as he begins to exit the water. As the handsome young man walks out of the lake the girls learn with disappointment that he is still wearing his jeans. They next are upset to see an older, less-attractive man exit the lake looking for his jeans. The girls watch as the still-shirtless young man walks toward his horse, and the tagline appears — "In 1873 Levi's Only Came Shrink To Fit. 501. The Original Jean" ("Creek"). Although no dialogue is used in the ad and no explanation of events or characters is given, the people and time period depicted in the ads are so iconic that the viewer is able to understand the context. The characters' dress and habits, the horse-drawn wagon, the majestic scenery, and the black-and-white film immediately provide clues that allow the viewer to create a back story based on an understanding of American mythology. These are pioneers in a wide-open land. They are the "men of hope and expectation, of enterprise and energy," described by Theodore

Roosevelt in his famous 1901 "Nation of Pioneers" speech (Roosevelt). Although the commercial's vision may not be historically accurate, it is important mythologically. The story that America was founded by rough-and-tumble, hardworking pioneers, who faced long odds but persisted and built a new society, is often told. The character of the pioneer resembles the cowboy in that both are rebellious spirits who create their own rules. In showing that pioneers preferred Levi's the company was attaching itself to another important historical symbol that held contemporary credence.

One more commercial from this series, which highlights Levi's usage of rebellious American historical mythology, is 1995's "Drugstore," a fast-paced ad set in what appears to be the early twentieth century. The grainy, over-exposed black-and-white ad has an eerie, voyeuristic feel that reminds one of a 1950s B-style horror film. The ad has two versions, which contain the same storyline but transpose the gender of the rebellious hero. In one ad the hero is a young man while in the other it is a young woman. The commercial follows the young hero as she drives through a gritty small town and purchases condoms from the owner of the local general store. The hero then sticks the tin of condoms in the watch pocket of her Levi's jeans and drives to a young man's house. Arriving at the residence, the young hero is greeted by her date's father, the same man that sold her the condoms. The man forbids his child to exit the house but the boy pushes his way past and leaves. The ad ends with a close-up of the store owner's angry, horrified face, as the tagline reads, "Watch pocket created in 1873. Abused ever since. 501. The Original Jean" ("Drugstore"). The mythological character of this commercial is the bored and rebellious small town American youth, trapped in a place and a life that she longs to leave. Obviously, by shooting two versions of the commercial, Levi's was attempting to be gender-neutral and to declare that rebellion has no gender. This is important because Levi's was again using a historical situation but changing the terms of the surrounding myth. Much like in the "Night and Day" ad, Levi's used a well-known story but changed the characters in order to declare that gender roles were no longer binding. In the traditional story it would be a male who bought the condoms and came looking for sexual fulfillment. In Levi's revised version each gender has an equal claim to a rebellious nature.

Besides challenging the issues of gender, this ad also differs from previous ads in its treatment of class structure. The gender-neutral James Dean-like character is much like the young man in the previously discussed

1992 commercial "Swimmer" except this ad contains no elements that refer to social class. In "Drugstore," the youths select companions who look very much like themselves in dress and mannerisms, and there is no hint that this coupling will change either life in any way. The tagline suggests that the watch pocket of the jeans is allowing the couple to commit "abuses" against the closed society in which they live. The sexual act that they appear to be destined to engage in is a deed of rebellion and individuality even though it is one of the world's most often experienced. The expressions of the store owner and the other customers as the youth buys the condom suggest that she is engaging in an outrageous behavior, even though it is not at all unusual. By having premarital sex and using contraceptives to prevent pregnancy, the young person is flaunting her society's rules regarding both sexual and biological normalcy. Levi's, by providing a secret compartment to hide contraband contraceptives, becomes an accessory to the act and a conspirator in the rebellion. This idea of small, everyday rebellions against a large monolithic system would undoubtedly appeal to young Poles. While many assuredly possessed the same youthful angst as their young brethren around the world, young Poles had also grown up in an oppressive society that would have limited their choices, leaving them searching for an outlet. Levi's uses the symbolic American rebel to tap into some of these frustrations and declare an understanding. Levi's once again is showing solidarity, with individuals and rebels in Europe in general and Poland specifically.

Contemporary Rebellion

While much of the early Levi Strauss advertising in Poland was produced for a mass European market, many later ads were created specifically for the Polish customer, often by Polish firms or Polish offices of international advertising agencies. One such campaign is a series of print ads created for the Polish market starting in 1996. These ads, designed to market Levi's Red Tab jeans, continue the theme of youthful rebellion but place the emphasis on contemporary youth instead of historical images. The common element of these ads is the red tab that is attached to each pair of Levi's jeans. This bright red label, with the word "Levi's" stitched in white, serves as an iconic logo for this campaign and others. In three of the print ads, shirtless young men and women are shown in various poses, advertising Levi's jeans. Each of the models' hair has been colored a striking bright red in order to match the hue of the Levi's Red Tab logo ("Red Tab 1, 2, and 3"). In taking on the qualities of the blue jeans, the model and the jeans have become interconnected and the line that separates wearer from clothing has become blurred. The models no longer merely wear the Levi's jeans but rather have become attached to the ideas of the product, and in return the product has become integrated into the wearer's life. The jeans have become a part of the user's daily existence and are no longer only an American myth or idea but increasingly a Polish one. The ads still declare that Levi's jeans are a product for individuals and rebels but they do not reference the brand's Americanness. Undoubtedly, a Polish ad viewer would be aware of Levi's American heritage, but no longer were advertisers stressing this linkage. These ads appear to mark a turning point for Levi's in Poland, where the blue-jean maker began attempting to become more universal. Before, Levi's jeans claimed to be a product of youthful rebellion and could prove it with an American historical pedigree in 1996 with its ads, Levi's seems content to remain "cool" but does not feel the need to label itself as American. No longer are rebellion and youthful coolness portrayed as only American traits. In these ads these qualities become universals that young Poles can embrace. Levi's was now offering Poles a symbol of something broader and deeper than American culture.

Three other print ads from this campaign seem to support the theory that Levi's was attempting to transform itself into a transnational idea. Each of the advertisements displays the head of a young man or woman marked with the bright redness of Levi's Red Tab. The first ad features the close-up faces of a red-headed couple, another displays a side view of the head of a young man adorned with red rooster-like plumage, while the last shows the side and back of a young woman sporting chicken-like feathers. In each of the ads the pictures are shown next to the Red Tab label and the words "Red Tab" and the Polish translation, "*Czerwona W Szwka*" ("Red Tab 4, 5, and 6"). Levi's jeans are featured in none of the ads and if not for the Levi's logo it would be altogether unclear what was being advertised. The storylines within the ads are debatable, which seems to be intentional. The ads are an unsettling mixture of brightness and grayness, a jarring jumble of creativity and apathy. Although the meaning of the ads is uncertain, one can certainly surmise that youth rebellion and individuality are a part of it. The latter two ads appear to have turned the models into a rooster and a chicken, possibly as a way to express their base, animalistic tendencies. The highlighting of these carnal desires may be a reference to a teenager's growing sexual desire or a young person's feeling of isolation and uncertainty. No matter what type of individualistic rebellion the ads are meant to convey, it seems clear that each attempts to garner universal understanding and appeal. In previously aired ads in Poland, Levi's linked itself to an understood American mythology. In these ads, the company embraces universally known animal traits in order to display its selling points. In the past Levi's marketed itself as a historically rebellious American company with ties to many of the great American myths and ideas. In 1996 the jeans maker portrayed itself as the keeper of individuality, not only an American idea but a universal one.

During the mid–1990s Levi's ads continued the practice of showing rebellion and individuality in a non-nationalistic, non-gender-based way, but usually with an unexpected twist. In a series of international commercials, Levi's focused less on its historical American past and more on its universal appeal. "Planet," a 1995 commercial, portrays the typical scene of a young woman rebelling against her parent's rules and wishes as the neighbors watch in horror. Although this sounds like a clichéd situation, the twist is that all of these events take place on another planet. The girl wearing Levi's jeans is an alien living in another society, but her life and experiences with her parents and neighbors mirror a stereotypical Earth teenager. Levi's is claiming not only to be international but rather truly universal ("Planet"). Concepts like the problems of youth, rebellion, and individuality are shown to be not American ideas but rather natural elements of life that all people share. In this ad even aliens understand the problems and complications of youth and the universal coolness of Levi's.

Likewise, in "Mermaids," a 1997 commercial, a man is rescued from drowning by three beautiful mermaids who try to steal his Levi's jeans. The man escapes with his clothing but it is clear that the mermaids desire the jeans much more than the man ("Mermaids"). In much the same way as "Planet," this ad shows the universal appeal of Levi's jeans. By showing that even legendary characters like mermaids understand the importance of Levi's and what they symbolize, the company is further distancing itself from being only an American product. Another example of this idea is a 1997 commercial, "Kung-Fu." This ad, created in a 1970s kung-fu-film style, follows a martial-arts hero as he is pursued by would-be killers. The action flows from a Chinese restaurant, to a rooftop, and a city street. Eventually the hero enters a laundry where a woman is about to wash a pair of Levi's jeans. In one quick motion the hero turns the jeans inside-out, hands them to the woman, and leaves the shop to continue the fight. The tagline appears, "Levi's 501. The Original Jeans. Best Washed Inside Out" ("Kung-Fu"). Again this ad takes a non–American rebellious mythology and links it to Levi's. While early 1990s ads used selected American settings and ideas, these ads from the mid–1990s embraced a more global vision of Levi's primary themes, youth, individuality, and rebelliousness. Levi's will most likely always be associated with its American past, but the company decided to not market that feature in its mid–1990s advertising. It also chose not to create ads that catered to individual nations or markets. Instead these ads show Levi's as an international brand marketing global ideas. This change to a marketing strategy that downplays the brand's American ties means that in places like Poland Levi's was attempting to become more locally acceptable. Unlike McDonald's, Levi's did not try to become more Polish but instead the brand wanted to gain status by becoming universal. Levi's hoped to develop its brand into one that could break the bonds of nationalism and become commonly accepted.

New Rebellion

Two other themes that dominated Levi's ads in Poland and Europe in the mid-to-late nineties were strong women and unusual storylines. These themes, evident in most of the Levi's advertising that has been discussed, became more prevalent in the latter half of the decade. As seen in previous ads like "Night and Day," "Campfire," "Planet," and "Drug-store," the role of women in society is one of the major elements in many Levi's ads. Even the Polish print ads from 1996 portray women as equally rebellious and outrageous as their male counterparts. While much of the reason for this stance probably can be traced to the large female market for jeans, it also speaks to an easy target for youthful rebellion, traditional gender roles. While in the past in Poland communist governments often encouraged women to work outside the home, the country remained primarily conservative. The nation's Catholic identity, coupled with strongly held

98

traditional views, helped to solidify highly structured, conservative gender roles. The fall of the communist government in 1989 marked a point in which many things, including gender roles, may have begun to change, but the change progressed slowly. Because of this, one can assume that the idea of more open gender roles would play well with many Polish youths who wished to rebel against perceived societal norms. Even though these commercials were not designed specifically for a Polish audience they almost certainly would have been seen as rebellious and individualistic to many young Poles.

One more mid–1990s commercial that showcases the idea of a non-traditional woman is a 1996 ad entitled "Washroom." In this commercial a woman who has just robbed a bank quickly enters a gas-station bathroom where a man holding a stick and wearing dark glasses is sitting. The woman, believing that the man is blind, takes off her clothes and her disguise, and hides them in the bag of money. Then, uncertain if the man is actually blind, she suggestively buttons her Levi's jeans and is unable to garner a reaction. Shortly after the woman leaves, a blind man emerges from the bathroom stall and takes his stick from the man in the corner. The tagline reads, "The original button fly. Seen in all the wrong places. Levi's 501. The Original Jean" ("Washroom"). Although the ad at first appears to be a male fantasy about secretly seeing a sexy woman undress, at closer inspection it has a very strong, nontraditional heroine. The ethics and morals of the woman, as a bank robber, may be questionable, but throughout the ad she appears to be intelligent and capable. She robs a bank and gets away without getting caught. She is quick-thinking enough to enter the men's bathroom when the women's is locked, and she assesses the situation with the dark-glasses-wearing man and even tests him, using her sexuality. While her occupation may be dubious, she displays all the traits of a capable career woman and defies categorization. In creating this character, Levi's was presenting another strong woman who rebels against society and touts her individuality.

Unusual Themes

The other major theme of Levi's in the mid and late 1990s is of oddly themed ads that often appear to have no meaning and no relation to the product. The most famous is a 1998 spot, "Hamster," that displays the death of Kevin the hamster after his exercise wheel breaks. The ad contains no visual depiction of Levi's jeans, and the connection between the rodent's death and the clothing is never made ("Hamster"). "Wives," another 1998 commercial, shows the life of a man with many wives and one model ship. It never is explained how these things connect to Levi's or what they means to the viewer ("Wives"). While past ads were akin to Hollywood films, these commercials appear to be more like experimental cinema. Other examples are 1998's "Mall," in which a man is riding the escalator in a shopping mall. At first the viewer only sees the top half of the man who appears to be behaving normally. Later the man is shown to be wearing no clothing on the lower half of his body ("Mall"). Another 1998 commercial, "Photocopier," has a copy machine printing out copies of the word "copy" as it counts down. When the machine reaches zero, it is hit by a large truck and demolished ("Photocopier"). All of these ads conclude with the tagline, "The original." It appears that Levi's was attempting to create anti-commercials that did not follow the generally understood rules of how to sell a product. As previously noted, the product was not shown or mentioned and the entire point was difficult to understand. By doing this Levi's was probably trying to showcase its rebelliousness and independence from another perspective. The ads, like Levi's jeans, do not follow the rules and instead are original. It does not matter if others understand them, what is important is that they feel right. This sentiment was likely crafted to appeal to young viewers' feelings of alienation and dissatisfaction with society. While the ads may be hard to understand as narratives, they do present Levi's themes of rebellion and individuality. The company seems to have mostly abandoned its use of mythology and Americana but still clings to its historical importance. The tagline, "the original," reminds consumers that the company has historical ties to youthful rebellion and individuality in an archetypal way that will never go out of style. The jeans maker advertises itself as having always been cool and remaining that way until the present day. In other words, even though Levi's was creating seemingly unusual ads it was using them to market the same message to its consumers.

Creating a New, Sexualized Image

As the twentieth century ended and the twenty-first commenced, Levi's found itself battling image problems in both the United States and

Europe. The company started to lose market share to newer brands such as FUBU and Diesel (Marsh 119–121). In Poland, brands such as Big Star, Wrangler, and Lee gained popularity and caused Levi's to rethink its approach to product design and advertising. One of the company's biggest changes was the summer 1999 launch of "Levi's Engineered Jean" (LEJ). This new style twists the seams of jeans in order to give the wearer more flexibility and freedom. The jeans are generally worn low and baggy, and Levi's touts them as an urban product. Notably, the jeans maker does not contend that LEJ is a new idea but rather asserts that the style is an enhancement of a natural occurring feature of Levi's jeans. The tag on the back of the jeans contains a veritable narrative: "In 1998, a Levi's Creative came up with a new way to construct the classic jean. The idea was simple. Deliberately use the unique and iconic feature of the 501 jean — 'The Leg Twist' — to create extra comfort in tomorrow's jeans" (Levi's Poland). Levi's once again chose to embrace its past and link its LEJ brand to its original jeans created in the nineteenth century. Advertising for the product displayed few ties to Levi's history, though, and generally focused on young couples in urban/suburban, sexualized settings. While past ads were flirtatious or coyly sexual, commercials for LEJ have often presented the product as a part of the suburban teenage mating ritual, or, in some cases, even as a sexual stimulant. This expansion of Levi's jeans' sexual role may be a reflection of a more sexualized culture or it might be an attempt to increase sales through titillation. Although the tagline for most of the ads includes the word "original," little is made of Levi's history or the mythology of the brand.

The sexualization of Levi's jeans advertising is evident in an international advertising campaign starting in the year 2000 with the tagline, "The Twisted Original." These commercials appear to focus more on the jean's role in interpersonal relationships and less on past themes such as history, mythology, and Americana. While the themes of rebelliousness and individuality can be found in the ads, they are less apparent. A good example of this campaign is "Undressed," a commercial from 2000. The ad focuses on a young, playful, naked couple that seductively dresses each other. After the two are fully dressed, their family returns home fully naked, catching the couple with clothing on ("Undressed"). The commercial presents a seemingly existentialist view of the "rules of society" but also portrays the sexual nature of clothing, jeans in particular. Another commercial, entitled "Dolls," shows two inflated, Levi's-jeans-wearing blow-up dolls that fall in love. After the male doll is blown into a fence and punctured, the female doll commits suicide by puncturing herself on the same fence. While the commercial seems to portray an offbeat love story, the subject of the narrative is a couple of blow-up dolls that appear akin to the sex-toy variety. At one point in the ad, the female doll even makes a face with a circular mouth that mirrors the pose of many sex dolls ("Dolls"). One must wonder if this is a shared joke that teenagers and young adults would understand more than older adults like their parents. In "Legs," from 2000, two pairs of jeans are separated at the factory and then find each other on the street one day. The jeans remove themselves from their owner's bodies and eventually wrap around each other, leaving their owners jeansless ("Legs"). The commercial is part modern-day fable and part visual example of the supposed sexual potency of Levi's jeans. The two pairs of jeans carry a pent-up sensuality that overtakes their owners and is eventually too powerful for them to handle.

Another international campaign for LEJ, with the caption "Twisted to Fit," expands the sexuality of the advertising. In 2001's "Temptation," a girl straddles and fondles a limp pair of Levi's jeans until they become still and erect. With the obvious statement of jeans as phallic symbol, the commercial again declares that Levi's are a carrier of sexual energy ("Temptation"). This connection between Levi's jeans and sexuality is also evident in another 2001 ad, "Flirt." In this commercial a young man and woman begin to silently show anatomical parts that match the twisted nature of their jeans while waiting in a subway station. Twisted hair, teeth, eyebrows, and navels are displayed, and then as the man undoes his pants, the lights go out. As the lighting returns the girl smiles in approval of what she has been shown, the message being that the man's sexual organ matched the twisted nature of his Levi's jeans ("Flirt"). In this way his jeans become a symbol for his penis. One last example is a series of three 2002 commercials for Levi's Worn Jeans. Each of these ads is titled "Rub," parenthetically described with the place that the action takes happens — "Rub (Shop Window)," "Rub (Hole in Wall)," and "Rub (Bowling Alley)." In each commercial young men and women sensually rub themselves against numerous objects in an urban environment. The tagline for the ads is, "Rub Yourself. Levi's Worn Jeans." The slogan and the visual are blatant references to masturbation and the sexual nature of the jeans. In all of these ads, Levi's jeans have become symbolic of sex organs or sex itself. While it could be argued that this interest in sex is an extension of the themes of rebellion and individuality, in the new ads one had to search for those themes when before they were readily apparent. In the early twenty-first century Levi's appears to be moving away from many of its older themes in order to focus on more sensational fare. Although the company still embraces its historical roots by declaring the LEJ an extension of its oldest brands, it chooses not to use that idea in much of its advertising. This may be a sign of changing tastes or new social norms but in the early years of the new millennium ideas like the Levi's role in American history are rarely mentioned.

Increased Urban Orientation

During the early years of the twenty-first century, Levi's international and local ads in Poland concentrated more on sexuality than other historical themes. This focus marked a shift for the company and seems to indicate a discernible effort to portray the jeans as more modern and youth-oriented. This trend of sexuality in Levi's advertising continued throughout the first half of the decade, but around 2003 it was joined by another seemingly new theme: urban life. While several previous ads had urban settings or city-dwelling characters, ads generally portrayed Levi's as a product for rural, small-town, suburbanite, or urban professional people. For example, the previously mentioned 1992 commercial "Night and Day" has a large metropolis as the setting, and the characters are urban professionals (the business woman) and skilled laborers (the mechanic). None of the characters seem gritty and street-smart. Many of Levi's past ads featured a boy or a girl from a lower socio-economic class but the characters rarely fit the twenty-first-century definition of urban, which is a product of the greater influence of rap music and hip-hop culture. While in the past "urban" may have only meant something that was related to the city, by the late 1990s the word had taken on connotations of hip-hop style and sensibilities. Baggy-pants-wearing youths, accessorized with flashy jewelry and cars, and listening to loud rap music became the new spokespersons for the concept of urban. As this understanding became part of the global culture, Levi's appears to have started using more urban characters and settings in its ads in an attempt to embrace trendiness of modern urban culture.

A 2003 international commercial, "Swap," displays Levi's focus on this new urban culture. As fast-paced music blares in the background, a group of youths menace several denizens of a city. Some of the ad's characters are fully human but others are human-bodied, mouse-headed adolescents that appear to be integrated into society. A gang of human and mouse-headed youths swagger aggressively through the city, asserting their dominance as they do. One female mouse-head forcefully evicts a suit-and-tie-wearing man from a phone booth, so that she can make a call. Eventually, the gang meets a wealthy woman in a deserted parking lot and, in exchange for a cash payment, the woman is given her cat that apparently has been kidnapped and held for ransom by the gang. The ad ends with the tagline, "Levi's Type 1 Jeans. A Bold New Breed" ("Swap"). Although the ad does not mention hip-hop culture or play rap music, it does employ many of the themes that are found in modern urban culture. The tone of the commercial has the same sense of menace that many "gangsta" rappers foster and exude. This idea of aggressive, street-hardened youths is one of the cornerstone elements of hip-hop and is found throughout "Swap." Also, the gritty urban setting of the commercial matches hip-hop's view of city life. In the ad, the city is bright, crowded, noisy, fast-paced, and dangerous. It is a place filled with predators and victims, and denizens of the city seem to understand of how life needs to be lived. This is not the ordered, civilized city of past ads but rather an urban jungle in which one has to fight and steal in order to survive. Additionally, many of themes of the commercial mirror hip-hop culture: the wealthy versus the underprivileged, one's right to disobey the law in order to continue to exist, and the sliding moral scale of contemporary urban life. Much of Levi's message in the commercial seems to be about race or nationality, as evidenced by the mouse-headed figures and the use of the word "breed" in the tagline. This inclusion of racial or ethnic differences mirrors many of the conversations about race that surround rap and hip-hop. While some could argue that many of themes that emerge from "Swap" could also be connected to other youth movements like punk or heavy metal, these youth factions do not fully address such a wide spectrum of ideas in the same manner as hip-hop. As "Swap" and other ads reveal, Levi's was embracing a new version of urbanism in the twenty-first century.

A 2004 Web site designed by Levi's for the Polish market also attempted to capitalize on the image and accessibility of hip-hop. The page that advertises Levi's 501 Anti-Form Jeans promotes a contest to compose a rap track. The page allows the user to select from a series of different words and three pre-programmed background beats in order to craft a 40-word rap. The site depicts several youths dressed in stereotypical urban outfits (i.e., baggy pants, sleeveless white shirts, leather jackets, etc.) and contains oddly juxtaposed words, often crafted in a free-form graffiti-inspired style (Levi's Anti-Form). The site is attempting to embrace the hip-hop movement and to give Levi's an urban image among youths in Poland. Interestingly, by focusing on hip-hop and rap Levi's begins to return to one of its earliest themes: being an American product. Although rap has been embraced by youth in many places around the world, it is still a quintessentially American art form that carries a connection to the United States in the minds of many. "Swap" was set in an American city, even though the ad was broadcast widely in Europe. The 501 Anti-Form Webpage is mostly in English even though it was designed for the Polish market by the Polish branch of an international ad agency (*iLeo Poland*). Even many of the words that would-be rappers can chose from are Americanisms, like "yo," "rap," and "hip-hop." Although the type of American culture differs greatly from previous versions, Levi's once again began to display its American identity in its urban-themed ads. In some ways, city streets were the new version of the mythic, untamed American west. Just as Levi's had wanted to be the symbol of the American frontier it also wants to be linked to the new myth of the new urban America.

Local Urban Culture

Another marketing avenue that displays Levi's early twenty-first-century attachment to the urban lifestyle is in store advertising. Posters, floor displays, and other advertising materials that were present in Levi's stores in Poland provide insights into the brand's connection with the theme of urban culture. Posters advertising sales within the store often picture youths dressed in baggy jeans, oversized hooded shirts, or other hip-hop-inspired styles. Several of the images are of black males, which stand in contrast to Poland's homogeneous white society. Additionally, printing or lettering on posters, displays, or handouts generally reflects a street-art aesthetic. The type is not uniform in size, color, font, or placement. The color and the size of the letters is changed often and the words are placed haphazardly, invoking the style of graffiti. The advertising often uses a mixture of Polish and English words that suggests a fusion of cultures and the reappearance of a mythologized America. Ironically, it is black America that is being idealized and marketed in the newest version of the myth, a group and culture that has appeared in very few ads in Poland in the past. Just as Levi's had previously linked itself to American icons and myths that were not readily available in Poland like the cowboy, the frontier, and 1950s America, now the company was presenting African-American urban culture as an alternative culture to young Poles.

Levi's use of an urban theme and its ties to African-American culture can be seen in two window displays from Levi's stores. These windows were used to showcase Levi's products and to entice shoppers to enter the store. The first display featured Levi's clothing in the foreground with a poster for 501 Anti-Form Jeans in the back. The poster presents one large image of a young black man and three small pictures of urban youths of various ethnicities of the left side. The large photo that dominates the poster is of a black man wearing baggy jeans and holding his left hand in the air away from his body in a way that is popular among rappers. The images on the side show the youths in various types of oversized jeans and urban dress, and in Polish the caption reads, "Choose your style. Your size. Big. Or Very Big" ("Choose Your Style"). The ad is using young black men and urban youths in familiar outfits and poses to promote Levi's as urban culture to Polish youths. Two of the four pictures on the poster are of black youths and the clothing and body positions suggest to the viewer that the young men of the ad are city dwellers. By promoting African-American urban culture in a country that lacks much diversity, Levi's is linking itself to the growing mythology that surrounds the idea of urban culture. The jeans maker is endorsing the new mythology of urban America much as it did with its rural predecessor in the past. It is asking Polish consumers to embrace elements of an urban African-American culture that is both unique and familiar.

A second Levi's store-window display that uses urban American mythology to promote the company in Poland is an ad for Type 1 Jeans. The window is pasted with the name of the product and the slogan "A

Bold New Breed," and announces that 3D glasses are available inside. Behind the products displayed in the window is a large poster with 3D cartoon artwork that shows a young black male dressed in Levi's urban gear fighting a much larger man dressed in a long flowing coat that resembles the Neo character in the film *The Matrix*. On the poster the long-coated man appears to be controlling a ray-like weapon that is blinding the black youth ("A Bold New Breed"). This ad uses the young black male as a hero and has him fighting an evil villain. In doing so, Levi's is not only portraying the urban youth as an individual, appealing to young buyers' sense of longing for freedom, but also as a comic-book-style hero who fights against larger and more powerful adversaries. This expands the mythology of the urban American, making him not only a popular and respected figure but also a hero. This transition mirrors the use of the cowboy as hero and further displays the change that is taking place, moving the American mythology from a rural setting to an urban one. Levi's is again linking itself to a mythological America that in many ways never existed. It is continuing to choose themes and myths that display the qualities of individuality and rebelliousness, but the characters and the locations that are used have changed. Before it was the American frontier, small-town and rural America, and the suburbs and their denizens that were the preferred locations and characters. At the start of the twenty-first century new locations and groups of people are becoming the focus of the myths. In many ways Levi's is merely doing what it had done since the beginning in Poland, attempting to link itself to classical ideas while proclaiming itself to be modern, and asking Poles to accept the brand as an icon of individuality and rebellion.

Urban Poland

Levi's did not attempt to create the myth of American urban culture, but rather the company adapted an idea that was already prevalent in Polish youth culture. During the late 1990s and the early twenty-first century, shortly before Levi's began using the theme in its advertising, rap music and urban culture started to be embraced by many Polish youths just as they had in other parts of the world. The popularization of rap in Poland is often credited to a radio show introduced in 1993 and hosted by Bogna Swiatkowska and DJ Volt. This radio broadcast played American rap and hip-hop and the disc jockeys explained the American contexts of the songs, often focusing on the problems and issues that confronted African Americans in the United States (Polish HipHop Scene). The radio show not only played rap music but also educated the Polish audience about black urban America and showcased links to the Polish urban experience. Soon hip-hop culture was spreading among Polish youths who created their own rap in Polish and organized "black parties" at local clubs and discos. By the middle of the first decade of the twenty-first century, rap and hip-hop had become so popular in Poland and so identified with America that the U.S. embassy in Warsaw welcomed hip-hop pioneer Afrika Bambaataa to its "America Presents" series to talk about the history of hip-hop (America Presents). Many Polish teenagers and young men and women identify with the stereotypical mythologized African-American experience and consider the trials of urban Polish life to be akin to the problems of the American inner city. Polish rappers, like the popular Peja, create lyrics about brutal living conditions in Polish *bloki* (housing projects) and the general difficulties of life. These Polish rappers seem to identify with their American counterparts as evidenced by one Peja track that includes the words "South Bronx! South, South Bronx!" as its only English lyrics in order to show solidarity with his perceived urban American brethren (Faruque). This is the marketplace into which Levi's launched its urban-themed ads, one in which the youth of Poland often identify with and respect their American counterparts and furthermore wish to emulate them. Like most of its past uses of American mythology, Levi's was building on desire for urban American culture within Poland. Once again the jeans maker was using an American myth to proclaim the company's product's desirability.

The New Icon

Levi's advertising continues to stress its products' urban appeal in the middle of the first decade of the new century but it also refocuses on solidifying its iconic status in a way that appeals to contemporary youths. In numerous ways Levi's advertisements from 2003 to 2007 reinterpret many of the same themes of fun, individualism, independence, and rebelliousness

108

within the new urban aesthetic. Although little is concretely presented about Levi's ties to historical Americanism, the themes and the products are portrayed as international/transnational with a strong American flavor. Thematically, the new advertisements are akin to those from the early and mid–1990s with the exception that Levi's now often downplays history. Instead the company wishes to present itself as a contemporary and fashionable brand that appeals to modern youths. In many ways this is the primary responsibility of Levi's advertising and marketing, to constantly represent and repackage the themes of Levi's for a new customer audience. While it would be easy to dismiss 2003–2007 Polish advertising as repetitive and uncreative because of its similarities to past advertising, that would be unfair. The purpose of these ads is to re-create the traditional themes of Levi's for a new generation. The company understands that much of what its customer base wants remains unchanged, even if this is unknown to the consumers themselves. In reintroducing classic themes of fun, independence, rebelliousness, and individuality in new ways, the company is staying on message and allowing a new generation of customers to hear it again for the first time.

Many of the Polish advertisements from the early years of the twenty-first century present a flirty sexual awareness that expresses not only the sexual desirousness of the clothing but the rebelliousness and individuality that they symbolize. As previously mentioned, sexuality is a recurring device in Levi's advertising. A large portion of the company's early and mid–1990s ads were sexually suggestive, while later ads often utilized more sexually intense storylines. Both varieties of ads were meant to connect Levi's to the ideas of nonconformity and individuality that sexuality often represents. Although sex is a universal fact of life for humans, adolescents are often discouraged from engaging in sexual relations, especially in a predominantly Catholic country like Poland, often making sex and discussion of it rebellious. While one cannot argue against the notion that one of the purposes of these types of ads is to titillate, one also cannot deny that Levi's is attempting to connect the youthful understanding of sexuality and individuality with its products. Once again Levi's is reusing a standard device to present a new take on its traditional themes.

A number of print ads from the early years of the twenty-first century display the use of sexuality to present Levi's themes. A series of four ads show different views of a shirtless young man and woman wearing their Levi's jeans backwards. In each ad the couple is entwined, the two partners wrapped around each other, hiding parts of the other's body. In what might be the most interesting of the series, the shirtless couple is shown from behind, looking into a mirror. While they are apart in the picture, the mirror image shows them intertwined. The ads have no tagline except "501" and the company's logo ("Backward Lovers 1, 2, 3, and 4"). The sexuality of the couple and the freedom that the jeans seem to provide are paramount in the ads. The couple is asserting their freedom and individuality by being blatantly sexual and wearing their jeans backwards. They make no apologies for how they dress or act and refuse to conform to the standards of Polish society, all themes from past ads that are being reused in a new way.

Another device that Levi's reemploys to highlight its themes of youthfulness, individuality, and rebelliousness is a focus on the equality of women. As with previous commercials "Night and Day," "Planet," "Drugstore," and "Washroom," the ads from this period highlight nontraditional women's roles. Just as the series of print ads with the backwards-jeans couple shows neither of the partners as dominant and seems to project equality, most of Levi's ads from this period show women as strong, powerful individuals and place them on equal footing as men. While Levi's ads are often sexually suggestive, the woman is not a sexual object, as she often is in ads for other products or brands; instead she is a full participant. The ads often emphasize that the company's products are designed to fit a woman's lifestyle and needs. This is emphasized in two print ads from the same campaign that features the tagline, "Naprawde Twoje" (They are really yours). Both ads show a woman wearing only Levi's jeans, and stress that Levi's products are designed to be a part of a woman's daily life. In one, a shirtless woman wearing Levi's jeans is lying in bed with her back to the camera, and the other ad shows a close-up of the top of the jeans and a woman's bare hip and side ("Naprawde Twoje 1 and 2"). In both cases the women are beautiful and sexually appealing but they show how comfortable and accessible the jeans are. They are a product that are comfortable and practical but also look good. The women in the ads are not sex objects but rather attractive women who wear jeans. Levi's is telling women that they do not need to choose style over function but that they can have both and that their needs matter, a message that is often hard to find in advertising and in society. Another series of print ads entitled

"Girls," shows a close-up of a young lady's face and does not feature a picture of any Levi's product ("Girls 1 and 2"). The "girls" in the ads are all beautiful, and each is different in appearance and style. The ads seem to contradict the notion of a standard type of beauty. While one could argue that all the women in the ads have model-like proportions and appearances, the theme remains valid nonetheless. Certainly, Levi's does not showcase every type of woman but for a brand that is advertising to youthful customers, any attempt to dispel standard beauty myths is unusual. Both of these series of print ads show the company's use of women in non-traditional ways. The way that women are portrayed in the ads may seem less than radical but in a traditional society like Poland or compared to other advertisements they are unique. As in the past, by showing women in varied and untraditional roles Levi's is presenting itself as progressive and unencumbered by the rules of the society. The company is trying to show itself as following the rebellious and individualistic path that it advertises.

One other way that Levi's attempts to readvertise many of its historic themes is by strengthening its iconic brand status. This may seem inconsequential compared to the concrete themes that have been previously discussed but it is important because many buyers purchase Levi's reputation not its jeans. This concept can be seen in a famous saying, that advertising sells the sizzle not the steak. In the same manner, Levi's needs to sell its reputation in order to sell its clothing. This is one of the main reasons that Levi's ads have focused on themes like rebelliousness, individuality, coolness, and historical Americanism in past and present advertising. Levi's wishes to separate itself from the competition by constantly recreating its status as an iconic brand. Three print ads in particular from this period demonstrate Levi's efforts at continued branding. All three do not contain a picture or a mention of a Levi's product, but rather combine the Levi's name with elements of everyday society. The first advert creates an image of a Christmas tree made from Levi's rivets, buttons, and stitching, with the star at the top replaced by the company's Red Tag logo ("Christmas Tree"). Levi's is using an understood symbol of the Christmas season to market the accoutrements of its products. The buttons, rivets, logo, and stitching are unique to Levi's brand of jeans and by showcasing them the company is separating itself from the competition. The second ad also focuses on the parts of Levi's jeans, showing a close-up as the buttons, stitching, rivets, and logo seemingly float in midair, with the tagline

"*Zaproszenie*" (Invitation) printed in red in the bottom right corner ("Zaproszenie"). The purpose of the invitation is not entirely clear, but Levi's is once again highlighting the uniqueness of its brand. The third print ad shows a drawing of a Polish streetcar from many different angles, much as one might find at a train station or streetcar stop. In this rendering the trains are covered with the Levi's Red Tab logo and a rendering of the company's button design ("Street Car"). Again, no jeans are shown but Levi's displays its logo and unique button in order to prove its distinctiveness and its connection to Polish youth. The jeans maker is accessing the same themes of individuality and fun by showcasing the brand's uniqueness. In these ads Levi's products are a part of everyday Polish life and appear to distinctively meet the needs of young Poles.

A prime example of Levi's advertising from this period that embraces all of these themes of historical ties, youthfulness, sexuality, and strong branding is an international television commercial from 2007. The ad, entitled "Dangerous Liaisons," features a young man and woman engaging in a romantic rendezvous. The ad begins with Little Annie singing "Strange Love" as the young couple dressed in 1870s Levi's clothing meet in a nineteenth-century apartment. The young lovers embrace and start to frantically remove each other's clothing, surprisingly finding subsequently newer eras' garments beneath. Not only does the style of clothing change as they "undress," but the couple's appearances and the apartment's furnishings also morph to match each new period. Beginning in 1870s Levi's work apparel, both sporting stringy long hair, the two kiss and undress and are transported to the 1950s, the young man now with short hair and neat clothes and the young woman featuring bleach-blond hair and a pink sweater. As the sexual tension heightens, the couple removes another layer of clothing and become sixties hippies with long hair and wild clothing. The next change finds the pair in the 1980s, with the girl showcasing crimped hair and a *Flashdance*-style shirt. Eventually the romantic duo find themselves dressed for today and the young man opens his shirt to reveal a bare chest. The girl hastily removes her shirt, and the tagline reads, "New 2007 Collection.... From the Original. Levi's" ("Dangerous Liaisons"). "Dangerous Liaisons," a 2007 international commercial, could easily have been made in the early 1990s. The ad uses most of the familiar themes: historical Levi's, youthfulness, and sexuality. Even the tagline, "New 2007 Collection.... From the Original," makes the case that Levi's wishes to be seen as both traditional and modern. Although Levi's employed many different marketing ideas and strategies from 1991 to 2007, the company always returned to its central message that Levi's is the original brand of rebellion and youthfulness. This commercial does not explicitly reference America either present or past but it does concentrate on the place of Levi's within youth culture. "Dangerous Liaisons" neatly sums up Levi's marketing approach in 2007 and in much of its time in Poland, a youth brand that emphasizes its ties to the past.

Summary

Levi's advertising in Poland from 1990 to 2007 is a story of adaptation without change. As with many companies, the clothing maker had to constantly readjust its image while maintaining its core identity. Because Levi's customers in Poland are primarily adolescents and young adults, the company was forced to remain trendy and "cool" while keeping the link to its historical image that made it unique. The themes of Levi's advertising in Poland in this period generally remained the same, although the context and the settings continued to shift and evolve. Levi's advertising began the 1990s with a focus on a mythologized historical America, and the company wanted to market itself and its products around the themes of rebellion, independence, and individualism by connecting to an idealized American past. By doing this, Levi's accentuated its American identity and reminded Poles of the mythical America that produced the cowboy, the pioneer, and the antisocial bad boy. Throughout the 1990s and into the twenty-first century, Levi's continued use the same rebellious and individualistic themes but often its use of American images waned. In the mid–1990s the company began to focus more on internationalism, declaring that the themes of individualism and rebelliousness were universal. Although Levi's never denied its jeans were an American product, it often attempted to downplay that element of its brand. This changed again at the beginning of the twenty-first century when the jeans maker embraced an urban American mythology that once again showcased American individualism and rebelliousness. While many of the examples and storylines have changed, Levi's desire to be the brand of rebellion and individualism in Poland has not. Unlike companies like Coca-Cola and

McDonald's, Levi's did not attempt to become Polish; instead the jeans maker wished to represent its brand as timeless and universal like the themes of rebellion and individualism that it adopted. Levi's portrayed itself as not wanting to be a part of Polish society, or any society, but rather marketed itself to those who wanted to feel rebellious. In doing so, Levi's was remarkably consistent in staying on message. The ways the company showcased its core themes changed often, but the themes themselves did not. Subsequently, Levi's was able to become whatever the buyer wanted it be, which seems to be a core statement not only about the company's products but about the company itself.

Levi's Print and Television Ads

Ad Title	Year Produced	Themes
Backward Lovers 1, 2, 3, 4	2003	Sexualized Youth
Campfire	1993	American Rebelliousness
		Strong Females
Christmas Tree	2004	New Icon
Creek	1994	American Rebelliousness
Dangerous Liaisons	2007	New Icon
		Sexualized Youth
Dolls	2000	Sexualized Youth
Drugstore	1995	American Rebelliousness
		Strong Females
Flirt	2001	Sexualized Youth
Girls 1, 2	2004	Strong Females
Hamster	1998	Unusual
Kung-Fu	1997	International Rebelliousness
Legs	2000	Sexualized Youth
Mall	1998	Unusual
Mermaids	1997	International Rebelliousness
Naprawde Twoje 1, 2	2004	Sexualized Youth
		Strong Females
Night and Day	1992	American Rebelliousness
		Strong Females
Photocopier	1998	Unusual
Planet	1995	International Rebelliousness
		Strong Females
Red Tab 1, 2, 3, 4, 5, 6	1996	International Rebelliousness

3. Levi's

Ad Title	Year Produced	Themes
Rub (Bowling Alley), (Hole in Wall), (Shop Window)	2002	Sexualized Youth
Street Car	2004	New Icon
Swap	2003	Urbanness
Swimmer	1992	American Rebelliousness
Temptation	2001	Sexualized Youth
Undressed	2000	Sexualized Youth
Washroom	1996	Strong Females
Wives	1998	Unusual
Zaproszenie	2004	New Icon

4

When the Chips Are Down: Frito-Lay Poland

When one thinks of classic American brands, companies like McDonald's, Coca-Cola, and Levi's may well come to mind. Frito-Lay most likely does not. The snack-food maker produces popular items including Lay's, Ruffles, Doritos, and Cheetos snack chips, but these are less likely to be thought of as iconic brands. Nonetheless, Frito-Lay is the largest company in the snack-food industry, an industry that is often symbolically and economically linked to the United States and to the American lifestyle. Americans consume and export billions of dollars of snack foods each year. The U.S. Department of Commerce International Trade Administration (ITA) reports that in 2003 about sixty-six billion dollars of snack foods were sold worldwide. The ITA states, "The spread of Western eating habits to other parts of the world continues as lifestyles in those parts of the world become busier, and traditional family meal times become a thing of the past. As a result, the demand for snack food continues to increase" (Snack Foods, 2003). As of 2005, Frito-Lay generates over $10.3 billion of revenue worldwide annually, making it the largest snack-food brand in the world (Hoover's). Although Frito-Lay may not yet be a universally known name, it is the leading manufacturer of products that are considered deeply American. As the ITA noted, the United States is exporting its lifestyle to many places in the world and Frito-Lay's type of snack foods are closely associated with this transformation.

Like many American companies, Frito-Lay has been in Poland since the collapse of the socialist government. The company began selling potato chips and other snack foods in Poland in 1991. The snack maker is owned by PepsiCo, which is known in the United States for producing soft drinks such as Pepsi and Mountain Dew. Upon entering the Polish market, PepsiCo purchased controlling interest in E. Wedel, a popular Polish confectionary company, and linked the candy maker's operations with Frito-Lay's (Historia Frito-Lay). Frito-Lay quickly became the market leader and by 2005 had garnered a 30.7 percent market share by selling an estimated 470 million dollars worth of salted snacks in Poland (Bogdanowicz). This market share increased in 2006 after the company purchased one of its chief rivals, Star Foods ("PepsiCo Inc. Acquires"). Frito-Lay's major market share and sales combined with its highly visible media presence indicate that Frito-Lay is a very recognizable name in Poland.

Advertising in Poland

One of the most important factors in marketing a product like those sold by Frito-Lay is packaging, in order to attract attention on a store shelf. A product's package serves as an advertisement that should not only be eye catching but also informative and seductive. Professor Carl Rollyson notes that while living in Gdansk, Poland, in 1979 he began to understand packaging in a new way. He notes that Poles during this period craved American products and the packaging had much to do with this:

> Returning to Poland I realized that packaging is more than surface; it broadcasts in an extravagant way the inner works of the product. What's inside seems magical because of what it covers.... This is foolish, but Americans love it, and the Poles were starved for it.... For Poles such American items mean participation in a world community of consumerism, a largely American community because everyone knew that the pursuit of happiness was written into our Constitution — not simply our Declaration of Independence, but our character (7).

Although much has changed since the end of the Cold War, it is evident that Frito-Lay designs packaging to appeal to what its consumer base desires. Frito-Lay uses many of the same colors, logos, and mascots on both its U.S. and Polish packaging. Both countries market Frito-Lay items that are packaged in bright and colorful bags that often feature a cartoon mascot or a picture of the product. In fact, an American who did not read

Polish would have little problem guessing the contents of a Polish Frito-Lay container merely from looking at it. Although the packaging is similar, there are several differences, the three main ones being language, size, and availability of promotional items. Understandably, Polish Frito-Lay packages are labeled in Polish. The types of words and slogans that are used are generally different from their American counterpart, though, and often are far more bombastic. Frito-Lay packaging in the United States generally contains few words and slogans and instead relies on colors, mascots, and pictures of the product. By contrast, Polish packages often contain slogans, promotions, and other types of written enticements. The American packaging focuses on the quality and desirability of the product itself while the Polish version emphasizes the fun experience that the product provides. A good example of this is Polish Lay's potato chip bags from 1997 during a *Star Wars* promotion. Because PepsiCo acquired promotional rights to the *Star Wars* films, Frito-Lay products across the world contained *Star Wars* references. Although both the American and Polish packaging showcase *Star Wars*, the Polish bag contains many more slogans and phrases, while the U.S. version appears plainer, more understated. Although there are probably many reasons for this one, of the most obvious is that Frito-Lay is creating a new market in Poland and must be more aggressive to appeal to new, younger buyers. American buyers no longer need to be convinced to try snack foods but rather have to be persuaded not to stop eating them. The idea of eating chips and other snacks is not yet ingrained in the Polish culture, and so the packaging had to be more visually and verbally aggressive to assure notice.

The second major difference between U.S. and Polish Frito-Lay packaging is that of product size. While potato chips and other snack foods are available in smaller single serving sizes, many U.S. consumers prefer buying 16-ounce packages or larger. These large bags are presumably intended to be eaten over a period of time and not all at once. Conversely, Polish chips generally come in smaller sizes and are marketed as a quick, one-time snack. The smaller sized package most likely is the result of a combination of factors, including item cost, buyer demographics, and food's cultural and social place in Poland. While Americans often eat chips with a meal or instead of a meal, Poles view snack foods as a treat and not a meal alternative. This is partly because many snack foods are new to the Polish market but also since sit-down-style family meals hold a more important place in Polish culture than in the United States. Although societal norms are changing, Poles tend to value the ritual that a family meal provides. A meal, such as dinner, is not merely a time to eat but an opportunity to embrace family, history, and tradition. It is a time to socialize and to strengthen bonds between family and friends. Traditional foods are generally served and the meal becomes a symbol not only to the Polish family but also to the nation (Shallcross 2–3). Because of the meal's social importance in Poland, Frito-Lay has little choice but to conform to societal norms. By introducing its products in smaller-sized packages, the company is advertising them as snacks that need not interfere with the normal meal. This packaging may change in the future if Polish consumers alter their tastes and ideas about eating but for now Frito-Lay is respecting Polish traditions.

The third way that Polish Frito-Lay packaging differs from the American style is in offering promotional items. These toys, collectibles, or prizes are often inside of the snack food's package and resemble the giveaways that are common in the United States inside many boxes of cereal. While Frito-Lay occasionally offers these promotional items in the United States for major movies like *Star Wars* or *Lord of the Rings*, they are relatively uncommon. In Poland these prizes are often collected by young and old alike. In addition to numerous *Star Wars* collectibles, Frito-Lay Poland has offered prizes featuring Pokemon, Chester Cheetah, football stars, and animal pictures. The packaging generally uses a large amount of space to promote the giveaway that is featured inside. This indicates that in Poland snacks foods are not yet a staple of the Polish diet and that their primary audience is children. Although adults may enjoy receiving some of the in-package giveaways, the low prices, flashy displays, and prizes show a marketing effort aimed at a young audience. This can be accounted for by the fact that many snack foods are new to the Polish market and Frito-Lay needs to create a customer base. In doing this it appears that one of the primary targets is children. This is understandable because children are more open-minded and adaptable to change and new experiences. They also are easily swayed by flashy gimmicks and are a substantial source of revenue if they can be converted into lifelong customers. This strategy is used by many companies worldwide that understand the value of children as customers. In Poland, this appears to be a way in which Frito-Lay can circumnavigate the restrictive influence of tradition. Adults may adhere strongly to Poland's history and traditions but children have not had so many of these ideas ingrained and those that they do know they may wish to rebel against. While some other companies like McDonald's and Coca-Cola embrace traditional society, it appears that for the short term Frito-Lay instead attempts to exist beside it. The company does not endeavor to support Polish values nor to change them but instead it courts young consumers who have not fully accepted society's rules and traditions. In the long term these young customers will grow up and possibly change Poland's eating habits to include more Frito-Lay products but for now Frito-Lay is not pressing for this change. In many ways this is a middle path between adopting Polish values and being a "cool" new western product. Frito-Lay is willing to adapt to become part of the Polish market but is also searching for consumers who want a new and different lifestyle.

International Youth

Frito-Lay's attention to the youth market and to creating new customers can be seen in its advertising from 1997 to 2007. Its television commercials, print advertisements, in-package giveaways, and store displays highlight the company's desire to craft itself as a symbol of cool youthfulness. Although most companies desire young customers, Frito-Lay bases most of its campaigns around children and teenagers in an attempt to make them the company's primary customers. In effect, Frito-Lay is building its reputation as an international alternative to traditional Poland cuisine. The construction of this theme can be seen in the previously mentioned advertising that accompanied the 1997 re-release of *Star Wars* and the 1999 release of *Star Wars: Phantom Menace*. As stated before, these campaigns were conducted worldwide among many of the subsidiaries of PepsiCo. Frito-Lay Poland's *Star Wars* marketing campaigns uses many of the same items and designs as the snack-food seller does in other nations. The campaigns were internationally marketed to appeal to young customers. Packaging features pictures of the films' characters, like Jar Jar Binks, the young Anakin Skywalker, and Yoda, that are attractive to young customers. *Star Wars* themed trading cards and coins were created as in-package giveaways in an effort to entice young collectors. Creative store displays were fashioned that used *Star Wars* themes and characters and would catch the eye of young buyers. While many companies, including McDonald's and Coca-Cola, have international advertising campaigns, most of them embrace local tradition and use international marketing to explore commonalities between cultures. Frito-Lay is sympathetic to Polish needs but instead of embracing traditional values it chooses to target the globalized youth market. Frito-Lay is still respecting Polish desires but has elected to market its products to new, young, transnational-thinking consumers.

The Frito-Lay Poland *Star Wars* campaigns display a different approach to advertising and marketing than ones used by McDonald's, Coca-Cola, or Levi's. Early in its Polish advertising and marketing campaign, McDonald's wished to be viewed as a part of Polish society, and then it expanded its scope to include international ties. Coca-Cola always marketed itself as an international product but desired to be seen as a family drink that could be enjoyed by all. Levi's expressed itself as an international youth brand but advertised its close ties to tradition and the recent past. Frito-Lay Poland by contrast, presents itself as an international youth brand that offered an alternative to traditional Polish culture. The *Star Wars* films were marketed and released across the globe to a fan culture that crossed national borders. Internationally, *Star Wars* fans have created a culture that is not grounded in nationalism or ethnicity but rather in knowledge and affection for the subject matter. An interesting example of the international cultural popularity of *Star Wars* is the 2001 United Kingdom census that reports that 390,000 Britons claimed the *Star Wars* Jedi faith as their personal religion (Richardson). This accounts for .7 percent of the British population, making it the fourth largest religion in the United Kingdom ("Jedi Knights Demand"). By using the *Star Wars* films to promote their products in Poland, Frito-Lay is aligning itself with a culture that exists simultaneously within and outside of Polish culture. While many fans of the *Star Wars* films are proud of some parts of their Polish heritage, they identify with international ideas that often run counter to Polish traditional perspectives. These consumers are Polish but they do not embrace many of the same cultural touchstones as their Polish compatriots. While not all of these "new" Poles like *Star Wars*, many do embrace newness, change, and international culture. This attitude can be seen in a previously mentioned 2004 article entitled "Cheap Eats" in the Polish newspaper *Warsaw Voice*. In the article, two students explain why they sometimes prefer fast food to more traditional Polish fare and how they like the new choices that international products provide ("Cheap Eats"). By marketing to this group of Poles, Frito-Lay is attempting to be seen as an international youth brand that understands the needs of the young population.

In order to present itself an international youth brand, Frito-Lay Poland had to devise themes that would appeal to its target audience of children, teenagers, and young adults. The idea of marketing a known cultural product like *Star Wars* is the first and most obvious. The *Star Wars* promotion is one example of Frito-Lay using international cultural icons as marketing tools. Another of these international cultural icons that was used in a 1999 television commercial was model/actress Pamela Anderson. The ad for the Frito-Lay product "Lay's Max" shows the buxom, scantily dressed Anderson aboard an expensive yacht when she sees several young men in another boat eating a bag of Lay's Max. The young men are dressed in a casually trendy but unsophisticated manner, and their boat is dirty, smoke-filled, and in obvious need of repair. Anderson, by contrast, appears to be immaculately dressed and groomed, and exudes all the signs of wealth. In order to get the chips, Anderson offers the men various things in trade such as champagne and jet skis. The young men counter Anderson's offers by pointing downward in a provocative way. The commercial cuts to a scene of Anderson scrubbing the men's boat while being fed Lay's Max chips. The ad ends with the tagline, "Co Zrobisz, By Je Miec?" (What will you do to get them?). The commercial is noticeably based on Pamela Anderson's sex appeal and her international status ("Pamela"). Anderson is well known throughout the world for playing C. J. Parker on the television show *Baywatch*. The series about beach lifeguards is one of the most popular in television history and is reported to have been watched by over one billion viewers in 140 countries (Classic TV Babes). The show turned Anderson into a world-renowned sex symbol and the personification of the California lifestyle (even though she is Canadian).

In the Lay's Max ad, Anderson is shown as sexy, flirtatious, wealthy, and uninhibited. The ad showcases her surgically enhanced body that is displayed in a skimpy outfit, and her affluence, by surrounding her with symbols of money and status. (Interestingly, the boat resembles the one used in an infamous home video shot by Anderson only a year prior.) Although the commercial is a farce — Anderson could easily afford to buy

122

the potato chips herself— its central idea is that the young men have power and influence in an international class system. The men are not presented as Polish citizens bound by the regulations and traditions of their society. Instead, they are shown to be unaffiliated people who create their own roles and rules. The men engage an international icon in a complex negotiation to acquire something that they desire. Even the bargained-for service is surprisingly nonsexual. While the young men do mirror the archetypical trickster characters that are prevalent in many societies, they do so in a manner that affirms their status as internationalists. The men do not rail against oppressive governments, or espouse nationalistic causes. Rather they are members of an international community and see themselves and Anderson as equals. In fact, by the end of the commercial, the men are displayed as more crafty and intelligent than Anderson and thus in some ways better than her. While other more traditional Poles may see themselves foremost as members and products of a nation and a tradition, the characters in the commercial — and presumably many Polish consumers — understand their place in the world differently. Although they still feel a kinship to Poland and its way of life, they also understand the world in a more complex and less traditional manner.

Another series of commercials that highlight Frito-Lay's marketing as an international youth brand features Krzysztof Hołowczyc, a popular Polish race-car driver. Hołowczyc is seen in a group of commercials for Lay's and Lay's Max that emphasize his desire for the product and his speed at acquiring what he wants. Although few know Hołowczyc internationally, he is popular in Poland among both racing fans and those who do not follow the sport. Hołowczyc's management claims that he is one of the ten most popular Poles, "recognized by 52 percent of the Polish population" (Krzysztof Hołowczyc). The commercials portray the driver as an international celebrity who is the equal to other famous athletes and icons. Most of the ads show Hołowczyc as not only internationally popular but also young, nontraditional, and willing to break society's rules. This message seemingly will appeal to Frito-Lay's young consumer who wishes to live a similar lifestyle. An example of this is a 2002 *reklama* entitled "Promo Football Stars." In this ad Hołowczyc is shown stealing the contents of several bags of chips while their owners watch soccer on television. Hołowczyc races around the room and devours the chips before the owners know their snacks are gone. The commercial then promotes in-package giveaways that feature soccer stars such as Michael Owen and David Beckham ("Promo Football Stars"). The ad presents Hołowczyc as being very talented and as internationally popular as world-renowned soccer stars. The race-car driver is never shown to be a Polish icon but rather is showcased as a global star. He is not portrayed as a figure of Polish tradition and nationalism but instead is referred to as a worldwide celebrity who exists outside of national boundaries. This type of pitchman nicely fits Frito-Lay's desire to present itself to the youthful international Polish consumer. Icons like Hołowczyc and Pamela Anderson show the company's desire to market to young, nontraditional Poles.

One other series of ads that highlight Frito-Lay's marketing to young international Poles is the company's use of the Japanese Pokemon characters. These animated figures became popular internationally during the 1990s and their trading cards and coins were often highly prized by many collectors worldwide. In a series of promotions, Frito-Lay Poland advertised Pokemon in-package giveaways in many of its products. These print and television ads emphasized Pokemon's international desirability and how the consumers were part of an extended global society. In essence the American company, Frito-Lay, marketed a Japanese product, Pokemon, to Polish customers blurring the lines between nations and cultures. When consumers in Poland eat Frito-Lay chips and play with Pokemon toys it does not make them less Polish but it does highlight this shift from traditional Polish ideas to a more international culture. Frito-Lay both encourages and displays this transition as it attempts to court young Poles who are ready to embrace a more global society. In using this marketing technique Frito-Lay also is able to benefit from economies of scale by targeting global youth with a standardized message. By employing these global icons, Frito-Lay is able to make standardized ads for a large portion of the world and to encourage a more transnational way of thinking within individual countries, a proposition that benefits the company but also attempts to change national cultures in places like Poland.

Several Polish Frito-Lay commercials display the chip maker's use of Pokemon as an international icon. These ads advertise Pokemon in-package giveaways that are available with many Frito-Lay products. The most striking element among all of the ads is that Pokemon is never explained in any way. While this may seem to be a pedestrian point, it is the most important aspect of the campaign. Between 1999 and 2007 Frito-Lay created at least eight different television commercials featuring Pokemon but the Japanese characters are never introduced, only displayed and referenced. The commercials' creators assume that Pokemon is already an understood and desired brand within Poland and that the characters need no further introduction. This means that the very basis of the Pokemon advertising is the assumption of an international consumer society. Frito-Lay is not marketing to traditional Poland but rather to a global market that Poland is merely a part of. This was also evident in the previously discussed Pamela Anderson and *Star Wars* ads. The appeal of Pokemon is not that it is an accepted Polish product but rather that it is *not* Polish. By desiring Pokemon, Polish youths become a part of an international society that enjoys the character-based toys and games. The consumers embrace a larger global peer group and display themselves as different from older Poles (but similar to collectors their own age). By presenting Pokemon not as a new product but rather as an understood entity, Frito-Lay acknowledges the power of the international youth culture. The snack maker is linking itself to a global consumer society that exists outside of Polish tradition.

Several Frito-Lay Pokemon television commercials display this understanding of the Japanese characters' international appeal and the global consumer society of which they are part. One of the most interesting is a 2001 *reklama* called "Promo Pokemon" that advertises an in-package giveaway called "Pokemon *tazo*." These *tazos* are small coin-shaped pieces that are used in a multi-player game. By collecting *tazos* a player gains potentially better pieces and has a higher chance of beating an opponent. The commercial begins by showing a crowd of children and teenagers entering a large arena. The ad is filmed mostly in black and white, with the only color items being the red bags of Frito-Lay chips and the *tazos*. The crowd is shown from above as it enters the building and then the scene changes, as the youths pump their Frito-Lay-laden hands into the air as if they were at a rock concert. Colorful *tazos* fall from above into the outstretched black-and-white hands of the crowd and the announcer explains how many varieties of the game pieces are available. The crowd then circles around two players as they use their *tazos* to engage in Pokemon combat. The spectators cheer as an exhilarated young man proclaims and celebrates victory. The announcer informs viewer which Frito-Lay's brands contain the tazos and how he/she can acquire them ("Promo Pokemon").

The major theme of the commercial "Promo Pokemon" is the society that is created by owning and using Pokemon products. The ad features only young people who appear to be between the ages of ten and sixteen; no adults are shown. Also, everyone in the commercial is excited about Pokemon. The game gives collectors a purpose and connects them. Nationality, politics, or tradition are unimportant in the ad; instead the main factors are age and a willingness to embrace a new culture. The commercial portrays the Pokemon collectors as a cross between athletes and rock stars, with players being cheered and honored like celebrities. This Pokemon competition could exist any place in the world and little would change about the participants or how they behave. Traditional factors like nationality, ethnicity, class, and gender are of little concern and instead the Pokemon game becomes the primary unifier and divider. Frito-Lay uses this understanding to be noticed by its customer base. If many young nontraditional Poles feel themselves to be aligned with different groups or products like Pokemon then Frito-Lay is seeking to capitalize on this self-expression. Frito-Lay is marketing itself as the brand of the new Polish outsider, the food of the nontraditional Pole. Although snack foods are often embraced by the young, and Frito-Lay is new to Poland, this is still a different approach than used by many other youth-oriented brands. In employing Pokemon and international celebrities in its advertising Frito-Lay is embracing consumers who desire a more globalized and less traditional society.

Another later example of a Frito-Lay Pokemon television commercial that embraces internationalism is a 2005 ad labeled "Chester Pokemon." As the title suggests this ad also features both Pokemon characters and the Cheetos cartoon mascot, Chester Cheetah. In the commercial Chester loudly extols the virtues of Pokemon *tazos* and promotes their availability in several of Frito-Lay's products. The ad shows a video of several of the featured *tazos* and also scenes of excited young Pokemon users. The Pokemon consumers in the ad are three boys and a girl who are dressed in bright children's clothing that could seen anywhere in the world. Each of them appears to understand both the rules of Pokemon and of international society. The children accept Frito-Lay chips, Pokemon *tazos*, bright T-shirts and blue jeans as parts of their lives. None of these things are Polish in origin but nonetheless they are an important part of the society in which the children live. These items are not historically Polish but they are understood and desired by many Poles. By connecting to these international products and icons Frito-Lay is choosing not to market itself as participating in Polish tradition but rather to highlight its unique qualities and to emphasize its global desirability. This strategy could benefit Frito-Lay in the short term by capitalizing on trendiness but also could allow the company to change Polish taste in the long term. Ironically, by not embracing existing Polish traditions Frito-Lay may be creating future traditions ("Chester Pokemon").

Antiauthoritarian Ads

Along with the theme of promoting internationalism over traditional Polish culture, Frito-Lay also created many ads that showcase an antiauthoritarian viewpoint. These ads appear to be designed to appeal to the same young target group that is the market for the nontraditional international ads. In fact, this group appears to be the general consumer of almost all of Frito-Lay products. The idea of antiauthoritarianism is closely related to the theme of nontraditionalism but it is different because it entails rebellion against an individual or powerful group, more than an idea or tradition. While nontraditionalism rallies against the established culture, antiauthoritarianism rebels against those viewed as authority figures. Interestingly, because of Poland's history antiauthoritarianism is not always seen as untraditional but rather can be viewed as an important Polish cultural element. It is a way for consumers and citizens to create a feeling of individuality and for younger customers to have perceived independence and take control of their lives and futures. Though these notions of independence, control, and individuality are often more perception than reality, they are important marketing devices that appeal to a demographic that often wishes to live a new lifestyle.

The most obvious symbol of antiauthoritarianism in Frito-Lay advertising is the Cheetos mascot, Chester Cheetah. As previously mentioned, Chester Cheetah is a cartoon cheetah that often appears in Cheetos worldwide advertising. He is the embodiment of the trickster that is prevalent in most cultures and in many advertisements, most notably in the United States in cereal advertising (Green 49–52). Chester's mission is to obtain Cheetos by any means necessary and this often includes elaborate schemes that involve stealing or conning to get the snack. The cartoon cheetah is presented as having the sole ambition of acquiring as many bags of Cheetos as possible and then enjoying them in a loud feeding frenzy. While in pursuit of his goal Chester adheres to none of society's established norms and respects no authority except that of the power of Cheetos. Chester is the archetypical antiauthoritarian because he recognizes no establishments except the ones he creates himself. By designing a character that adheres to few rules and morals Frito-Lay is declaring the needs of the individual to be paramount over the role of well-established conventions. The company is advertising its products as outlets for individual expression and antiauthoritarian sentiment.

A typical Chester Cheetah advertisement is a 1999 television commercial entitled, "Factory." In this ad Chester breaks into a Cheetos factory by sneaking past a stereotypical, overweight, sleeping guard. Chester then sabotages the factory, breaks some of the equipment, and creates a new variety of Cheetos that he labels "Super Cool." In the commercial Chester disregards the sole authority figure, who is portrayed as inept (the sleeping guard). He also violates several laws (breaking and entering, trespassing, vandalism, destruction of property, and theft) and proves that he can run the factory better than its owners by creating a better quality and more desirable product ("Factory"). This ad can be dismissed as a typical child's fantasy of grandeur in which a youth believes that he or she is more capable of operating things than those in authority, but it should be considered that this fantasy is being provided by a major international corporation. Furthermore, the company is not only promoting criticism of authority in general but is creating an ad that assails the producer itself. Frito-Lay has created a character that rails against authority, and the victim in this commercial is the creator. Much like Job questioning God, Chester doubts Frito-Lay, and he goes further by taking the work of re-creation upon himself. By subjecting itself to ridicule, Frito-Lay is proclaiming that no authority is above notice and that everyone in power is suspect, no matter how large or important. This proclamation suggests to young consumers that they know best about the world, no matter what those in authority may claim.

Another Cheetos commercial from 2001, titled "Cheetos *Wrozka*," again showcases Chester's antiauthoritarian stance. In this ad the cartoon cheetah visits a fortune-teller and asks her to tell his future. She consults her crystal ball and informs him of new changes to the shape and taste of

Cheetos. Chester then ties her up, destroys her crystal ball, and creates a room full of Cheetos to consume ("Cheetos *Wrozka*"). Like the previous commercial, this one depicts Chester as destructive and antiauthoritarian. Although he comes to the fortune-teller because she is an authority on the future, he rebels against her by assaulting her and destroying the tools of her trade. Chester shows the fortune-teller little respect and chooses to take whatever path easily leads to the acquisition of his prized Cheetos. While the fortune-teller may represent a fringe element of society to some, to others she symbolizes an ancient connection to the earth and the keeper of timeless traditions. Chester disregards whatever respect she has earned and seems to treat her as an impediment that prevents him from eating Cheetos. This ad again displays the traits and themes that define Chester Cheetah as an advertising device, and links them to Frito-Lay's brand image. Chester, like many of the previously mentioned international icons, is nontraditional, but he goes much further and becomes antiauthoritarian and even antisocial. While the Frito-Lay brands could never be called antisocial, the advertising is suggesting that consuming Frito-Lay products is an antiauthoritarian act. The company's Chester Cheetah ads rally against authority figures, including Frito-Lay itself, in order to embrace the rebellious consumers. If McDonald's wants to be seen as Polish and Coca-Cola wants to be part of the Polish family, then Frito-Lay wants to connect with Poles who see themselves as disenfranchised.

One other campaign highlights Frito-Lay's use of the theme of antiauthoritarianism in its advertising. In two television commercials from 2001 for Lay's Max Chili Hell and Cream Heaven, the chip company shows teenagers engaged in antiauthoritarian activity that is unknown to their parents. One ad features a mother talking about her son while the other has a father discussing his daughter. Both commercials are comical looks at how traditionally minded parents are unaware of the antiauthoritarian lives that their offspring lead. The commercial "Lay's Max Czarus" is named after Czarus, the ad's central figure. The *reklama* begins with a shot of a conservatively coiffed and dressed middle-aged female smilingly describing her son, the aforementioned Czarus. Throughout the ad the woman describes Czarus's wonderful attributes while intercut video footage displays the young man's true actions. The woman opens by saying, "I am a happy, proud mother. Czarus is a lovely child. He is elegant and nice." The image changes to a video of the wild-haired youth, dressed in punk-rock-style black clothing, being fed Lay's Max chips by two sexy, scantily clad young women. The shot then reverses to show Czarus wearing black-rocker style boots and reveals that he and his lady friends are lounging at a bar. His mother continues, "A real romantic," as the shot focuses on one of the beautiful women checking her watch while standing next to a beat-up car that rocks up and down suggestively. "Well-mannered. People just love him," mom says, while Czarus terrorizes pedestrians by riding a motocross-style motorcycle through a busy walkway and pushing a man into a water fountain. "I'll tell you a secret. He sings. In a choir." The young man screams loudly into the camera, apparently the lead singer of a metal band called The Hur. "And when he comes back, he always brings me a present. But he doesn't like to boast about it." Czarus hands a cat to his mother that he has recently taken out from under a car. Throughout the commercial he has been seen eating Lay's Max Chili Hell but now he takes a bag of Cream Heaven out of his mother's cabinet. Czarus hugs his mother and the announcer states, "Lay's Chili Hell and Cream Heaven. Because everyone has two faces" ("Lay's Max Czarus").

The other commercial in this campaign follows the same format of a parent talking about a child, this time a father extolling his daughter's virtues. The ad, "Lay's Max Marysia," details the exploits of the daughter Marysia. The father, a bald, bespectacled, neatly dressed man, comments to the camera, "My daughter Marysia? Little girl. Lovely child. Never had problems with her. People just love her." The girl is shown aggressively kissing a young man in a movie theater and then the outside of a car is shown rocking sexually, as in the first commercial. "You might say very grown up for her age, although a little shy, but isn't it girlish." Marysia is then shown getting her bellybutton pierced by a large tattooed man in a dark parlor. "She's even got a job. In a bank." Marysia is shown pole dancing next to a neon sign that reads "Va Bank." "I am the happiest father in the world." A conservatively dressed Marysia sits on her father's lap, giving him a hug, as the announcer says, "Introducing Lay's Chili Max Hell and Cream Heaven. Because everyone has two faces" ("Lay's Max Marysia").

These two ads portray the theme of antiauthoritarianism by showcasing the division between parents' view of their children and the lives the children actually lead. This may seem like merely an ad about nontraditional actions but it becomes antiauthoritarian by showing how the children react to their parents. The ad's young actors rebel against their parents but do so secretively. Czarus and Marysia do not tell their parents that they are defying them but instead create a secret existence that runs counter to parental authority. While many of the things that the two young people do appear to be harmless, the commercial does send the message that the parents are too naïve and trusting, while the children are wise and worldly. In the ad's version of Poland, the authorities are wrong. The parents' and the children's views of society are vastly different, and Czarus and Marysia are not attempting to change their parents or the traditional culture but only wish to live in an already existing new culture. In other words, the two teenagers are not trying recreate Polish society. They do not need to; their society has already changed even though their parents do not understand this. While this view is antiauthoritarian, it is not wholly untraditional. Many Poles claim that acts of rebellion against authority are part of Poland's heritage. Numerous examples of this include several uprisings during Poland's stateless, partitioned period, the 1944 Warsaw Uprising, and the Solidarity movement. Frito-Lay's antiauthoritarian advertising provides an outlet for youths seeking to rebel against the powerful, an idea that is not new or unique within Poland.

While Polish culture may at least marginally condone antiauthoritarianism, Frito-Lay ads concretely support the idea. The main moral of the ad campaign for Lay's Chili Max Hell and Cream Heaven seems to be that it is acceptable to lie to one's parents and live a double life. The most important part of both ads may be the tagline, "because everyone has two faces." Just as Chester Cheetah's destructive actions are condoned and even encouraged, the advertiser justifies Czarus and Marysia's behavior by declaring that it is human nature to act this way. By doing this, Frito-Lay is attempting to become an antiauthoritarian product. The advertising campaign proclaims that it understands the problems of being a teenager and the need to lie to one's elders about one's true life. While few teens live such double lives most feel that they are misunderstood by the older generations and alienated by society. In this campaign Frito-Lay shows that it understands the life of common Polish teenagers and sympathizes with their plight. The company declares that it is natural for teens to have antiauthoritarian impulses and that they should not be embarrassed by this. While youths may be misunderstood by their parents and society, Frito-Lay connects with them and understands how difficult their lives truly are.

By creating antiauthoritarian advertising Frito-Lay is providing its young audience a means to rebel against those with power. This is almost certainly a way for Frito-Lay to connect itself to the youthful escapist fantasy of taking authority and power away from those in control. The Chester Cheetah and Lay's Max ads provide a link between the youthful feelings of powerlessness and isolation and the powerful presentation of the company's products. The ads allow Frito-Lay to become a member of a specific group within Poland that feels the need to contest authority or to create a new lifestyle. While this idea is similar to the Levi's theme of youthful rebellion, it is different because Levi's claims buying its products is a mark of individuality but Frito-Lay connects with youths and serves as a conduit for their frustrations. Levi's are a symbol of being an individual, but Frito-Lay says it understands what it is like to be young. Levi's ads cater to what one wants to be. Frito-Lay ads affirm what one is. By linking itself to many youths through the idea of antiauthoritarianism, Frito-Lay wishes to become a part of the experience. It hopes for its products to become the snack food of youth and to be seen as another vehicle for being different and yet being a part of the group, an irony of both youth and advertising.

Adventurous Youth

While Frito-Lay uses the themes of internationalism and antiauthoritarianism, it also creates commercials and products that are designed to fit seamlessly into consumers' lives. The company wants to become a part of Polish society not by changing to fit the culture's norms, but by convincing consumers to buy its products because of their desirability, after which, over time, they will become commonplace. Telling evidence of this is that Frito-Lay appears to have shifted its marketing strategy very little from the mid–1990s through 2007. While it is easy to track a chronological change in advertising in Poland for companies like McDonald's, Coca-Cola, and Levi's, it is much more difficult to do this for Frito-Lay because the themes remain mostly the same for the duration of the period of study. Frito-Lay does not seem to have numerous campaigns that blend its product into Polish society like McDonald's and Coca-Cola, or commercials that attempt to rely on historical tradition like Levi's. Instead the company appears to wish to remain trendy and to focus on the youth market and gain lifelong consumers. Previously mentioned ads have shown Frito-Lay's use of trendy ideas marketed toward Polish youth and have identified themes and ideas that connect to the snack-food maker's desire to entice the youth market. While the themes and ideas of internationalism and anti-authoritarianism are important to Frito-Lay's marketing strategy they also are only a part of the larger theme of appealing to young customers. These consumers appear to be the basis of Frito-Lay's marketing in Poland and the driving force behind the brand's acceptance.

The idea of creating ads and products that appeal to young consumers is by no means unique to Frito-Lay and is used to some degree by all of the companies in this study. What is distinctive about Frito-Lay's idea of youth marketing is the age range of youths that the company targets and the constant re-creation of the product. While McDonald's targets pre-teenage children with advertising featuring its spokesman Ronald McDonald and commercials about birthday parties and Happy Meals, it does this in connection with a greater number of ads that are designed to appeal to adults. As evidenced by McDonald's advertising, the company actively markets its products toward adults and has designed entire campaigns meant to appeal to adult consumers. McDonald's advertises with a mind toward preteen and teenage consumers, but only as one group within Polish society. Levi's, the other youth brand in this study, usually pursues teenagers and young adults as consumers and does not generally market its products toward children under the age of twelve. Levi's generally markets toward an audience of teenagers and twentysomethings that can afford the company's products. Conversely, Frito-Lay almost exclusively directs its ads toward children, teenagers, and young adults. This age range provides Frito-Lay with a different primary consumer than the other companies in this study. Largely because of this consumer base, Frito-Lay often re-creates or modifies its products to appeal to young consumers. The company frequently introduces new in-package promotions and regularly changes its products' shapes, sizes, colors, and other attributes. While it is not unusual for a company to introduce new products or to slightly modify existing ones, it is rare for this to happen frequently to the company's well-known brands and products. This can disrupt the continuity of a brand and upset customers by removing familiar structure. It is almost unimaginable that McDonald's would significantly change its Big Mac, and many still remember the customer backlash when Coca-Cola introduced "New Coke" to the United States. Even Levi's, as it continues to create new products for fickle young consumers, still makes its 501 blue jeans in the same manner that it has for decades.

Because Frito-Lay's primary audience in Poland is the young consumer, many of the themes and elements contained in its ads are necessarily meant to appeal to this sector of society. Many of the aforementioned commercials contain ideas and devices that obviously were created to attract young customers. These include the use of celebrities, Pokemon, sports stars, and the cartoon character Chester Cheetah. The company continually reinforces its image as a youth brand by re-creating its marketing and advertising campaigns but remaining clear in its main theme that it can connect to youthful needs and desires. Another one of the themes that Frito-Lay uses to appeal to young Poles is that of the adventurous, exciting life. This often-used advertising device attempts to link a product with a fun and desirable lifestyle. In these types of ads, young consumers are shown engaged in exciting activities or living desirous lives. Frito-Lay employs this theme in order to show that its products fit into an exciting and adventurous lifestyle. Although it is not stated that Frito-Lay products create this desirable lifestyle, a correlation between good times and the snack foods is implied. In other words, Frito-Lay does not claim that its products will change a consumer's life for the better but the idea is certainly suggested.

An example of a Frito-Lay commercial that features a desirable adventurous lifestyle is "Szczyt," a 2001 commercial featuring the previously discussed Polish race-car driver Krzysztof Hołowczyc. The ad features a fast-paced instrumental soundtrack, along with exaggerated action sequences that give the commercial the feel of a James Bond spy film. The ad begins with Hołowczyc, dressed in a suit and tie, spotting a young man eating Frito-Lay chips. The race driver eyes the youth and then begins chasing him down streets and narrow alleyways. The chase continues along a highway and up a mountain. When the young man reaches the mountaintop, Hołowczyc stands waiting. The race driver grabs the bag of chips as the announcer comments, "Try to reach the Everest of chips" ("Szczyt"). While very few viewers actually wish to be involved in the dangerous worlds of espionage or law enforcement, the fantasy of being an action hero is very appealing to many. Hollywood earns billions of dollars internationally each year producing films that cater to desires for fun and adventure. Although the young man is not the commercial's protagonist and does not achieve any desired goal, Frito-Lay chips do provide him with an opportunity to engage in adventurous and exciting behavior. Again, the viewer does not really wish to be chased, attacked, and have his food stolen, but it is a compelling fantasy for those who see their lives as mundane. Additionally Frito-Lay puts the excitement within both international and Polish cultural contexts. The commercial's storyline resembles spy films that were largely made during the Cold War. These films generally operated on a template in which a well-dressed urbane hero was chased and fought a villain in order to acquire some important item. In the ad, Krzysztof Hołowczyc serves as the hero who must chase down and obtain the valuable bag of chips. Hołowczyc, a Pole, would have likely been the villain in a Cold War spy film that pitted East versus West. In this commercial stereotypes have been redefined and now Hołowczyc stands as a symbol of the international hero. In doing this flip-flop, the ad not only provides an adventurous outlet but also places Poland within a new international context. No longer is Poland a gray, dark nation as it was seen during the Cold War, but rather it is a land of adventure, excitement, and heroes. In this advertising Frito-Lay is once again not trying to quickly change society but stressing how Poland has already changed. The snack maker is embracing the "new" Poland and marking itself as a "cool" product. In providing these messages Frito-Lay not only links itself to youthful adventurousness but also continues using the same ideas of internationalism and nontraditionalism.

Two commercials from 2002 take the idea of youthful adventurousness further and seem to suggest that Frito-Lay's products and giveaways can change a person's outlook on life. Both advertise trading cards featuring soccer stars, available as in-package giveaways in Frito-Lay products. The ads take the form of a newscast that informs people about a growing soccer obsession within Poland. In both ads a fake broadcaster tells the nation about strange events occurring. Most Poles would recognize the faux newscaster as a caricature of famous Polish telejournalist Bogusław Wołoszański, who hosted news shows from the 1970s into the twenty-first century. Wołoszański's most famous show, "Sensacje XX wieku" (Sensations of the Twentieth Century) outlined and commented on important historical events. The actor portraying the announcer in the commercial resembles Wołoszański in voice, dress, and appearance and has many of the same mannerisms. By using the reference to a famous television personality, Frito-Lay is placing the ad well within the context of Polish society and history.

The first commercial, "Lays *Obsesja Piłkarska* 15" (Lays Obsession is Growing), shows the Wołoszański character discussing the growing Polish preoccupation with soccer. As an older woman walks across the park carrying her groceries, the announcer proclaims, "Soccer obsession is growing. It's even conquering the most resistant. Here is the evidence." After saying this, the announcer runs toward a soccer ball, showing that even though he is wearing a shirt, tie, and leather jacket, he is also dressed in red soccer shorts, long sports socks, and athletic cleats. He then strongly kicks the soccer ball which is caught by the older woman who kicks it back in a goalie's style. The ad ends with a display of the soccer cards available in Frito-Lay products ("Lays *Obsesja Piłkarska* 15"). The second ad, "Lays *Obsesja Piłkarska* 30," uses the same format and announcer but shows new examples of the growing mania. The first scene shows a leather-clad motorcyclist sitting in a park eating Lay's chips. A serious-looking, conservatively dressed middle-aged man kicks the biker's helmet like a soccer ball and runs away with it over a hill. The next scene displays a mother walking through the park with her young son, apparently coming home from the grocery store. The child eats a bag of Lay's as the woman bounces a head of cabbage like a soccer ball on her unskirted knee. The commercial cuts to the newscaster standing in front of a formally dressed couple. The man is wearing a three-piece suit and tie while the woman is dressed in a long red gown. The newscaster states, "This is a real obsession, which is increasing because of stickers, cards, and soccer balls [in Frito-Lay packages]." During this speech, the well-dressed man soccer-kicks a street lamp's glass globe, causing it to explode, as his girlfriend cheers ("Lays *Obsesja Piłkarska* 30").

In these two commercials the theme of youthful adventurousness is not only used but is portrayed as spreading in a virus-like manner. Each of the commercial's scenes features adult characters acting in a youthful, free-spirited way because of Frito-Lay's in-package giveaways. The mature characters' actions are unexpected and unconventional, and the viewer is meant to be surprised and amused by the adults' youthful antics. Their behavior is so odd that it is declared newsworthy by the commercial's creators.

An announcer who is well known for broadcasting major events of the twentieth century is parodied in order to reinforce the significance of the actions being recorded. The commercial is clearly implying that its products can make even dull and stodgy adults youthful and fun. If Frito-Lay chips can turn old women, nerdy men, mothers, and upper-class couples into adventurous young adults, then what might they do for its already youthful customer base? Additionally, Frito-Lay again ignores the traditional Polish social order in favor of a society driven by youthful urges. Older women and mothers, normally revered in Poland, are shown to be subjugated to the desires of the younger generation. This break from tradition strongly follows Frito-Lay's overall campaign to showcase its youthfulness and to encourage the rise of internationalism that is featured in many ads across the entire period until 2007. In these two ads the theme of youthful adventurousness not only is used to portray the fun that youths could have with Frito-Lay products but also the ways that the entire society could change if it only embraced fun.

Another commercial that illustrates Frito-Lay's idea of youthful adventurousness overtaking mature adults is a late 2002 ad that features an Albert Einstein impersonator. The ad, called "Twistos Einstein," shows the scientist creating havoc in a supermarket by playing with common items and interacting in a juvenile manner with people around him. Einstein eventually eats a young lady's Frito-Lay Twistos, and is then escorted from the store by security. Before leaving, the physicist gives his famous stuck-out-tongue pose and appears to have reverted to a state of intense childishness ("Twistos Einstein"). In the commercial Einstein is presented as the rare adult who never allowed himself to altogether leave childhood behind. Einstein acts as the popular conception dictates, the aloof scientist who plays with the world around him and creates scientific discoveries. He is shown as the uncommon adult who embraces youthful adventurousness and never gives in to the dullness of adult life. In Einstein's life, even a mundane task like grocery shopping can provide fun, adventure, and new discoveries. Einstein serves as an international role model for those who wish to remain adventurous even after their youth has faded.

One additional ad from 2005 shows youthful adventurousness mixed with technology to become seemingly more commonplace. This ad, entitled "Lay's Appetite Computer," displays a fast-paced, highly technological lifestyle that is made even more energized by teenagers. The commercial begins with a young man using his computer to instant message an unseen woman. The man electronically asks his female correspondent if she wants to talk and she replies that she cannot now because she needs to go get a snack. The young man smiles to himself, grabs his book bag, and races out of his apartment. The commercial mostly features scenes of the young man adventurously maneuvering through the city and overcoming any obstacles that he encounters. When chased by a pack of dogs, the young hero grabs meat from a street butcher and tosses it toward his canine pursuers. When faced with a dead-end alley, he scales the wall. When he tears his shirt, he uses the back entrance to a laundromat and takes another. Finally he arrives at what appears to be a library or cyber café where he spots a beautiful young woman. He offers her a bag of Lay's Appetite chips and comments, "You said that you were hungry." The announcer then extols the virtues of the chips, and the ad ends with the tagline, "*Chcesz Troche*" (Do you want some?) ("Lay's Appetite Computer").

The previously mentioned commercials have shown youthful adventurousness sparking a traditional society, and used high-tech youth lifestyles as its basis. The roles of adults in the last ad are as bystanders or background players, as the ad focuses on the young man and woman and their relationships to each other and their youth-oriented society. The commercial embraces the use of new technology that is shown to be both fun and adventurous. Not only do the main characters communicate via a computer messaging program that many adults would probably not understand, but they also finally meet in a bright, cheerful building, surrounded by computers and young technophiles. More importantly, though, the commercial uses the narrative structure of a video game, one that many viewers under the age of thirty would understand. The commercial follows the narrative of a standard quest game, in which the user must conquer obstacles and solve puzzles in order to complete a task. Often the goal is to save a person who has been captured by a hostile force. One example of a popular game to use this structure is Super Mario Brothers, a video game in which the player must master many hurdles and difficulties in order to save a kidnapped princess. This same structure is evident in "Lay's Appetite Computer" where the young man must scale different obstacles in order to rescue his "princess" from hunger. Furthermore, as with many video games, the girl is not shown until the end of the ad — she is only included as an object to be rescued. Even her typewritten words at the beginning of the commercial as reminiscent of written pleas by captured females featured at the start of games like Super Mario Brothers and Donkey Kong. The characters in the ads are not only using technology in their lives but also their stories are being presented in a computer-game-inspired manner. This shows an adventurous existence in which one's life can be fun, challenging, and productive like a video game. Unlike traditional Polish life in which one is often unsure of winners and losers, this imaginary lifestyle provides a concrete and desirable outcome. In the end, the obstacles are conquered and the princess is rescued. By creating this narrative Frito-Lay is not only presenting adventurous youthfulness but is also invoking a technologically driven society in which any outcome is possible.

Summary

In many ways analyzing Frito-Lay advertising in Poland is a study of both youth marketing and the introduction of new ideas. The company helped to create a new snack-food category in Poland and quickly became the field's leading name. Frito-Lay chose to not market itself as traditionally Polish. Instead the company advertised itself as the youth-oriented brand of those who wanted new and exciting ideas and products. The company used ads that promoted Frito-Lay's international ties, its acceptance of worldwide youth culture, its understanding of young people's need to rebel against authority, and the idea of adventurous youth. Since Frito-Lay's major theme from its beginning in Poland until 2007 was promoting itself as a youth brand, its ads show little change over time. While McDonalds, Levi's, and Coca-Cola ads displayed shifts in how their themes and ideas were presented, Frito-Lay's ads were remarkably consistent in their presentation. From the beginning, Frito-Lay marketed itself as a youth brand that did not run counter to Polish traditionalism but was another option that Poles could explore. Frito-Lay advertised to those consumers who were already exploring new views of Poland and the world and were contemplating changes in both society and their lives. By promoting youth-oriented brands, Frito-Lay was declaring its compatibility with the group's desires and open-mindedness. As its core customers age this may change, but for the time being Frito-Lay has aligned itself with the desires of the younger generation of Poland.

Frito-Lay Television Commercials

Ad Title	Year Produced	Themes
Cheetos *Wrozka*	2001	Antiauthoritarianism
Chester Pokemon	2005	Internationalism
Factory	1999	Antiauthoritarianism
Lay's Appetite Computer	2005	Adventurous Youth
Lay's Max Czarus	2001	Antiauthoritarianism
Lay's Max Marysia	2001	Antiauthoritarianism
Lay's *Obsesja Pilkarska* 15	2002	Adventurous Youth
Lay's *Obsesja Pilkarska* 30	2002	Adventurous Youth
Pamela	1999	Internationalism
Promo Football Stars	2002	Internationalism
Promo Pokemon	2001	Internationalism
Szczyt	2001	Adventurous Youth
Twistos Einstein	2002	Adventurous Youth

5

Red, White, and Cola: Coca-Cola Advertising in Poland

In 2004 the Polish Peasant Party (PSL) was considering changing its name in order to better connect with the local electorate. This discussion prompted party convention delegate Jan Bury to comment, "The PSL is a brand like Coca-Cola, it's a big deal; whoever wants to change it, has no concept at all or is being counterproductive" ("Heard in Passing"). It is telling that the Polish party chose to think of the changes in terms of rebranding and the brand Bury thought of was the American icon Coca-Cola. Arguably, Coca-Cola is the most recognizable American product worldwide. The American soft-drink company, which was founded in Georgia in the 1880s, has grown to become both a positive and negative international symbol of the United States. Although the Coca-Cola Company produces over 400 brands in more than 200 different countries, the soft-drink maker is still primarily known for its first product, the widely popular Coca-Cola Classic ("Brand Fact Sheet"). Many of Coca-Cola's products are ubiquitous throughout the world, but international popularity is paired with some negative reactions. For example, public demonstrations against the company's products have taken place in several countries and opponents have invented concepts and phrases, like "Coca-Colonization," that put forth the view that the beverage company is disrupting local cultures. While Cola-Cola has both supporters and detractors, the company continues to expand internationally. The soda producer's history in Poland is a long and often confusing one that reflects the difficulties that faced American corporations that wished to operate in the country during the socialist period. Coca-Cola first entered the Polish market in 1957 when it was showcased at the International Fair in Poznan. Afterward, the soft drink was produced outside of Poland and was only available for hard currency at specialty stores like the previously discussed Pewex. In 1972, Coca-Cola signed an agreement with the Polish government that allowed the beverage marker to bottle its products in Poland. Existing breweries were used to produce and package the soft drinks and the first Polish-made bottle of Coca-Cola was created on July 19, 1972. This method of production continued until 1991 when Cola-Cola expanded its Polish operations and created a new Polish Coca-Cola company (Coca-Cola Poland) and two independent bottlers (Warszawa Coca-Cola Bottlers Ltd. and Bydgoszcz Coca-Cola Bottlers Ltd.). This change allowed the corporation to take control of all business operations and marked the first time that Coca-Cola was able to act independently ("Polish Coca-Cola is already ... 10 years old!"). Since 1991, Coca-Cola has continued to expand, opening new bottling plants and other means of production in Poland. Coke's operation in Poland has become so developed that many of the items that are produced within the country's borders are shipped to nearby countries for sale.

Early Polish Coca-Cola Advertising

It is important to note that although Coca-Cola was available on a limited basis in Poland in 1957 and was bottled in the country from 1972 onward, the soft drink was not highly touted by the socialist authorities. In fact, Coca-Cola was the object of several socialist advertising campaigns that attempted to portray the product as evil, stating, "The enemy tempts you with Coca-Cola" and "Coca-Cola means liquid imperialism" ("Polish Coca-Cola is already ... 10 years old!"). These anti–Coke slogans tried to portray the soft drink as an American symbol, as previously discussed in chapter 2. In a theoretical socialist context, a symbol of a capitalist country is a negative thing, but in socialist Poland it also served as symbol of resistance. By equating Coca-Cola with the supposedly negative aspects of the United States the Polish authorities were unintentionally linking the company with America's positive virtues. Many Poles who were dissatisfied with the state would note the government's dislike of the product and its American pedigree. These factors, coupled with Coca-Cola's limited availability, would make the product even more desirable to many and created a lasting impression that would exist even after socialist rule ended. It is reported that by September 1972, Warsaw's largest store was selling over 1,500 bottles of Coca-Cola a day. A Polish newspaper editorial of the time opined, "This innocent soft drink, which until recently could be found only in encyclopedias, has found its way into almost every home. For many years, Coca-Cola has had a reputation of being the symbol of American life or of repulsive dollar imperialism.... It finally reached Poland not as a sinful thing but as a fruit of peaceful coexistence" (quoted in Witzel and Young-Witzel 166). During the socialist years Coca-Cola was a product that was both expensive and difficult to acquire and additionally was denounced by the authorities as unsavory, capitalistic, and American. Although these campaigns were meant to impede Coke's sales, they actually helped to create a market for the soft drink during and after the Cold War.

The one other overarching factor that should be mentioned in connection with Coca-Cola's early advertising is that of the company's highly recognizable red-and-white color scheme. To most Americans a red-and-white Coke can conjures up images of the sugary soda and little else. Although the trademarked logos, colors, and designs are distinctive, they symbolize little more than a cold beverage. Conversely, in Poland, Coca-Cola's colors are national symbols with deep historical and traditional meaning. They are the colors of the Polish flag and the hues that Solidarity used to represent the Polish nation. The red and white of the nation symbolize a connection to the past, a link between modern Poland and the nation's often turbulent history. Besides possibly the Polish eagle, no other symbol is as highly regarded or understood within the nation as the Polish red and white. Certainly one could not contend that Coca-Cola attempted to create trademark colors that would appeal to Poles. Coca-Cola's use of the colors red and white dates back decades before the company's entrance into Poland. Although both Coke and Poland independently adopted the symbolic red and white, this coincidence is potentially very advantageous for the soft-drink producer. While Coca-Cola has never marketed itself as a Polish national symbol, the company may enjoy a subliminal association that its corporate colors provide. Poles may be drawn to Coca-Cola for nationalistic reasons without completely understanding the connection. This lucky association began providing free brand support to Coca-Cola even before the first true advertising campaign commenced.

Because Coca-Cola has been available in some form or another in Poland since 1957, there was a preliminary amount of advertising produced prior to 1990. Since officially the state was hostile to the beverage company (even though both parties signed an agreement in 1972), today very little of this advertising remains and it is difficult to acquire. Besides the socialist anti–Coke advertising and the company's red-and-white logo, one other important socialist-era device worth noting is a slogan created by the well-known Polish poet and songwriter Agnieszka Osiecka. The slogan *"To jest to"* (Coke is it) is extremely famous within Poland and its translation has been used in many countries worldwide. Reports of when the slogan began vary but it seems that Osiecka composed it in the early 1970s around the time that Coca-Cola began bottling in Poland ("Polish Coca-Cola is already ... 10 years old!"). The slogan seemingly gained popularity after winning a radio contest and being featured in a 1982 campaign that was used in many places throughout the world (*Służiński*). The slogan has remained and is still featured on much of the Coca-Cola signage throughout Poland. Although the slogan's simplicity and catchiness are undoubtedly the main reasons for its enduring appeal, much has been made of Osiecka's contribution to Coca-Cola's advertising. Osiecka remains a popular and esteemed figure and her connection to Coke gives the brand both an air of respectability and a relationship to Polish culture. To have one of the most recognizable product slogans in Poland produced by a well-regarded artist forges a bond between Polish culture and Coca-Cola. The soft-drink maker's advertising cannot be seen as merely American imperialism when well-known Polish wordsmiths are crafting the slogans. While this is only one slogan, it does show the start of a relationship between Poland and Coca-Cola that started long before the end of the Cold War. Coca-Cola's place in Polish society would continue to develop and change, but the foundation was laid well before 1990.

Post-socialist Period

Many would claim that Coca-Cola first officially entered the Polish market in 1991. Although the company had been selling its products in

Poland for decades through franchisees and distributors, the year 1991 marks Coca-Cola's first direct investment in distribution and production facilities ("Historical Background 1991–1996"). Now instead of relying on intermediaries the company was able to take control of every aspect of Polish operations. This means Coca-Cola was not only able to expand production but also to remake its image in the Polish market. Very little information is available about Coca Cola's Polish advertising from 1990–1992, possibly because the company was using worldwide campaigns within the Polish market, ones that required little development and change. This is a common practice among many companies and may have been necessary in Poland while Coca-Cola was concentrating on building its Polish operations. It is likely that the company attempted to build its infrastructure and assess the Polish market before designing a complex campaign for Poland. Additionally Coca-Cola appears to have experienced an initial honeymoon period that allowed for a certain amount of goodwill toward the company because of Coke's symbolic connection to the United States. In his book *For God, Country and Coca-Cola*, Mark Pendergrast claims that "crowds gathered to cheer the arrival of the first Coca-Cola trucks in Warsaw, reminiscent of the welcome given the liberating U.S. tanks of World War II" (391). Although U.S. tanks did not liberate Warsaw during World War II, the point that Coca-Cola trucks are seen as symbols of America and Cold War liberation cannot be ignored. Coca-Cola was entering the Polish market in a new way and was already had many symbolic associations even before the company begun to advertise in earnest.

Coca-Cola and Universal Christmas

One Polish ad that does exist from 1990 is a print ad displaying the classic Coca-Cola Santa Claus grasping an armful of gifts, with the words *Wesołych Świąt* (Merry Christmas) placed underneath. The painted image of Santa Claus dressed in red coat and hat with white fur trim is so well known that no labels are included to inform the viewer of his identity (*"Wesołych Świąt"*). It is assumed that Polish viewers, like their American counterparts, will understand St. Nick's symbolic value and importance without assistance. This ad and the understanding behind it are significant in several key ways, the most important being that this commonly accepted image of Santa Claus is in many ways a creation of Coca-Cola advertising. The character of Santa Claus, or Saint Nicholas, is based upon the life of a Christian bishop who lived in Asia Minor during the fourth century. St. Nicholas eventually became the patron saint of children in several countries and was transformed into an object of folklore and legend. Until the twentieth century there was no generally accepted version of Santa Claus's appearance. Various folklore and popular culture sources created images of St. Nicholas that were vastly different in height, weight, dress, and appearance. In 1931, Coca-Cola paid the artist Haddon Sundblom to create a portrait of Santa Claus for the company's advertising. The finished product featured the modern idea of St. Nick dressed in Coca-Cola red and white (Louis and Yazijian 97–98). It should be noted that most of the elements of Coca-Cola's Santa are unoriginal; they are generally borrowed from other sources. What Coca-Cola did do was standardize the look of Santa Claus through its advertising, creating one image of the "jolly old elf" that is accepted worldwide (Witzel and Young-Witzel 107–8). This standardization is important because it not only displays the power of advertising but also universally links Coca-Cola to both Santa Claus and the Christmas holiday itself. Since 1931 Coca-Cola has continuously used Santa Claus in its advertising and this image continues to be one of the most popular of Coca-Cola's logos. The Coca-Cola Santa Claus has become so traditional that many worldwide consumers purchase Christmas decorations with Coca-Cola ads featuring St. Nicholas. Because of this connection to Santa and Christmas it is not surprising that a Polish ad from 1990 features St. Nick. Coca-Cola is using one of its most popular and well-respected icons as a focal point for this early ad. This is a show of strength and an understanding of how important the image of the Coca-Cola Santa Claus is in international popular culture.

By using an accepted symbol of both Christmas and Coke in an early Polish ad, the company was appealing to traditional family values and invoking images of happy children, joyous adults, and religious tradition. This was a strong selling point in a predominantly Catholic country like Poland, where Christmas images invoke not only family but also religion. In many ways this ad is a precursor to the many Coca-Cola campaigns that will follow in the next seventeen years. The image and prose are timeless and nothing about the ad requires either thought or explanation. This

146

is the ad's appeal; the image and phrase are so culturally symbolic that Coca-Cola does not have to produce additional prose or information. The soft-drink maker was connecting itself to Christmas and all of its understood implications. Although other companies could try this approach, Coca-Cola is uniquely capable of utilizing its historical links to Santa Claus and Christmas advertising. This connection between Christmas and Coca-Cola seems to be an early step in what will become one of the company's primary marketing themes, Coca-Cola's connection to everyday family life. In this ad no families are displayed and no slogans are presented that would indicate the inclusion of a familial theme. Nonetheless, it can be assumed that these associations are prominent within the viewers' minds. As in many societies, Christmas in Poland is generally a time for family gatherings and the renewing of familial bonds. This simple ad invokes many of those ideas and the image of Santa Claus connects Poland, Christmas, and Coca-Cola, an impressive feat for a single image and two words to accomplish.

Coca-Cola continued to use images of Santa Claus and Christmas in Poland throughout the years from 1990 to 2007. These images continually represent ideas of Coca-Cola's connection to the Polish family. A 1994 print ad showed Santa Claus toasting a polar bear with a bottle of Coke. The Coca-Cola logo appears in the top left-hand corner as an ornament and the ad's text reads, "*Wesołych Świąt i Szczęśliwego Nowego Roku*" (Merry Christmas and Happy New Year). The polar bear in the ad is a new character from the international "Always Coca-Cola" campaign ("Polar Bear"). The polar bear first appeared in a television commercial entitled "Northern Lights" that featured a group of bears watching the aurora borealis while drinking bottles of Coke. The commercial proved popular, and many other similar ones have been produced, including ones containing a bear family selecting a Christmas tree. While the Coca-Cola polar bear ads first showed adult bears relaxing and drinking Coca-Cola, they soon become about family and even connected to Coca-Cola's image of Christmas. In this 1994 Polish print ad, Coca-Cola was once again attempting to establish kinship with the idea of Christmas and family. The featured Santa Claus looks much the same as in the 1990 print ad and again revives notions of home and family. In this ad he is newly juxtaposed with a cuddly, furry polar bear that raises the ad's cuteness factor and presents a modern Christmas character to balance the tradition of Santa Claus. Once again Coca-Cola was using Christmas to advertise itself as family-oriented. Coke was not only the "official sponsor" of the holiday season but also of the Polish family.

The theme of Christmas and family is continued in a 2003 television commercial entitled "Christmas Caravan." This ad shows a caravan of Christmas-decorated Coca-Cola trucks journeying across the country to deliver Coke to a small town. "Christmas Caravan" is an international ad that has added Polish scenes for the local market. In the Polish version of the commercial the trucks are shown traveling through the cities of Warsaw, Gdansk, and Krakow. As the caravan passes through mountain areas bridges magically become wrapped in glowing Christmas lights and outdoor pine trees are transformed into multicolor lighted Christmas trees. Wherever the trucks go, the joy of the Christmas season follows, including a small town where the caravan is met by local residents filled with Christmas cheer. At the end of the ad, when the caravan travels to another town, viewers are shown the back of a truck that features a picture of Santa Claus holding a bottle of Coke and the slogan "Always Coca-Cola" ("Christmas Caravan"). In this commercial Coca-Cola is not only providing soft drinks to Poland but also many of the important elements of the Christmas season. As the trucks travel through the country they bring with them the magical joyousness of the holiday season. The caravan of Coca-Cola trucks travels to each city and small town to ensure that everyone has access to the important beverage and the Christmas spirit that accompanies it. When the trucks arrive they not only bring Coca-Cola, they also bring Christmas. As in other Polish Coca-Cola Christmas ads, this commercial promotes the company's connection to Christmas and thus to Poland and the country's families. While the commercial is bright and cheerful it is also is the opposite of flashy and cosmopolitan. The ad is an attempt to connect Coca-Cola with feelings of nostalgia and memories of Christmases past. Like previous ads this one is also used in various international markets and shows Coca-Cola's connection not only to Polish Christmas and family but to those ideas globally. Coke is able to communicate the idea that the company is not only the local sponsor of Christmas but the international one as well.

Another Coca-Cola Poland advertisement that continues the theme of the soft drink maker's Christmas sponsorship is a 2005 holiday Web site. This electronic ad has several classic games that feature Christmas imagery, Coca-Cola icons, and company sponsorship. The Web site contains six games in a leveled system that forces the player to gain a minimum score on a lower level game before advancing to the next game. The opening-level game is a Coca-Cola Christmas rendering of the popular Chinese game Mahjong. This Coca-Cola version of the game has playing tiles that feature pictures of bottles of Coke, toys, and elves. The electronic game board is bordered by images of Santa Claus, elves sledding, Christmas trees, and other wintry scenes. The Web site's design utilizes both classic images and games but offers few connections to Poland. The message is that games, Coca-Cola, and Christmas are universal and need no direct ties to any one country. The Web site uses the modernity of the Internet to provide traditional content and understood symbols and values. If many flashy modern ads can be labeled "eye candy," then the images and games contained within this Web site are "eye comfort food" (Adverblog). Once again Coca-Cola had positioned itself as the international sponsor of Christmas and the family. This reasonable way of reaching a traditional society like Poland was also a way of connecting Coca-Cola to worldwide family values. From 1990 to 2007 in Poland, Coca-Cola continually used the ideas of Christmas and family to showcase itself as another universal concept.

Omnipresent Average Coca-Cola

Much the same as Coca-Cola used Christmas as a standard element of its image and branding, the company has also attempted to make its logo physically present in as many places as possible. Since its earliest days, Coca-Cola has utilized copious amounts of advertising that often make the soft drink maker's logo appear to be omnipresent. Billboards, neon signs, supermarket displays, restaurant signs, and market nameplates are only a few of the forms of Coca-Cola advertising signage that have become so common internationally that they are rarely considered. Most consumers see Coca-Cola advertising in so many places that they no longer cognitively perceive it. Unlike McDonald's, Levi's, and Frito-Lay, which want their products to be considered as special purchases by the consumer, Coca-Cola does not wish to hold a vaunted position in the buyer's mind. Coca-Cola does not desire to be associated with a night out on the town or become the symbol of youthful rebellion. Rather the soft-drink maker wants its products to be a common yet essential part of everyday life. This is evident in the previously discussed Christmas ads, where the company attempts to be an ever present yet crucial part of the holiday season and thus both Polish and world society. Coca-Cola's use of signage is another element in this strategy. While McDonald's wants to become a part of Polish society and Levi's wishes to be symbol of youth, Coca-Cola wants its products to be a universal part of daily life. This is made evident by the ubiquitousness of the company's logo in Polish society. One can hardly walk down a street in a Polish city or town without seeing Coca-Cola logos on windows, shop signs, table umbrellas, wall menus, lighted signs, and elsewhere. These physical ads are so commonplace that they are accepted without notice. They no longer register in many people's minds as ads but have instead become a seemingly unimportant part of the landscape. Although these physical ads may be unimportant in the daily lives of many, they are serving their purpose in making Coke commonplace and universal in Polish society. If Mark Pendergrast's claim of cheering crowds for the first Coca-Cola truck in Warsaw is true, then much has changed in Poland. In the early years of the twenty-first century, typical Poles are unlikely to even notice Coca-Cola trucks unless the trucks hit them.

If Coca-Cola has truly become both less noticeable and more of an everyday part of Polish society, then how has physical advertising helped in this transformation? Although many factors, such as politics, changing Polish societal and cultural attitudes, other types of advertising, and generational differences are involved in this change, it is reasonable to assume that physical advertising played a role because of its ever present position in Polish society. Coca-Cola would most likely stop spending the large amount of money this advertising costs if it was not producing desired results. The first thing to notice about Coca-Cola's and most other brands' physical advertising is that it is designed to both stand out and blend in simultaneously. The ads almost always are a functional part of everyday life that feature a brightly colored easily identifiable logo. The viewer should recognize the logo but give the ad itself very little thought. This is a very different approach from many other types of advertising that attempt to attract attention, but also to create a buzz among consumers. Television, radio, print, and other types of ads all struggle to be both memorable and engaging. But these physical ads are not meant to be remembered or even really thought about. They are background noise that would only be considered if they disappeared. They perform their intended function if few reflect on them but many accept them as normal. By becoming commonplace the ads help the product to gain an unquestioned role in the fabric of society. By using a large number of physical ads in Poland, Coca-Cola is attempting to become a routine part of Polish life. While other products strive to be extraordinary, Coke merely wants to be everyday.

Because of the astonishing amount of Coca-Cola physical advertising in Poland it is difficult to select only a few examples to analyze. Since this type of advertising's primary goal is to be commonplace then it seems fitting that the most ordinary of these ads be considered. To some, these ads may seem pedestrian or devoid of narrative, but they are underappreciated. One of the most common kinds of Coca-Cola physical ad is the store sign that features a bright red object with the words "Coca-Cola" written in white on it. Often additional slogans or icons appear on the sigh, but the red-and-white Coca-Cola is the staple. These ads are used internationally in almost all of the countries where Coca-Cola is sold, but they are often changed to include the local language. This is true in Poland, where many of the signs contain Polish slogans. These physical ads that contain the Coca-Cola logo very often serve another more functional purpose besides advertising. An example of this is a red, white, and black 1994 ad featuring a can of Coca-Cola, a fork, a knife, and a plate. The crudely drawn ad features "*Pchac*" (Push) under the logo, which makes it clear that the ad is intended to hang on doors to inform customers how to get inside. Another ad from 1996 is a lighted, round store sign that features the Coca-Cola logo, a picture of a bottle of Coke, and the word "*Zawsze*" (Always). An additional 1990s ad showcases the Coca-Cola logo as it serves as a menu for a Polish restaurant. What these ads share is that they generally go unnoticed at least on a conscious level. Although one of these ads may seem incapable of producing a narrative, when taken as a whole they produce an image of a brand that is universally accepted without much thought. Much like the ads themselves, Coca-Cola is attempting to become an ever present yet unconsidered part of Polish society.

When using both Christmas ads and physical advertising in Poland, Coca-Cola is creating an image of a universal brand. The soft-drink maker wants to become a part of Polish society, not only as a product but as a part of everyday life. This theme is also present in one of Coca-Cola's early

Polish advertising campaigns, "Always Coca-Cola." This Polish extension of an international campaign was launched in spring 1993 and is considered to be the first example of a coordinated Coca-Cola advertising campaign in Poland ("Historical Background 1991–1996"). Although advertisements for Coca-Cola existed previously in Poland, this marks the first time that the company used such an extensive campaign. "Always Coca-Cola," translated into Polish as "*Zawsze* Coca-Cola," is an ad campaign that emphasizes the brand's timelessness and everyday appeal. The international campaign originally consisted of twenty-seven commercials, each focusing on different types of consumers ("Highlights in the History of Coca-Cola"). The campaign has been wildly successful worldwide, winning numerous awards, including a spot on *Ad Age's* 100 Most Important Advertising Campaigns ("Top 100 Advertising Campaigns"). Because the "Always Coca-Cola" campaign is a worldwide tool, the ads have not been crafted for Polish audiences and are examples of the company's interest in a global strategy. While Coca-Cola may translate certain words or slogans for the Polish market, mostly these ads reflect little thought being given to the individual country. This fits in well with Coca-Cola's theme of universality and indicates that the company's television advertising was similar in almost every market. This campaign says very little about Coca-Cola's connection to Poland but it does reassert the soft drink maker's desire to be a common part of everyday life in every region of the world.

The "Always Coca-Cola" campaign's theme of universality is evident in the previously discussed Coca-Cola polar bear ad, "Northern Lights," the most famous ad from the campaign. The ad, showing polar bears drinking Coca-Cola at the North Pole, is designed to strongly appeal to international consumers regardless of nation of origin. The bears have a high "cute quotient" that makes them attractive to many different kinds of consumers. Most notably the bears are a retro, traditional device, providing consumers with the feeling that the bears have been a part of Coke's advertising for generations, even though they have been created recently. This character identification seems to be confirmed by the bears' popularity and their usage in Christmas advertising alongside Santa Claus. While many brands employ lovable mascots, the polar bears are different because they instantly become identifiable and yet do so in a low-key and unassuming manner. "Northern Lights" and the other Coca-Cola polar bears ads that follow do not utilize up-tempo music or flashy effects; instead the ads quietly portray the simple pleasures of everyday life. In "Northern Lights" and subsequent ads, the bears enjoy their family, friends, and natural surroundings. There is nothing nationalistically unique about these ads, no one place or group of people would have a special connection to the content. The subjects of the ads — friends, family, and everyday pleasures — can be understood by any consumer. The ad was created to have mass appeal and to restate Coca-Cola's connection to the remarkable yet common things in life. "Always Coca-Cola" was designed as an international reminder that Coca-Cola is (or wants to be) a part of the fabric of many societies. Though little of this content is unique to Poland it does reconfirm Coca-Cola's message in the early 1990s. The company is working hard to become a common part of everyday life.

While Coca-Cola was conducting the "Always Coca-Cola" campaign worldwide, it was specifically attempting to portray itself as a good neighbor within the Polish market. Many of company's ads from the 1990s reflected Coca-Cola's interest in helping Polish charities or providing aid to victims of calamities. These ads fit the company's strategy of become an average part of Polish society. If something greatly affected Poland, then that should in turn concern Coca-Cola and the company would be expected to pitch in and help. Charitable sponsorship and corporate disaster fundraising are far from unique to Coca-Cola in Poland. Numerous companies in many different countries, including Poland, are deeply involved in local charitable efforts. This is generally thought of as a "win-win" investment that provides positive advertising for the company and a beneficial contribution to society. Coca-Cola's efforts were noteworthy because their charitable contributions became a major part of local advertising. Coke's "good neighbor" policy provided a local connection to its international campaigns and helped the company to further integrate into Polish society. This is evidenced by an internally produced history of Coca-Cola Poland that notes that during 1995, "In Qtr. 4 we also launched a heavy X-Mas campaign tied-in with a PR-effective charity program" ("Historical Background 1991–1996"). Notice that Coca-Cola is linking its charitable efforts to its traditionally popular Christmas advertising. In this advertising the company is able to show that it truly has the Christmas spirit and does in fact promote the good feelings that surround the holiday season. Also note that Coca-Cola is well aware of the positive results that its charitable advertising provide. The advertising is referred to as "a

PR-effective charity program." Coca-Cola is using charitable advertising to promote itself as a normal part of Polish life.

Advertising featuring Coca-Cola's charity in Poland is a popular concept that was used many times by the company. In 1994 Coca-Cola began sponsoring Special Olympics Poland and the company was careful to note this fact in many of its press releases and official publications. Coca-Cola helped to fund the 2001 Special Olympics European Football Tournament in Warsaw and the company's logo graced many of the games' facilities. This sponsorship linked Coca-Cola to both charity and sports, which further helped to define the company's status as a normal part of Polish life. The soft-drink maker also fused television sponsorship and charitable giving to create a 2001 event revolving around the Easter holiday that also connected to a Polish television show. In this promotional event Coca-Cola gave stuffed Easter bunny toys to orphanages in Poland for Children's Day. The idea for the advertising/charity event originated from a contestant on the Polish version of the voyeuristic reality show "Big Brother," of which Coca-Cola is a leading sponsor. The contestant apparently commented on air that he wanted to give his Cola-Cola Easter bunny to an orphan. The company recognized the value of the promotion and expanded the idea to include orphanages across the country ("The Coca-Cola Business in Poland"). Following one of Coca-Cola's general patterns, this promotion was linked to a holiday and showed the company as a caring part of everyday Polish society. In a predominantly Catholic country like Poland, giving orphans a gift associated with a major Christian holiday can only be good public relations. It is difficult to think of the downside of an event that includes orphaned children, Easter, Children's Day, and toys. Add to this mix a reality television show that is popular among younger Poles and the PR opportunities only grow. In this promotion, Coca-Cola is a good neighbor and an everyday part of Polish life but it is also is hip enough to understand current trends and to listen to young Poles' ideas. With this event the company was able to be a part of normal Polish life for older and younger Poles, an impressive achievement.

Cola-Cola has sponsored many other charity projects and community programs in Poland, including the Terry Fox Run to raise money for cancer research, charity auctions for children living in orphanages, and the Annual Charity Ball of Journalists. Each of the events helps the soft-drink producer to remain in the public eye and reinforces the company's desire to be seen as a daily part of Polish life. One other advertising promotion from 2001 to 2002 showcased how Coca-Cola uses various methods of advertising to display the universal appeal of its charitable contributions. In the summer of 2001, heavy rains caused catastrophic flooding in many parts of Poland. Many areas not totally recovered from previous flooding in 1997 suffered yet more damage (Warsaw Prepares Flood Defenses). Agencies of the European Union, charities like the Red Cross, and donors from numerous countries contributed money to the relief fund. Coca-Cola also provided support for the flood victims in various ways. One of these was to partner with the Polish Humanitarian Organization (PHO) and sponsor relief projects like "Lets Bring the Joy," that donated mini-buses, sports gear and equipment, juice, Christmas gifts, and trip sponsorships to various schools and children affected by the flooding (Assistance for 2001 Flood Victims). This sponsorship was advertised on an in-store Coca-Cola display that used the red-and-white "Always" logo. The top portion of the sign retained the word "*Zawsze*" but "Coca-Cola" was replaced with "*Możesz Pomóc*" (You Can Help). The bottom of the sign said that Coca-Cola was working with the PHO to help children in places like the Bieszczady Mountains. The company used a clever new version of its logo to inform the public that it is "always" helping needy children in Poland. As in other charity efforts, Coca-Cola was not embarassed to advertise its role as donor. These signs would be seen by many that entered shops and stores and would reassure that once again Coca-Cola was acting as a normal part of the community. The company was working with relief agenices and helping unfortunate children, as any good citizen would.

In addition to the helping relief agencies by donating money and advertising space, Coca-Cola also used advertising to raise money for charity. Like other forms of charitable advertising, raising money for various causes also provided the company with a method to bolster its public image and continually reestablish itself as a brand. In 2001 Coca-Cola created a special limited-edition aluminum can to be auctioned off to raise money for flood relief. These special numbered cans were limited to a production run of two hundred and were meant to be collectors items for those interested in Coca-Cola merchandise. The colorful cans are decorated with child-like crayon drawings of a house, trees, and the sun. The can's caption reads, "*Nadzieja nie tonie*" (Hope cannot be flooded) suggesting that Coca-Cola and the buyer are helping to sustain hope in Poland. The drawing on the can forces one to think of the children who have been harmed by the flooding and the slogan pushes one toward action by reinforcing the idea that the better things in life will always prevail. Coca-Cola was attempting to rally moral support for the flood victims and to raise money for rebuilding. To accomplish these goals it used its very familiar can and logo. This means that Coca-Cola the corporate citizen and Coca-Cola the product could not be separated. The soft-drink maker's charity effort was placed on the product itself, forcing the two to be thought of as one entity. Coca-Cola is auctioning off its products and recognizable logo to help charity, which created a more personal impression than only giving money, at the same time that it helped the company's image. Coca-Cola used this charitable fundraising as an opportunity to again present itself as an average member of Polish society. Like any good citizen was giving part of itself to help others that were suffering in the community.

Coca-Cola was not only advertising its status as an everyday part of Polish life by illustrating its charitable efforts. It also was emphasizing its universal appeal by advertising its sponsorship of common and popular parts of Polish society like sporting events. Sports sponsorship is a common vehicle of advertising for many companies worldwide. The sponsors gain credibility and recognition by aligning themselves with popular teams or events. Coca-Cola uses this approach in many markets worldwide and sponsors a variety of sporting activities. In Poland the company most noticeably sponsors multiple soccer teams and leagues but also is involved with other sports. Much like charitable advertising, sports promotion gives the company an opportunity to declare itself a part of society's fabric. Many sports fans in Poland rabidly follow their favorite teams and Coca-Cola's affiliation with these teams and the leagues that they play in gives the company credibility as a member of society. The soft-drink maker has even mixed charity and sports in events like the Coca-Cola Cup, a youth soccer tournament founded in 1999 that has featured nearly three thousand teams a year from elementary schools across Poland. The winning team receives a soccer-based trip to another country and often gets to compete against other youth teams in Europe (Coca-Cola Cup). The tournament appears to grow every year and Coca-Cola has devoted a Web site to news and information about the Cup. The Coca-Cola Cup is one of many sporting events the company sponsors that project the value and strategy of Coca-Cola's efforts. Much like holiday advertising and charitable promotion, sports sponsorship has helped Coca-Cola brand itself as an average, universal part of every-day life. The company is able to seem omnipresent without being cast as an overbearing colonizing force. Coca-Cola has worked hard to become a common part of Polish society and not the outside invader that some believe it to be. One cannot speak for all Poles, but it appears that many have accepted the company as a part of their daily lives.

From the mid to late 1990s until the present, Coca-Cola has contin-ued to use much the same strategy as it had in previous years. Numerous holiday campaigns, including those for Christmas and Easter, have been launched, maintaining the company's connection to such advertising. Santa Claus and the polar bears remain focal points in many ads, as the com-pany continues to stress its link to important holiday times and traditions. The soft-drink maker also keeps building advertising campaigns around previously discussed ideas like charity promotion and sports sponsorship. Coca-Cola has also engaged in numerous sports promotions, including a 1996 Olympic-based campaign entitled "Go for the Gold." These ideas, along with a continued reliance on physical advertising, showcase Coca-Cola's confidence in its basic theme of being an everyday part of Polish life. From 1990 to 2007 the company worked hard to assert its brand as fundamental, so common that it almost goes without notice. This major theme seems to be so ingrained in Coke's strategy that it will most likely be used for the foreseeable future. In the early years of the twenty-first century the company did add other significant marketing and advertising themes. These not only illustrate a change in Coca-Cola's marketing strat-egy but also demonstrate an effort by the company to meet unresolved needs within the Polish market. While Coca-Cola has had great success with its continuing theme of universality, it also must address Polish cul-tural needs that are not being fulfilled.

Uniquely Coca-Cola

In August 2000, the world's largest advertising billboard was placed in the center of the Polish capital of Warsaw. The billboard, a part of the "Coca-Cola, What a Feeling" campaign, earned a spot in the *Guinness Book of World Records* and dwarfed the surrounding neighborhood ("The Coca-Cola Business in Poland"). This enormous outdoor advertisement is one of the first ads to utilize other themes beside the well-marketed connections to family and the universality of Coca-Cola. This addition of new advertising themes came at a time when Coca-Cola had been produced independently in the Polish market for around ten years. In the fast-moving world of advertising it is remarkable to work with a theme for this length of time. Certainly, Coca-Cola had many different campaigns and selling points during these years but it is exceptional that the company remained so focused on this governing theme. By contrast, McDonald's, Levi's, and Frito-Lay all changed or evolved their major themes several times during this ten-year period. In this context it is remarkable that Coca-Cola expanded its advertising scope in the year 2000. The billboard chosen to display this ad was also remarkable for its size. The outdoor ad was roughly 7874 square feet, a massive structure by anyone's definition ("The Coca-Cola Business in Poland"). The billboard was almost entirely red and white, and it featured a giant bottle of Coke and part of a beautiful woman's face. The background of the billboard was Coca-Cola red, as were the skin of the attractive woman and the bottle of Coke itself. The only parts of the woman that were not red were her white lips and blue eyes. Additionally, the outline of a Coke bottle can be seen in the middle of her tightly pressed lips. Behind her it appears that the billboard is sweating condensation like the outside of a cold Coke bottle. The billboard's slogan reads "*Odkryj na nowo wszystkimi zmysłami*" (Rediscover with all your senses). A Coca-Cola bottle-cap logo is placed in the ad's top righthand corner, in case anyone was unaware of the sponsor.

The billboard was significant because it seemed to be the antithesis of Coca-Cola's previous ideas of commonness and normality. Coca-Cola's main theme in Poland had been that it was a reliable part of daily life, but this ad was different. Everything about it — its size, the color scheme, and the slogan — demands to be noticed, making it exceptional. While Coca-Cola's past ads embraced the idea of a common respectable community this ad glorified glittery, self-promoting individualism. One can generally see Coca-Cola's previous advertising strategy in Poland as being akin to elevator music, ever present yet unobtrusive. This giant billboard broke away from that mold, and expresses the bling-bling attitude of hip-hop culture more than the instrumental version of a Barry Manilow tune. While Coca-Cola's image and logo seemed to be everywhere in the past, it was almost always small and inconspicuous. This outdoor ad prided itself on being the largest in the world and featured an excessively bright image and an indulgent slogan. Why would a company that values classical themes like family holidays and everyday goodness create such an ad? The most obvious answer is that Coca-Cola was worried about its place in the Polish market and needed to change advertising strategy in order to increases sales. According to data compiled by the market research group Snapshots International, the growth rate of Poland's carbonated soft drink market drastically shrank from 1998 to 2001. Between 1997 and 1998, sales for carbonated soft drinks rose 11.5 percent in Poland. In 1999, sales only increased by 2.8 percent. In 2000, sales were up 3.3 percent and in 2001 they shrank by 2.9 percent. Coca-Cola controlled 39.5 percent of the Polish market, but sales appeared to be stagnant or even beginning to decline ("Snapshots International"). It looks as if the company may have been forced to rethink its strategy in the Polish market.

As has been stated, it is not unusual for a company to change advertising slogans; this happens with great regularity. Also, Coca-Cola did not abandon its marketing approach but augmented it with new themes and ideas. What is noteworthy is how long Coca-Cola went without changing its marketing and then the direction that the company chose to pursue. If Coca-Cola's theme of commonplace was aimed at a family market, then its new brash approach would seem to be designed for Polish youth. Coca-Cola's new advertising screams, it needs to be noticed, much the same as many of its young customers. Each of the other companies in this study, McDonald's, Levi's, and Frito-Lay, rely heavily on youth-focused advertising in Poland, and one could argue that Coca-Cola's past advertisements would also appeal to younger Poles. This means that youth-focused advertising is a common and seemingly productive practice. If Coca-Cola wished to both grow the carbonated soft drink market and its share of it, then it would make sense to market to customers without as many preset notions or habits but with disposable income. The company's main rival in Poland, PepsiCo, for years had run advertisements that were bright, flashy, sexy, loud, and hip. These Pepsi ads looked to appeal to young Poles who wanted to be cool and different from the older generation that Coke represented to some. The cache that Coca-Cola has inherited from being a socialist-era symbol of rebellion had all but disappeared by the year 2000 and a new generation was growing up with little or no memory of the Cold War period. Coca-Cola's success was slowing and Poles were beginning to ask for something different. It was up to Coke to provide them with new visions of what the soft drink is or might be.

Coca-Cola as Uniquely Exciting

The enormous billboard in the Polish capital of Warsaw is an example of Coca-Cola as a provider of good times and excitement. Unto itself this theme is unexceptional. Many companies attempt to brand their products as instruments of a fun, party lifestyle. Coke's main competitor, Pepsi, has been utilizing this strategy internationally for decades. What is striking is how the theme of an exceptional experience is the inverse of Coca-Cola's older theme, commonplaceness. Because the soft-drink maker was using both themes in different campaigns in 2000, it was marketing itself as both common and exceptional. Notice the slogan from the Warsaw billboard, "Rediscover with all your senses." The ad is asking consumers to forget what they think they know about Coca-Cola and to try the product again. No longer is Coca-Cola only marketed as a safe part of everyday life but now also as a chance to enjoy life to the fullest. The soft drink is seen to be big, bold, and fun, and consumers are urged to understand that it is more than merely a part of everyday life. In other places Coca-Cola was marketing itself as a part of everyday life, but here as an exceptional product that could bring excitement to customers' lives. As the millennium began, Coca-Cola Poland seems to want to be both new and extraordinary, and traditional and common. While it may be unable to be all things to all people, Coca-Cola was trying.

Coca-Cola's theme of exceptionalism showcases the company's desire to modernize its image and to induce consumers to take notice of the soft drink. This is seemingly a difficult task because for years the company has worked to become an omnipresent yet unremarkable part of Polish society. In effect, at the start of the twenty-first century, Coca-Cola was battling the marketing image that it itself created. Note that this campaign was seemingly a reaction to the needs and desires of Polish customers. Although often masked by business terms like sales growth, market share, and branding, this change in Coca-Cola's advertising strategy displays the company's social interactions with Polish citizens and consumers. Yes, the soft drink maker was changing in order to increase sales, which undoubtedly is Coca-Cola's primarily objective in everything it does. The company was altering its advertising approach in response to a perceived need within Polish society, though. Many critics would contend that these changes in presentation are merely cosmetic alterations. Some would claim that Coca-Cola is creating and selling the same product in Poland and has only changed the marketing. While this is undoubtedly true on certain levels, it also misses the larger cultural implications of the advertising and marketing alteration. By changing its long-running Polish advertising narrative Coca-Cola was attempting to interact differently with Polish society. The company was paying attention to needs and desires within Poland and attempting to conform to some of these. From a narrative viewpoint of the social and cultural relationship between Coca-Cola and Poland, it is unimportant that Coca-Cola's products changed little physically. What is important is the communication between Coca-Cola and Polish society. The new ads showed that the company understood it was not meeting the needs of a large number of Polish consumers. This advertising change was an attempt to better communicate with different types of Poles and to establish a new dialogue between Coca-Cola and some Polish citizens. This understanding of Coca-Cola's role in Poland and the company's marketing and advertising strategy as a constant ongoing communication with Polish society is very different from the views of those who see the company's actions as monolithic imperialism.

As mentioned, by the end of the year 2000 Coca-Cola was seeing a slowing of growth in the soft-drink market that would soon become a decline. The company apparently interpreted this as a sign of dissatisfaction by younger Poles and used new advertising in an attempt to reach them. While sales data and market-share reports indicated that Coca-Cola's market was becoming stagnant and needed to focus on younger consumers, a nonscientific sampling of public opinion apparently supported this view. As with many other western products that entered Poland shortly after the end of socialism, Coca-Cola had a fairly substantial honeymoon period in which the product was accepted as new and exciting. Coca-Cola was an antisocialist symbol in Poland during the Cold War and this provided the brand substantial interest among Poles who desired Coke's symbolic appeal. The company offset this "coolness factor" by enlisting advertising that displayed Coke as a regular and trustworthy part of everyday life, knowing that the brand could not depend on being a novelty for the long haul. Because Coca-Cola typically embraced middle-of-the-road conservative values and ideas it did not often appeal strongly to teenage and twentysomething Poles who were the core customers of many brands. This group is known to be a fickle buying demographic that needs to be constantly courted and embraced in order to remain loyal. Coca-Cola's changed advertising theme indicates that the company understood that their marketing was not working with a younger audience. Even Polish consumers seemed to understand that Coca-Cola was missing what should have been one of its primary audiences.

When asked their opinions of Coca-Cola, most Poles, young and old, respond that the soft drink is primarily a young person's beverage that is generally enjoyed by older Poles only on special occasions or when out in public. This seems to contradict Coca-Cola's marketing of the product as an everyday part of Polish life. A random survey of several Poles finds that older and younger Polish consumers differ greatly in their views of American products, including Coca-Cola. Poles forty-five and older tend to see "new" products like Coca-Cola as supplements to Polish culture that should be used sparingly and only on specific occasions. These older drinkers think of Coca-Cola as a beverage for celebrations, parties, and meals that take place outside the home. Younger Poles tend to see Coke as a drink for celebrations but also as an everyday lifestyle choice. The soft drink reflects positively on the user and showcases new Polish values. While it is probable that some respondents exaggerated or changed their answers to fit understood social values, it is telling that almost each respondent indicated a gap in views between older and younger generations. This type of thinking highlights some of the divisions in Polish society and culture that likely led to the changes in Coca-Cola's advertising.

Youthful Individualism

Coca-Cola's new themes of fun and individualism are evident in much of its Polish advertising from the early years of the twenty-first century. The company used several types of commercials to convey the idea that Coca-Cola is a vibrant and fun drink that appeals to a youthful audience. One idea that has been commonly used is that of Coca-Cola's youthful energy transforming normal adult society into something exciting. Common traditional settings that are generally thought to be boring are changed into exhilarating places and events. The idea of these ads is that Coca-Cola can turn even the dullest places into havens of excitement. One early television ad that showcases these ideas is a 2002 commercial called "Hot Five Promo." In it Coca-Cola partners with the youth brand MTV to create a cross promotion for both companies. In the commercial a Polish fireman sees a passenger train painted with the Coca-Cola logo that appears to be on fire. The fireman jumps onto the moving train and then realizes that it is only hosting a hot party. Scantily clad young women and men are dancing to loud music and drinking Coca-Cola. The announcer informs the viewers that Coke drinkers who collect twelve bottle caps can get a free MTV music CD. The party continues until other firemen board the train, and the first fireman becomes embarrassed that he forgot to cancel the fire alarm ("Hot Five Promo").

The "Hot Five Promo" commercial displays the idea that Coca-Cola can make any situation or location exciting and fun. The soft drink transforms a boring train ride into an adventurous party, complete with sexy young people and popular music. Only Coca-Cola, it is suggested, can provide this kind of party atmosphere and only young people can understand it. The firemen, though brave and hard-working, mistake the good-time atmosphere of the party for a dangerous situation and try to rescue the youths. The young people on the train understand this world of fun and excitement better than the older people in society and recognize the importance of Coca-Cola. The youth of the commercial are smarter than their adult counterparts and are always in control of the situation, unlike the fireman who is twice wrong within the thirty-second ad. If before Coca-Cola was portrayed as a keeper of conservative values, now it is an agent of change. It is a beverage that can change the social order and create a society in which life is more exciting and less plodding. It is Coca-Cola, along with MTV, that provides the means to transform a normal dull day into an exciting party. It is Coca-Cola that can make even public transportation enjoyable and can allow the young to take over the very infrastructure of society. No longer are firefighters and other public servants of the world in power, now things are controlled by teenagers wearing fashionable clothes, listening to MTV music, and drinking Coca-Cola. According to the ad, the revolution has come again and this time it is a soft drink that is remaking Polish society.

Another ad, "Grandpa Titled," also from 2002, follows the same theme of a youthful remaking of society. In this television commercial for the Coca-Cola-owned soft-drink brand "Lift," two young granddaughters make a banner for their grandfather. The dignified grandfather lives in a large, well-decorated house that suggests that he not only has money but also upper-class status. The house's size and regal decor, along with the appearance of the grandfather, hint that he may be of noble background. This idea is further suggested by the grand manner with which the grandfather strokes his moustache. Several Poles have commented that when they viewed this commercial, the grandfather's moustache and how he touches it made them think of the nobility in the classic Polish novel and film *With Fire and Sword*. This well-known Henryk Sienkiewicz novel, and the film adaptations that followed, are set in seventeenth-century Poland and feature several characters of Polish nobility that look similar to the commercial's grandfather. All of these factors seem to confirm that the grandfather is descended from Polish nobility, although no offical noble class exists in present-day Poland. In the commercial, the young preteen granddaughters playfully imitate their grandfather's habit of stroking his moustache as they make a banner for him that proclaims how much they love him. The ad ends with a shot of the grandfather's back and the heart-shaped hole in his sweater, allowing the viewer to realize that the girls made the banner from their grandfather's clothing ("Grandpa Titled").

"Grandpa Titled" is designed to highlight generational differences in Poland. The stately Polish grandfather is contrasted to his granddaughters who appear much more modern and western in appearance and action. The girls are dressed in colorful outfits that could be seen on preteens anywhere in the world. Although the children are portrayed as loving and sweet, they also separate themselves from their grandfather's generation by making fun of his moustache and using his sweater as material for their banner, the message being that they can find fun and excitement anywhere and that they embrace different values than previous generations. Their grandfather appears to be a wealthy man of noble descent who is clinging to many of the ways of the past. His clothing and his house are from a different era and his manners are courtly and regal. He is the very symbol of the older generation of Poland. His granddaughters by contrast are fashionable in both manners and appearance. They also are smarter than their grandfather; they alone know that they destroyed his clothing in order to create his gift. They have tricked the adults and are creating a new way of life vastly different from their grandfather's. Although the Coca-Cola owned beverage Lift is portrayed as a family drink in the ad, it also is clear that the new members of the family are much more adventurous and fun than the older ones. The younger generation is embracing the excitement and good times that Coca-Cola brings and even the children of Poland's first families are not immune.

One other example of Coca-Cola's advertised ability to help create a reorganized fun-driven, youth-centered society is a 2003 commercial, "Breakdance." The ad for the Coca-Cola brand "Sprite" features urban street dancers, skateboarders, and bicyclists performing tricks to a hip-hop beat. The youths, dressed in baggy urban clothing, rap about their lives and the freedom that comes with performing and drinking Sprite. The rap lyrics provide an outlet for the youths to express their opinions about society and to proclaim both their independence and distrust of traditional societal roles. Some of the lyrics: "Do you want to express yourself? Do you need a source of your passion? Make your own style! There are a million ways. And each of them is best. What unites them is thirst and passion!" ("Breakdance"). In this ad Coca-Cola blatantly suggests that Sprite provides an opportunity for excitement and fun. The soft drink can not only alleviate Polish youths' physical needs but also can help fulfill their emotional and psychological thirsts as well. Sprite, it is suggested, understands the need for rebellion and change and encourages youths to follow their own paths and remake society in whatever way they deem best. Coca-Cola is allying itself with spirited youths who believe they can change the world around them into a place of fun, excitement, and purpose. This message is far different from that of universal normality that Coca-Cola clung to for almost ten years.

Humorous Youth

Coca-Cola's new themes of individuality, fun, and excitement are not only seen in ads about young Poles changing society but also can be viewed in ads that concentrate on Polish youths participating in silly yet exciting situations. These humor-based ads are a staple in the advertising world and are used by all of the companies in this survey. What makes these amusing ads noteworthy is the sheer amount of them used from 2002 to 2007 and their differences from Coca-Cola's other themes and ideas. These ads not only differ greatly from Coca-Cola's previous campaign of universal normality but they also contrast with the aforementioned ads that concentrate on ideas of an exciting and fun youth-dominated society. In those ads young Poles are presented as strong and able leaders who are often wiser and craftier than older generations. These ads portray Polish youths as not only equal to older Poles but generally better. By comparison, the humor-based ads still focus on the ideas of fun and excitement within Polish society but they typically depict Polish youths as bumbling, silly, or amusing in some other way. While the previous ads show young Poles to be fun, exciting, and capable of changing society, these ads often focus on youthful buffoonery and offer little in terms of societal change. In effect, one kind of ad is declaring youths to be a threat to the adult establishment while the other contends that young Poles are altogether harmless. Because both types of ads were created simultaneously, one can assume that Coca-Cola is attempting to gain as wide of an audience as possible by appealing to different advertising tastes. Coca-Cola is producing advertising that both rebels and reassures, the company's way of having its cake and eating it too. It showcases how Coca-Cola is using different approaches to reestablish itself in the Polish market. Not content to only create one approach to showcasing its new theme, Coca-Cola utilizes various ideas and methods in its campaign.

The idea of Coca-Cola's connection to an exciting, fun and humorous way of life in Poland is contained in many commercials from the early years of the new millennium. One of the most memorable is a summer 2003 ad entitled "Summer Promo 30." This television commercial uses the good-time ideas of summer, the beach, and friends to promote Coca-Cola. The ad features five young men and women walking down a beach and singing a catchy song. The youngest of the group is sent to buy some Coca-Cola but when he returns the Coke bottles are missing their caps. It is soon revealed that the young man has taken the caps in order to spend them on prizes in Coca-Cola's new promotion. The ad ends with the young man being chased across the beach by the other members of his group ("Summer Promo 30"). The commercial is reminiscent of the structure and tone of many music videos. The ad contains no dialogue but utilizes a catchy tune by the artist DJ Bobo called "Chihuahua." The group of youths is portrayed as a band that is engaged in entertaining hijinks. This idea of a music group in funny and silly situations is reminiscent of the Beatles' film "Help," the Monkees' network television show, and scores of music videos featured on MTV in both the United States and Europe. The ad is a Polish creation but elsewhere in the world Coca-Cola has used the same song and structure. Although the ad appears to be a routine copy of international music videos, many Poles have commented that they believe it to have meaning within the Polish market. They claim the word "Chihuahua," that is repeated again and again in the song, sounds to them like the Polish word "*ciałała*," which means "to collect something without spending it." This ties in nicely to the message of the ad, that customers should collect Coca-Cola bottle caps to obtain prizes. Coca-Cola has produced an entertaining commerical that connects to the local culture and seems to provide youth appeal.

Notice how different the "Summer Promo 30" commercial is from its previously mentioned counterparts. The ad is a major change from Coca-Cola's original strategy of portraying itself as a common brand and is quite different from the youth-based ads that show young adults changing the world. The ad, and others like it, shows youths in a safe and understanding light. They are not capable young people displaying their abilities to lead and create. Rather they are shown as a caricature of the idea of the carefree, cavorting young person. This staple of popular culture promotes the idea that youth is fun and safe and has few of the real problems that face adults. The troubles that do occur are trivial, fun things that never seriously threaten to ruin the good times that the youths seem to perpetually experience. When the youngest band member steals the others' Coke bottle caps he has not really caused a problem but rather has created a way to have a new kind of fun. This type of commercial is a safe alternative to more serious ads about excitement for both young and older viewers who do not want to think of a changing society. It is an escapist vehicle for those who desire the idea of excitement but do not wish to think of the consequences. As Coca-Cola pairs this type of ad with the others that show youth in a more serious light, they seem to engage the question of what it means to be young. Certainly, Coca-Cola argues that to be young means to have fun and live an exciting life, but leaves the rest of the question open to public opinion. Are young Poles ambitious citizens who are poised to lead the country at the start of the new century or are they silly adolescents who are too young to understand the world's problems? Coca-Cola allows members of Polish society to answer these questions for themselves and to accept the ideas of youth that they deem worthy and to reject all others. The company defines youth as broadly and in as many ways as possible and then asks Poland to choose which version it prefers. While this is certainly a smart business practice for Coca-Cola to attempt to be as many things to as many people as possible, it also shows a partnership between the company and Polish society. In order to sell products in Poland, Coca-Cola must respect Polish public opinion and constantly change in order to meet the needs of the populace.

Many other ads from 2002–2007 connect Coca-Cola to the idea of humorous, silly excitement. Some of these ads are Polish versions of international ads while others are made locally. These commercials include 2003's "Beach Titled," in which a young man plays a funny trick on his friends to get more Fanta, "Tattoo," a 2004 commercial showing young men and women tricked into being tattooed with Asian characters from a lunch menu, and 2004's "Fanta Orange Straw," in which young men think they are being clever but in reality are being conned by several beautiful young women. A series of 2005 "Bamboocha" commercials portray a comical Pacific-island culture and the 2005 "Thirst never wins" Sprite campaign shows two young people engaged in pointless activities in order to show how much they like the soft drink. These ads and others utilize the idea of humorous yet safe excitement to create a distinct impression of Polish youths. Because Coca-Cola has a strong desire to connect to excitement and fun, it re-creates a kind of advertising that can be both eye-catching and uncontroversial. While Polish youths may be the target audience for this campaign, other Poles could be convinced that they too want to experience the exciting lives that Coca-Cola seems to offer. The ideas of these ads connect to the myth of the lucky yet foolhardy person that is prominent in Polish culture. Polish literature and culture is replete with stories and myths of characters that bumble through an exciting yet unexamined life. Usually, through luck and lack of pretense, these individuals are able to gain everything that they and the hearer of the tale could ever wish for. Coca-Cola uses this familiar type of character to sell its new ideas in Poland, understanding that the company cannot merely claim to be a part of Polish culture but rather that Coke needs to actually find a way to become so.

International Poland

One other advertising theme that was beginning to come to the fore at the start of the twentieth century was that of an international Poland. In previous advertisements Coca-Cola had expressed its perceived place within Poland and had begun to strongly court young consumers but had rarely shown Poland as an international entity. In 2006–07, Coke began to use a global marketing campaign in Poland that showcased the nation's cultural importance. The international campaign titled "The Coke Side of Life" portrays Coca-Cola as a fun, youthful, and exciting product that sometimes creates experiences that border on magical. Several international commercials were created and additional local content was produced to make the ad campaign more culturally relevant. In a March 2006 press release, Coca-Cola highlighted the global/local cultural aspects of the campaign by saying, "Because Coca-Cola is a global brand with local connections and meanings, 'The Coke Side of Life' offers each country an opportunity to interpret their own moments of happiness and the brand's role in those. Working with markets around the world, we have collaboratively coauthored an integrated creative platform that can be adapted to fit different market needs. And we are inviting countries to add to the effort through joint global initiatives" ("Welcome to The Coke Side of Life'").

While many other international Coca-Cola advertising campaigns had been used in Poland, "The Coke Side of Life" is one of the first that emphasizes an international community and Polish society's place in the company's view of the world. One of the most comical is a global television commercial produced for the 2006 FIFA World Cup in soccer. The ad portrays the international shared value of soccer and the importance of this global community. The commercial begins with a visual of the words, "We all speak football (soccer)" written inside an empty Coca-Cola bottle and then shows scenes of natural enemies watching soccer and celebrating when a goal is scored. The rivals in the commercial are a fly and a fly swatter, a lumberjack and a tree, a scientist and a white rat, a chicken and a cook, a hippie and a bar of soap, and a cactus and a red balloon. As the goal is scored, all of the former adversaries embrace and forget about their differences as a joyful Bach instrumental is played. The last scene shows a husband and wife in bed, drinking a bottle of Coca-Cola as the important goal is scored. The pudgy, bald husband leaps out of bed to celebrate as does a more attractive man who has been hiding in the closet. Both men eye each other momentarily and then embrace as the words "We all speak football" again fill the screen (FIFA World Cup Germany 2006). This humorous ad attempts to portray an international society of which Poland is a part. The commercial reflects upon shared experiences and common desires that are understood and sponsored by Coca-Cola.

While promoting international values in commercials like the above-described World Cup ad, "The Coke Side of Life" campaign also attempts to mix a perceived global culture with traditional local cultures. The best example of this is a series of ads that are central to the advertising campaign. These print ads display how desirable "The Coke Side of Life" is in some cultural, artistic, or other local manner. The various advertisements generally show brightly colored objects splashing out of a bottle of Coca-Cola and creating an eye-catching visual. Many different versions of this "Coke Side of Life" ad have been created, and several are very provocative and classically artistic in nature. A Polish adaptation of the ad envisions the city of Krakow springing from the bottle. The brightly colored spires and rooftops of local landmarks like Wawel Castle are easily identifiable, as is the city's symbol, the dragon, which can be seen escaping from the open Coke bottle. The mixture of multiple bright and dark colors creates an inviting representation of Krakow's skyline and symbols that both celebrates the city and its connection to Coca-Cola. The tagline reads, "Krakow po radosnej stronie życia" (Krakow on the happy side of life). While one can argue the artistic merits of the ad, it is clear that Coca-Cola is attempting to embrace both the local and the global ("Krakow po radosnej"). This marketing focus can certainly be seen as an extention of Coca-Cola's twenty-first century emphasis toward youthful advertising but it also highlights the company's desire to be simultaneously global and local. Much like McDonald's, Levi's, and Frito-Lay, by 2007 Coca-Cola was beginning to advertise itself as a local version of a global brand.

Summary

Arguably, Coca-Cola is the most well-known American brand worldwide. Since its humble beginnings as a nineteenth-century, Georgia medical tonic and drug-store refreshment, the soft drink has grown to generate nearly unprecedented global sales and establish immense international popularity. The company has an equally exciting history in Poland, where prior to 1990 it often served as a capitalist/anticapitalist symbol. Coca-Cola entered the post-socialist years as a highly regarded symbol of both the United States and the changes that were taking place within Poland. Although Coca-Cola may have been trendy at the beginning of 1990s, the soft-drink maker soon shaped an advertising campaign that presented Coca-Cola as a trustworthy, traditional, and ever present member of Polish society. In order to do this the company created a symbolic position in Polish society and fashioned advertisements that focused on both traditional values and the common everyday qualities of Coca-Cola. The beverage maker crafted ads that displayed its traditional association with the Christmas season in general and Santa Claus in particular. These television commercials and other types of ads were meant to broadcast the message of both time-honored values and everyday commonplaceness. They often showcased the Coca-Cola Santa, loveable new characters like the Coca-Cola polar bears, or traditional characters with Coca-Cola accessories, like Santa's elves. To reinforce this message Coca-Cola created numerous physical advertisements that produced a seemingly ever-present identity for the soft drink. Shops, restaurants, cafes, city streets, and numerous other Polish places brimmed with signs, menus, umbrellas, and many other kinds of physical Coke ads. Coca-Cola was ostensibly everywhere but in a manner that was meant to blend into everyday life. The company also attempted to become a daily part of Polish life by sponsoring sporting events, associating with local charities, and becoming a member of humanitarian organizations. From 1990 until 2000 the company produced very little advertising that shocked, titillated, or contained an aggressive approach. Instead Coca-Cola embraced common values and situations and campaigned to become a part of the everyday life of post-socialist Poles. Unlike other American products, like Frito-Lay, Levi's, or even sometimes McDonald's, for ten years Polish Coca-Cola ads did not even occasionally yell, but constantly whispered.

For nearly a decade Coca-Cola almost solely marketed itself as a common Polish product that could be and (should be) used as a part of everyday life. This advertising theme continued throughout 1990–2007 and will probably continue to be used by Coca-Cola for many years to come.

In the year 2000, the soft-drink maker started to shift much of its advertising from the theme of commonplaceness to the idea of exceptionality. This important transformation of theme is displayed in ads that the company generally targeted towards young and young-minded Poles. Coca-Cola was changing much of its marketing approach in Poland to meet the needs of younger and unhappy potential customers. This transition displays an important element of cultural interaction between the company and Polish society. Much like the other American companies in this study, Coca-Cola had to create a dialogue with Poland in order for both parties to prosper from the relationship. The company altered its advertising message after almost a decade in order to appeal to Poles who were being left out of the conversation between Coke and Polish consumers. Although this shift in message is commonplace in the advertising industry, it is nonetheless noteworthy because it displays the too-often-overlooked interaction between society and company. By producing narratives that reflect the tastes and values of its Polish audience, Coca-Cola demonstrated its dependence on the local population, a point often overlooked or understated by many when thinking about "Coca-Colonization."

Coca-Cola Television Commercials

Ad Title	*Year Produced*	*Themes*
Breakdance	2003	Exceptionalism
Christmas Caravan	2003	Traditionalism
FIFA World Cup Germany 2006	2006	Internationalism
Grandpa Titled	2002	Exceptionalism
Hot Five Promo	2002	Exceptionalism
Polar Bear	1994	Traditionalism
Summer Promo 30	2003	Exceptionalism
Wesołych Świąt	1990	Traditionalism

Conclusion

Once, while having an argument with an acquaintance in Poland, I was asked to name one valuable thing that the United States had given the world. I quickly answered "rock and roll" and she responded that the music had developed into an art form under British tutelage. Unable to convince her otherwise, I moved on to other American cultural inventions, only to be disagreed with at every turn. "Movies!" "The best movies are made in Europe where not every film needs to have a car explosion, a happy ending, and a sequel." "Television!" "You think *Dynasty* is a contribution to society?" "Blue jeans!" "The fashionable ones are made in Paris." As our verbal sparring about American culture continued while we walked down the street, I finally pointed to a local McDonald's and asked, "What about that?" She looked at me incredulously and said, "How can you try to take credit for McDonald's? McDonald's is as Polish as it is American. Everyone that works here, produces for here, and shops here is Polish!" Although my friend was undoubtedly biased and slightly irrational, her main argument that American culture is no longer only controlled and dictated by American interests is true. American culture no longer exists, if it ever did, in a pristine form that is governed and directed by only U.S. influences. Once American culture began to spread internationally it became subject to local cultural forces that influenced, revised, and changed it. While many forms of global and transnational culture may have begun in the United States, and may be directed by U.S. corporations or interests, this is not a complete understanding of transnational cultures but rather only a beginning. The idea that one monolithic, centrally controlled, international culture is taking over the planet is over simplistic. In places like

Poland, American companies and organizations market their products to local customers in a variety of ways. Though all companies advertise and market differently, each must find ways to connect with the local community and culture. These transnational local encounters not only change the producing culture but also alter the product and the receiving culture.

The purpose of this study is to locate and define narratives that exist within Polish advertising for American products and to show how these narratives interact with local Polish culture and how these interactions affect both the products and Polish culture over time. In order to do this I have analyzed Polish advertising for four American companies McDonalds, Coca-Cola, Levis, and Frito-Lay, from 1990–2007. These ads have been viewed as narratives and used to chronicle and understand the ideas, themes, and mythologies that are present in various types of Polish ads. These advertising narratives have revealed much about both Polish and American societies and their shared ideas, experiences, and mythologies. Each of the companies in this study has used different methods and themes in their advertising and each has had to find a way to successful interact with Polish culture. In doing this, commonality is defined and new ties are created that illuminate past connections and showcase new ones. I do not propose that these Polish advertising campaigns produced by four American companies are earth shattering. Nor can I state that these ads are entirely typical of campaigns used in various countries of the world. Rather, I assert that the narratives produced in these Polish ads display a small example of a much larger international occurrence, the development and strengthening of transnational cultures. These ads showcase some of the ways that various cultures interact both locally and transnationally. Ad producers must cooperate and identify with local cultures while also creating and servicing transnational identities. No longer can the world afford to think of culture merely in static nationalistic terms, especially when referring to cultural brands produced by multinational corporations. In the twentieth-first century, local cultures exist and even thrive, but they do so alongside transnational cultures that do not belong to a single place.

Many scholars and writers will claim that globalization represents a threat to traditional local cultures, that it tends toward corporate-controlled, monolithic global cultures. In this understanding of globalization, businesses and organizations invade local areas, assert dominance, and induce the society to become part of an internationalized lowest-common-denominator culture. In doing so, many of the traditional cultural values that make local society unique disappear and the world loses something exceptional. Undoubtedly, part of this understanding of globalization is true. Globalization requires various cultures to interact in new ways and often forces them to compete for cultural acceptance. Older traditions are placed alongside relative newcomers, and because of this many of the older ways are less frequently adhered to or sometimes are even lost. Any time that traditions and cultural aspects are lost we must question the changes and their effects both locally and globally. This process is not as one-sided as it could appear, though. Products and ideas rarely invade a society but rather they are generally introduced and marketed in an attempt to convince local consumers to try and eventually accept them. Some scholars would claim that this is a form of cultural colonization, and that advertising and marketing are forces that convince local citizens to desire things that they do not need and push them to abandon long-held beliefs and customs. This view does not give the local populace enough credit for understanding the complexity of the choices that it makes nor does it allow for the idea that some of these changes may be beneficial to both producer and receiver.

The idea of devaluing the capabilities of a local culture is especially true when discussing Poland, since a certain bias often appears to exist when referring to Polish culture and eastern and central Europe in general. Often "western" writers and thinkers seem to believe that the former socialist states of Europe are less forward thinking and viable. Although few would admit this, there are long-standing prejudices that eastern Europeans are less advanced and less prepared to handle the complexities of globalization. According to historians like Larry Wolff, this western understanding of eastern Europe may date back to the Enlightenment when many Europeans saw the eastern Europe as a dark reflection of the west. Many current accounts of Poland are founded on the same idea that the society is unprepared to deal with international forces and global cultures, and should be protected by outsiders who understand the intricacies of the situation much better. Poland will undoubtedly make both positive and negative choices, but for scholars to suggest that Polish society is unable to grasp the impact of these choices and the changes they will elicit is both capricious and insulting. To assert that Polish society cannot understand and select the most viable options for itself is in affect a declaration of its unfitness to operate within the context of globalization, an understanding that appears to be both biased and flawed.

The underlying premise of this study contradicts the notion that members of Polish society are victims of globalization and are unprepared and unable to combat the destructive forces of a new international culture. Instead, I assert that Polish advertising narratives showcase a complex communication between Polish citizens and international companies. This relationship is not an equal partnership but it also is not the one-way imposition of culture on Polish society that many scholars report. Companies like McDonald's, Levi's, Frito-Lay, and Coca-Cola spend much time, effort, and money to understand what countries like Poland need and desire. The companies then create advertising narratives that attempt to blend new products and services with existing cultural traditions and mythologies. In this paradigm the outside culture brings change to countries like Poland, but it is only the change that is acceptable to the local culture. Often this means that the new products and cultures are blended with the local culture to create a new cultural understanding that changes both the local society and the product. Generally this is an ongoing process that never ends because the needs and desires of the local society are constantly changing and the outside culture must adjust to remain viable. This process is neither charitable nor egalitarian. Rather both sides press for changes and outcomes that work in their best interests. The companies' main objective is to make as much profit as possible, while Polish citizens wish for changes that make their lives better and more fulfilling. While some economists may claim that this is a perfect example of market forces creating a greater good, I do not. I suspect that Polish society loses as much or more than it gains, but that is undeterminable and in the end left to the Poles alone to decide. The point of this study is to show that the process is more equitable than many scholars contend, that Poles have a high level of influence over outside cultures that enter Poland, and that American companies operating in Poland are heavily influenced by the needs of Polish society.

The four companies that comprise this study showcase various examples of American corporations communicating with Polish society. In many ways McDonald's is the company that has transformed itself the most during this seventeen-year period. While the cultural acceptance of its brand is one of McDonald's primary goals in Poland, the fast-food giant changed advertising and marketing themes several times. McDonald's quickly attempted to define itself as a company that understood and respected Polish culture and values after introducing itself to Poland in 1992. This can be seen in architectural advertising in restaurants in important Polish places like Warsaw, Krakow, and Zakopane, and the ongoing theme of Polishness in McDonald's commercials. In these advertisements McDonald's was branded as a western company that understood and valued Poland. One can never be certain what a strategy has accomplished but later commercials showcase a cultural awareness of the products that, coupled with McDonald's expansion and sustainability, indicates a high level of success. This means that a substantial number of people seem to have accepted McDonald's as a part of Polish society. It is debatable whether McDonald's advertising was a mirror or molder in Poland but it is obvious that the company became more widely accepted within Polish society. Around the year 2002, McDonald's apparently altered its approach, and instead of only focusing on its image as a good Polish citizen it expanded its identity to be considered more international. This evolution directly followed movements within Poland that showed the nation to be more viable internationally and more open to transnational exchanges. As 2007 ended, Poland was a member of NATO and the European Union, and becoming an internationally powerful presence, and McDonald's was promoting its ties to Poland and its international stature. This is a tale of how McDonald's was able to be both local and international, an American company that was able to come to in Poland in 1992, show itself as culturally sensitive to Polish society, and then change itself to market its international status.

By contrast, Levi's 1990–2007 Polish advertising represents cultural adaptation without change. Like many other companies, the jeans maker had to constantly readjust its image while maintaining its core identity. Since most Polish Levi's customers were teenagers or young adults, the company was obliged to remain exciting and fashionable while simultaneously preserving the idea of being a historic symbol that separated it from other brands. The themes of this period's Levi's advertising in Poland mostly went unchanged, but the settings and context continued to shift and develop. Levi's launched its Polish advertising in the 1990s by concentrating on an idealized mythological American past while the company used the themes of rebellion, independence, and individualism to market itself and its products. This helped Levi's to emphasize its American qualities and to remind Poles of a storybook America featuring the cowboy, the pioneer, and the antisocial bad boy. During the 1990s and into the twenty-first century, Levi's continually used rebellious and individualistic themes but its use of American images subsided. Beginning in the mid–1990s, the jeans maker started to highlight its status as an international brand, asserting that the themes of individualism and rebelliousness were universal. While Levi's never denounced its American origins, it chose not to focus its advertising on this part the brand's background. The start of the twenty-first century saw this focus again adjusted when the company again embraced an urban American mythology that showcased American individualism and rebelliousness. Although specific examples and storylines changed, Levi's aspiration to be the brand of rebellion and individualism in Poland did not. Levi's, unlike companies such as Coca-Cola and McDonald's, never attempted to become Polish. Rather the clothing maker desired to portray its brand as timeless and universal like its adopted themes of rebellion and individualism. Levi's branded itself as not being a part of Polish society, or any society, but instead marketed itself to those who wanted to be antisocial. By doing this, Levi's was outstandingly reliable in staying on message. The company often changed the ways it presented its core themes, but the themes themselves never dramatically changed. Because of this Levi's was able to transform into whatever the buyer wanted it be, which is at the heart of a company that oxymoronically wants to be a rebellious and individualistic corporation.

Frito-Lay advertising in Poland is a study in both youth marketing and the introduction of new ideas. The company introduced the snack-food category into Poland and then rapidly grew into the most prominent brand. Unlike McDonald's and Coca-Cola, Frito-Lay did not advertise itself as traditionally Polish. Rather it marketed new and exciting brands to young consumers who craved change and acceptance. The snack-food maker created advertisements that publicized Frito-Lay's international ties, its understanding of young people's need to rebel against authority, its acceptance of worldwide youth culture, and the idea of adventurous youth. Because Frito-Lay's main marketing point in Poland from the early 1990s until 2007 was endorsing itself as a youth brand, its advertisements display few changes over time. While McDonalds, Levi's, and Coca-Cola ads display shifts in how themes and ideas are presented, Frito-Lay's ads are remarkably consistent in their presentation. Since its introduction into Poland, Frito-Lay presented itself as a youth brand that was not against traditional Polish culture but instead was an alternative for young Poles. The company marketed itself to those customers who had already begun investigating different views of Poland and the world, and were considering changes in both society and their lives. Frito-Lay became a youth-oriented brand and asserted its compatibility with the group's needs and desires. As its central customers mature this may change, but for the time being Frito-Lay has associated itself with the desires of the younger generation of Poland.

From 1990 until 2000, Coca-Cola almost exclusively marketed itself as an ordinary Polish product that could and should be a part of everyday life. This marketing approach persisted throughout 1990–2007 and Coca-Cola will most likely continue to use it for years to come. In the year 2000 the company began to change the theme of much of its advertising from the idea of commonplaceness to the theme of exceptionality. This important thematic transformation is showcased in ads generally created for young Poles. Coca-Cola was shifting a large portion of its Polish marketing to match the desires of younger, unsatisfied prospective customers. This move highlights a significant factor of cultural interaction between Coca-Cola and Polish society. The soft-drink maker, much like the other American companies in this study, had to create a dialogue with the citizens of Poland in order for both parties to grow from the relationship. Coca-Cola changed its main marketing theme after almost a decade in order to appeal to Poles who were being left out of the conversation between Coke and Poland consumers. While this shift in message is routine in the advertising industry it is nevertheless remarkable because it displays the too-often-overlooked interaction between society and business. By producing narratives that reflect the tastes and values of its Polish audience, Coca-Cola demonstrated its dependence on the local population, a point often overlooked or understated by many when thinking about "Coca-Colonization."

In his book *Smile When You're Lying*, Chuck Thompson recalls a visit to the former East Germany after the end of the Cold War. Thompson reflects upon the past and tells a German resident how part of him misses the Cold War period. He comments, "I can't help but have a little regret whenever I visit Eastern Europe. In an abstract way I hated you, or at least your government for a good portion of my life." He goes on to explain, "The straightforward morality of a Cold War struggle against a professional and worthy foe dedicated to science and economic equality, at least as they interpreted it? I sort of miss it" (290). Many Americans and Poles, although they will probably not admit it, also miss the security of the Cold War mentality. Although the political, economic, and cultural changes in the world since 1990 have been positive for many, they also have been frightening. In many ways, the world is less understandable than it once was and it is often unclear if changes should be perceived as good or ill. The questions about globalization, transnationalism, and cultural colonization that this book addresses are not easily answered. Although I contend that many scholars oversimplify the process of globalization and cultural exchange in their work, some readers will disagree with my assessment. In the end, I only hope to be another voice in the growing dialogue that surrounds these complicated issues. While this study examines the advertising narratives of only four companies in one country, it provides another view about ideas and issues that are increasingly important in the early years of the twenty-first century. These Polish advertising narratives allow for another point of view involving globalization and its effects on a local culture. In viewing these advertising narratives in Poland from 1990 to 2007, we are able to see how a newly capitalistic society reacted to cultural changes and what affect these reactions had. This is a small but interesting part of the overall idea of globalization that promises to remake the world that we live in.

Works Cited

"Adam Małysz." *In Your Pocket*. 2006. http://www.inyourpocket.com/poland/zakopane/en/feature?id=55661 (page discontinued April 19, 2008).

AdForum. 2006. Bartle Bogle Hegarty and the Levi's Campaign in Europe in the 1980s. AdForum. 8 January 2007. http://www.adforum.com/creative_archive/2003/AW1136_WFA_Areel_detail.asp?ID=33082&TDI=VDUubxAp&PAGE=1&bShop=False&awcat=&ob=brand&awid= (page discontinued April 19, 2008).

Adverblog. *Merry Xmas, from Coca-Cola Poland*. November 29, 2005. Adverblog. http://www.adverblog.com/archives/002210.htm (accessed April 19, 2008).

Agro Wakacje. http://www.agrowakacje.pl (accessed April 19, 2008).

America Presents Archives 2005. U.S. Dept. of State, United States Diplomatic Mission to Warsaw, Poland. http://warsaw.usembassy.gov/poland/ampresents_calendar_2005.html (accessed April 19, 2008).

Anderson, Benedict. *Imagined Communities: Reflections on the Origin and Spread of Nationalism*. London: Verso, 1983.

Ash, Timothy Garton. *The Polish Revolution: Solidarity*. Third ed. New Haven: Yale University Press, 1999.

"Assistance for 2001 Flood Victims." *Polish Humanitarian Organisation*. 2002. http://www.pah.org.pl/7483.html%22 (accessed April 19, 2008).

"Backward Lovers 1." Levi Strauss & Co. Print advertisement. 2003.

"Backward Lovers 2." Levi Strauss & Co. Print advertisement. 2003.

"Backward Lovers 3." Levi Strauss & Co. Print advertisement. 2003.

"Backward Lovers 4." Levi Strauss & Co. Print advertisement. 2003.

Barańczak, Stanisław. *Breathing Under Water and Other East European Essays*. Cambridge, MA: Harvard University Press, 1990.

Beller, K. "Solidarność" (Solidarity anchor). 1980. In "Some Like It Red: Polish Political Posters, 1944–1989." *The Art of Poster*. http://www.theartofposter.com/RED/Red.htm (accessed April 19, 2008).

"Bimber." Print advertisement. 1945.

Boczar, Danuta A. "The Polish Poster." *Art Journal* 44, no.1 (Spring 1984), 16–27.

Bogdanowicz, Ewa. "Salted Snacks Market." *U.S. Commercial Service Warsaw*. August 2006. http://commercecan.ic.gc.ca/scdt/bizmap/interface2.nsf/vDOWNLOAD/ISA_4979/$file/X_4424889.DOC (accessed April 19, 2008).

"A Bold New Breed." Levi Strauss & Co. Print advertisement. 2002
"Brand Fact Sheets, Coca-Cola Company." Coca-Cola Company. http://www.virtual vender.coca-cola.com/ft/index.jsp (accessed April 19, 2008).
"Breakdance." Coca-Cola television advertisement. 2003.
"Campfire." Levi Strauss & Co. television advertisement. 1993.
"Cheap Eats," *Warsaw Voice*, March 17, 2004. http://www.virtualvender.coca-cola.com/ft/index.jsp (accessed April 19, 2008).
"Cheetos *Wróżka*," Frito-Lay television advertisement. July 30, 2001.
"Chester Pokemon," Frito-Lay television advertisement. December 9, 2005.
"Choose Your Style." Levi Strauss & Co. print advertisement. 2002.
"Christmas Caravan." Coca-Cola television advertisement, 2003.
"Christmas Tree." Levi Strauss & Co. print advertisement. 2004.
Cieślak, Zofia. Personal interview. November 22, 2006.
"Classic TV Babes." TV Acres. http://www.tvacres.com/sex_babes_baywatch.htm (accessed April 19, 2008).
"The Coca-Cola Business in Poland." Company document, 2001.
"Coca-Cola Cup." http://www.cocacolacup.pl (accessed April 19, 2008).
"Creek." Levi Strauss & Co. television advertisement. 1994.
Cristodero, Damian. "They Came to See the Polish Batman." *St. Petersburg Times.* November 2, 2006. http://www.sptimes.com/2002/02/11/news_pf/Olympics/They_came_to_see_the_.shtml (accessed April 19, 2008).
Część I—Szklane Domy. 2006. *http://jezyk-polski.eza.pl/materialy/lektury/zeromski _przedwiosnie/1.htm* (site discontinued April 19, 2008).
"Dangerous Liaisons." Levi Strauss & Co. television advertisement. 2007.
Davies, Norman. *God's Playground: A History of Poland, Volume II.* New York: Columbia Press, 1982.
Davies, Norman. *Heart of Europe: The Past in Poland's Present.* New York: Oxford University Press, 2001.
de Mooij, Marieke. *Global Marketing and Advertising: Understanding Cultural Paradoxes.* Thousand Oaks, CA: Sage Publications, 1998.
Dobbs, Michael. *Down with Big Brother: The Fall of the Soviet Empire.* New York: Alfred A. Knopf, 1997.
"Dolls." Levi Strauss & Co. television advertisement. 2000.
"Drugstore." Levi Strauss & Co. television advertisement. 1995.
"Dziadek." McDonalds television advertisement. February 2, 2002.
"Engel." McDonalds television advertisement. April 11, 2002.
"Factory," Frito-Lay television advertisement. June 10, 1999.
FAOSTAT. Food and Agriculture Organization of the United States. http://faostat.fao.org (accessed April 19, 2008)
Faruque, Zinnia. "Hip Hop Fridays: Poland's Experience of Rap Echoes America's," *Black Electorate.com*, December 2, 2005. http://www.blackelectorate.com/articles.asp?ID=1522 (accessed April 19, 2008).
Ferster, Karol. "*Prawo Głosu*" Print advertisement. 1952.
"FIFA World Cup Germany 2006." Coca-Cola television advertisement. 2006.
"Flirt." Levi Strauss & Co. television advertisement. 2001.
Friedman, Thomas. "Where U.S. Translates as Freedom." *New York Times*, December 28, 2003.

Works Cited

Fox, Francis. "Poland and the American West." In *Western Amerykanski: Polish Poster Art and the Western*. Kevin Mulroy, ed. Seattle: University of Washington Press, 1999.

Frith, Katherine Toland. "Undressing the Ad: Reading Culture in Advertising," in *Undressing the Ad*, Katherine Toland Frithm ed., New York: Peter Lang, 1998, 1–14.

"Girls 1." Levi Strauss & Co. print advertisement. 2004.

"Girls 2." Levi Strauss & Co. print advertisement. 2004.

"Grandpa Titled." Coca-Cola television advertisement. 2002.

Green, Thomas. "Tricksters and the Marketing of Breakfast Cereals." *Journal of Popular Culture* 40, no. 1 (2007), 49–68.

"Hamster." Levi Strauss & Co. television advertisement. 1998.

Hanson, Phillip. *Advertising and Socialism: The Nature and Extent of Consumer Advertising in the Soviet Union, Poland, Hungary and Yugoslavia*. White Plains, NY: International Arts and Sciences Press, 1974.

"Heard in Passing." *Warsaw Voice*, November 24, 2004. http://www.warsawvoice.pl/view/7095 (accessed April 19, 2008).

"Highlights in the History of Coca-Cola Television Advertising." Library of Congress. http://memory.loc.gov/ammem/ccmphtml/colahist.html (accessed April 19, 2008).

Hilscher, Hubert. "Nie ma dla nas sprawy drozszej niz polska ludowa." Print advertisement. 1972. In *Polski Plakat Polityczny*. Warsaw: Krajowa Agencja Wydawnicza, 1980.

Historia Frito-Lay. Frito-Lay. 2007. http://www.fritolay.pl/historia.htm (accessed April 19, 2008).

"Historical Background 1991–1996." Coca-Cola Company document, 1996.

Hobsbawm, Eric. *Invention of Tradition*. New York: Cambridge University Press, 1983.

Hoover's. "Frito Lay, Inc." http://www.hoovers.com/frito-lay/ — ID__48009 —/free-co-factsheet.xhtml (accessed April 17, 2008).

"Hot Five Promo." Coca-Cola television advertisement. 2002.

iLeo Poland. "Golden Drums 2003." http://www.arcww.com.pl/portoroz (accessed April 19, 2008).

"I'm lovin' It." McDonalds television advertisement. January 2, 2004.

International Networks Archive. "The Magic Bean Shop." 2003. http://www.princeton.edu/%7Eina/infographics/starbucks.html (accessed April 19, 2008).

Jasiński, Jarosław. "KPP- PZPR." Print advertising. 1978. In *Polski Plakat Polityczny*. Warsaw: Krajowa Agencja Wydawnicza, 1980.

"Jedi Knights Demand Britain's Fourth Largest 'Religion' Receives Recognition." *Daily Mail*, November 16, 2006. http://www.dailymail.co.uk/pages/live/articles/news/news.html?in_article_id=416761&in_page_id=1770 (accessed April 19, 2008).

Krajewski, Andrzej. "Odstrzał." Print advertisement. 1973. In *Polish Poster Gallery* http://www.poster.com.pl/movie-western-1.htm (accessed April 19, 2008).

"Krakow po radosnej stronie życia." Coca-Cola print advertisement. 2006.

Krzysztof Hołowczyc & Hołowczyc Management. http://www.holowczyc.pl/eng/popularnosc.php (accessed April 19, 2008).

"*Kto pije*." Print advertisement. Date unknown. In *Socjalizm On-Line* http://www.socjalizm.info (accessed January 24, 2007; advertisement no longer available).

Kubik, Jan. *The Power of Symbols Against the Symbols of Power: The Rise of Solidarity and the Fall of State Socialism in Poland.* University Park, PA: Pennsylvania State University, 1994.

"Kung-Fu." Levi Strauss & Co. television advertisement. 1997.

"Lay's Appetite Computer." Frito-Lay television advertisement. March 22, 2005.

"Lay's Obsesja Piłkarska 15." Frito-Lay television advertisement. March 27, 2002.

"Lay's Obsesja Piłkarska 30." Frito-Lay television advertisement. March 27, 2002.

"Lay's Max Czarus." Frito-Lay television advertisement. May 15, 2001.

"Lay's Max Marysia," Frito-Lay television advertisement. May 15, 2001.

"Legs." Levi Strauss & Co. television advertisement. 2000.

Lengren, Zbigniew. "Amerykańska reklama obuwia." Print advertisement. 1952.

Lepkowska-White, Elzbieta. "Polish and American Print Ads: Functional, Individualistic, Collectivist, and Experiential Appeals." *Journal of Global Marketing* 17, no. 4 (2004), 75–92.

Levi Strauss Poland. http://eu.levi.com/default.aspx?lang=pl&country=PL (accessed April 19, 2008).

Levi's ANTI-FORM. Levi-Strauss Poland. http://www.arcww.com.pl/portoroz/levis/index.html (accessed April 19, 2008).

Lewandowski, Marek. "1 maja Święto Solidarnośći Robotniczej" (Solidarity, People.) Print advertisement. 1981. In *The Art of Poster* http://www.theartofposter.com/poster.asp?id=7858 (accessed April 19, 2008).

Longhurst, Kerry. "From Security Consumer to Security Provider — Poland and Transatlantic Security in the Twenty-First Century." In *Poland: A New Power in Transatlantic Security.* Marcin Zaborowski and David H. Dunn, eds. Portland, OR: Frank Cass, 2003.

Louis, J. C., and Harvey Z. Yazijian. *The Cola Wars.* New York: Everest House, 1980.

"Mall." Levi Strauss & Co. television advertisement. 1998.

Mark, Margaret, and Carol S. Pearson. *The Outlaw and the Hero: Building Extraordinary Brands Through the Power of Archetypes.* New York: McGraw-Hill, 2001.

Marsh, Graham, and Paul Trynka. *Denim: From Cowboys to Catwalks: A Visual History of the World's Most Legendary Fabric.* London: Aurum, 2001.

McCracken, Grant. "Culture and Consumption: A Theoretical Account of the Structure and Movement of the Cultural Meaning of Consumer Goods," *Journal of Consumer Research* 13, no. 1 (June 1986), 71–84.

McDonald's. http://www.mcdonalds.com (accessed April 19, 2008).

McDonald's Poland. http://www.mcdonalds.pl (accessed April 19, 2008)

"McDrive." McDonalds television advertisement. May 1996.

"McKielbasa." McDonalds television advertisement. January 31, 2003.

"McPolska." McDonalds television advertisement. May 15, 2002.

"Mermaids." Levi Strauss & Co. television advertisement. 1997.

Młodożeniec, Jan. "Niebieski żołnierz." Print advertisement. 1972. In *Polish Poster Gallery.* http://www.poster.com.pl/movie-western-1.htm (accessed April 19, 2008).

"Mother's Day." McDonald's television advertisement. May 25, 2005.

Mueller, Barbara. *Dynamics of International Advertising: Theoretical and Practical Perspectives.* New York: Peter Lang, 2004.

Muth, Michael. "Marketing Still Inconsistent in Poland." *Marketing News* 29, no. 1 (January 2, 1995).

Works Cited

Mysyrowicz, Witold. "Symbol i rzeczywistość." Print advertisement. 1983.

"Naprawde Twoje 1." Levi Strauss & Co. print advertisement. 2004.

"Naprawde Twoje 2." Levi Strauss & Co. print advertisement. 2004.

"NATO aby zniszczyć ziemie." Print advertisement. 1983.

"NATO Zagrożeniem pokoju." Print advertisement. 1983.

"Nie pije." Print advertisement. Date unknown. On *Socjalizm On-Line*. http://www. socjalizm.info (accessed January 27, 2007; advertisement no longer available).

"Nie ulegaj pokusie" Print advertisement. Date unknown. On *Karta*. www.karta.org.pl (accessed February 1, 2007; advertisement no longer available).

"Night and Day." Levi Strauss & Co. television advertisement. 1992.

"Olympic Weeks." McDonald's television advertisement. July 14, 2004.

"Pamela," Frito Lay. Television advertisement. June 15, 1999.

Pendergrast, Mark. *For God, Country and Coca-Cola: The Definitive History of the Great American Soft Drink and the Company That Makes It.* New York: Basic Books, 1993.

"PepsiCo Inc. Acquires Polish Snack Manufacturer." *AM Online*, January 5, 2006. http: //www.amonline.com/web/online/VendingMarketWatch-News/PepsiCo-Inc-Acquires-Polish-Snack-Manufacturer/1$15198 (accessed April 19, 2008).

"Photocopier." Levi Strauss & Co. television advertisement. 1998.

Pietrzak, Michał. "Bimber z tradycjami ma byc legalny." *Dziennik Online* September 23, 2006. http://www.dziennik.pl/Default.aspx?TabId=124&ShowArticleId=107 24 (accessed April 19, 2008).

"Planet." Levi Strauss & Co. television advertisement. 1995.

Poland — Polish Geert Hofstede Cultural Dimensions Explained. 2003. http://www.geert-hofstede.com/hofstede_poland.shtml (accessed April 19, 2008).

"Polar Bear." Coca-Cola print advertisement, 1994.

"Polish Coca-Cola is already ... 10 years old!" Coca-Cola Company document. 2002.

Polish HipHop Scene. 2000. Tytus. 19 June 2006. <http://enigma.art.pl/liquide.html>.

"Potato Print." McDonald's television advertisement. May 17, 2004.

"President Woodrow Wilson's Fourteen Points." http://www.lib.byu.edu/~rdh/wwi/ 1918/14points.html (accessed April 19, 2008)

"Promo Football Stars." Frito-Lay television advertisement. March 27, 2002.

"Promo Pokemon." Frito-Lay television advertisement. July 30, 2001.

"Quality." McDonald's television advertisement. March 14, 2001.

"Red Tab 1." Levi Strauss & Co. Print advertisement. 1996.

"Red Tab 2." Levi Strauss & Co. Print advertisement. 1996.

"Red Tab 3." Levi Strauss & Co. Print advertisement. 1996.

"Red Tab 4." Levi Strauss & Co. Print advertisement. 1996.

"Red Tab 5." Levi Strauss & Co. Print advertisement. 1996.

"Red Tab 6." Levi Strauss & Co. Print advertisement. 1996.

Richardson, Tim. "Jedis Reach for the Stars in UK Census." *The Register*. February 14, 2003. http://www.theregister.co.uk/2003/02/14/jedis_reach_the_stars (accessed April 19, 2008).

Rollyson, Carl. "Freeze-Frame Poland 1979: Polish Cowboys and Marlboro Men." In *Coca-Cola Culture: Icons of Pop.*" Roger Rosen and Patra McSharry Sevastiades, eds. New York: Rosen Publishing Group, 1993.

Roosevelt, Theodore. "Theodore Roosevelt: Speech at the Minnesota State Fair." *T.R.*

The Great New Yorker. 2006. http://www.trthegreatnewyorker.com/Statesman/ S — D%20SPEECH%20AT%20MINNESOTA.html (accessed April 19, 2008).

"Rub (Bowling Alley)." Levi Strauss & Co. television advertisement. 2002.

"Rub (Hole in Wall)." Levi Strauss & Co. television advertisement. 2002.

"Rub (Shop Window)." Levi Strauss & Co. television advertisement. 2002.

Sanford, George. *Poland: The Conquest of History*. Amsterdam: Harwood Academic Publishers, 1999.

Sarnecki, Tomasz. "Solidarity, High Noon." Print advertisement. 1989. In *The Art of the Poster*. http://www.theartofposter.com/RED/Red.htm (accessed April 19, 2008).

Senft, Joe. "The Polish Consumer: Is Your Advertising Effective?" Economic Outlook. http://www.masterpage.com.pl/outlook/consum.html (page discontinued April 19, 2008).

Shallcross, Bożena. "Home Truths: Towards a Definition of the Polish Home." In *Framing the Polish Home: Postwar Cultural Constructions of Hearth, Nation, and Self*. Athens: Ohio University Press, 2002.

"Shoot Out." Print advertisement. 1971. *Movie Goods*. http://www.moviegoods.com/ movie_product.asp?master_movie_id=3892&mgaid=western-movie-posters (accessed April 19, 2008).

"Skoki." McDonald's. Television advertisement. January 1, 2002.

Śliwka, Karol. "Polska Rzeczpospolita Ludowa" Print advertisement. 1974.

Służyński, Maciej. "*Slogan reklamowy.*" Signs.pl. September 10, 2005. http://www. signs.pl/article.php?sid=3118 (accessed April 19, 2008).

Snack Foods, 2003. International Trade Administration, Office of Consumer Goods. www.ita.doc.gov/td/ocg/snacks03.pdf (accessed April 19, 2008).

Snapshots International. "Poland Carbonated Soft Drinks Report 2002." London: Snapshots International, 2002.

Stachurski, Marian. "Rekord Annie." Print advertisement 1958. In *Western Amerykanski: Polish Poster Art and the Western*. Kevin Mulroy, ed. Seattle: University of Washington Press, 1999.

"Street Car." Levi Strauss & Co. print advertisement. 2004.

"Summer Promo 30." Coca-Cola print advertisement, 2003.

"Swap." Levi Strauss & Co. television advertisement. 2003.

"Swimmer." Levi Strauss & Co. television advertisement. 1992.

"Szczyt," Frito-Lay. television advertisement. July 30, 2001.

"Temptation." Levi Strauss & Co. television advertisement. 2001.

Thomas, William I., and Florian Znaniecki. *The Polish Peasant in Europe and America: Monograph of an Immigrant Group*. Volume 1 and 2. University of Chicago Press, 1920.

Thompson, Chuck. *Smile When You're Lying: Confessions of a Rouge Travel Writer*. New York: Henry Holt, 2007.

"Top 100 Advertising Campaigns." *AdAge*.com. http://adage.com/century/campaigns. html (accessed April 19, 2008).

Treutler, Jerzy. "Jak, Zdobyto Dziki Zachòd" Print advertisement. 1965. In *Western Amerykanski: Polish Poster Art and the Western*. Kevin Mulroy, ed. Seattle: University of Washington Press, 1999.

Tutak, Ryan James. "The Race is On: Competition for the CEE Car Market." Beyond

Works Cited

Transition, 2001. World Bank. http://www.worldbank.org/html/prddr/trans/may jun99/pgs25–27.htm (accessed April 19, 2008).

"Twistos Einstein," Frito-Lay television advertisement. February 4, 2002.

"Undressed." Levi Strauss & Co. television advertisement. 2000.

"Untitled." McDonald's television advertisement. March 1997.

Wandycz, Piotr. *The United States and Poland.* Cambridge, Mass: Harvard University Press, 1980.

"Warsaw Prepares Flood Defenses." CNN.com, July 31, 2001. http://archives.cnn.com/2001/WORLD/europe/07/30/poland.floods/index.html (accessed April 19, 2008).

"Washroom." Levi Strauss & Co. television advertisement. 1996.

Watson, James. *Golden Arches East: McDonald's in East Asia.* Stanford, CA.: Stanford University Press, 1997.

"Welcome to the Coke Side of Life.'" Coca-Cola Company, March 30, 2006, press release. http://www.thecocacolacompany.com/presscenter /nr_20060330_coke_side_of_life.html (accessed April 19, 2008).

Weschler, Lawrence. "The Graphics of Solidarity." *Virginia Quarterly Review* 82, no. 1 (Winter 2006), 111–129.

"*Wesołych* Świąt." Coca-Cola print advertisement, 1990.

Wieckowski, Michał. "Solidarność 1 maja 3 maja." Print advertisement. 1981. In *The Art of Poster.* http://www.theartofposter.com/poster.asp?id=9114 (accessed April 19, 2008).

"WiesMac." McDonald's television advertisement. January 7, 2000.

Witzel, Michael, and Gyvel Young-Witzel. *The Sparkling Story of Coca-Cola: An Entertaining History Including Collectibles, Coke Lore, and Calendar Girls.* Stillwater, MN: Voyageur Press, 2002.

"Wives." Levi Strauss & Co. television advertisement. 1998.

"World Children's Day." McDonald's television advertisement. November 10, 2005.

World Heritage List. UNESCO. http://whc.unesco.org /pg.cfm?cid=31 (accessed April 19, 2008).

World Potato Congress. 1999. http://www.potatocongress.org (site discontinued April 19, 2008).

"*Zaproszenie.*" Levi Strauss & Co. print advertisement. 2004.

"*Źle tankujesz*" Print advertisement. Date unknown. On *Socjalizm On-Line* http://www.socjalizm.info (accessed January 22, 2007; advertisement no longer available).

Index

189

Index

Index

United States Army 36
United States Constitution 117
United States Department of Commerce
   International Trade Administration (ITA)
   116

Voice of America 24

Wandycz, Piotr 23
Warsaw 23, 43, 58, 61, 62, 63–64, 84, 108,
   143, 145, 148, 150, 154, 155, 157, 160, 177
Warsaw Coca-Cola Bottlers Ltd. 142
Warsaw Pact 87
Warsaw Uprising 43, 131
Warsaw Voice 67, 121
Washington, Dinah 90
"Washroom" 99, 110, 115
Watson, James 62
Wawel Castle 170
Western film posters 47–54

White House 24
"WiesMac" (ad) 70–71, 85
Wilson, Woodrow 22, 23
With Fire and Sword (Sienkiewicz) 47, 164
"Wives" 100, 115
Wolff, Larry 175
Wołoszański, Bogusław 135–136
"World Children's Day" 83, 85
World Cup of soccer 80, 81, 169
World Potato Congress 74
World War I 17, 18, 21, 22, 23, 30
World War II 18, 45, 64, 145
Wrangler 101

Yoda 120

Zakopane 63, 66–67, 69, 84, 177
Żeromski, Stefan 62–63
Znanecki, Florian 20

193